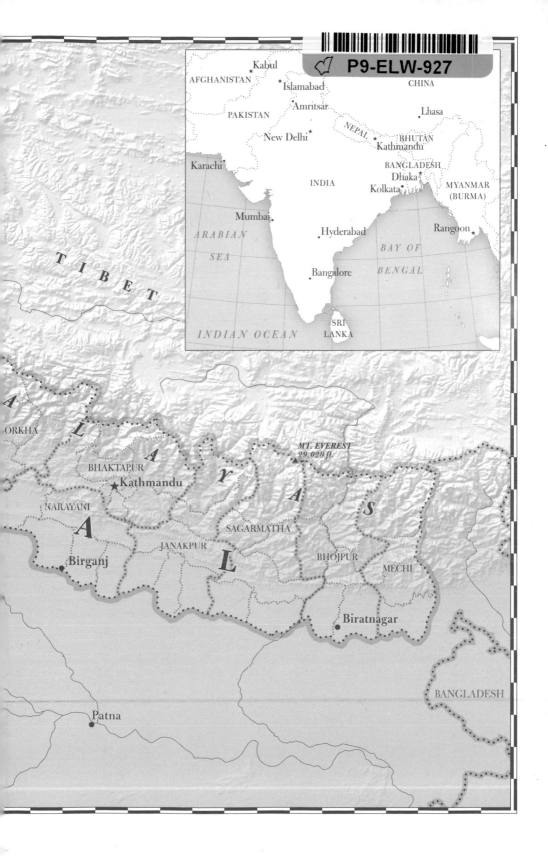

P9-ELW-927

Kabul
AFGHANISTAN
Islamabad
CHINA
Amritsar
PAKISTAN
Lhasa
New Delhi
NEPAL
BHUTAN
Kathmandu
Karachi
BANGLADESH
Dhaka
INDIA
Kolkata
MYANMAR
(BURMA)
Mumbai
Hyderabad
Rangoon
ARABIAN
SEA
BAY OF
Bangalore
BENGAL
INDIAN OCEAN
SRI
LANKA

TIBET

ORKHA

HIMALAYAS

BHAKTAPUR
Kathmandu

MT. EVEREST
29,028 ft.

NARAYANI

SAGARMATHA

JANAKPUR

BHOJPUR

Birganj

MECHI

Biratnagar

Patna

BANGLADESH

Little Princes

Little Princes

*One Man's Promise to Bring Home
the Lost Children of Nepal*

Conor Grennan

WILLIAM MORROW
An Imprint of HarperCollins*Publishers*

HarperCollins books may be purchased for educational, business, or sales promotional use. For information please write: Special Markets Department, HarperCollins Publishers, 10 East 53rd Street, New York, NY 10022.

FIRST EDITION

Designed by Lisa Stokes
Endpaper map by Nick Springer Cartographics LLC

Library of Congress Cataloging-in-Publication Data has been applied for.

ISBN 978-0-06-193005-8
ISBN 978-0-06-204985-8 (international edition)

10 11 12 13 14   OV/RRD   10 9 8 7 6 5 4 3 2 1

03131 8908

For Lizzie

Contents

A Note on the Crisis in Nepal

THE DECADE-LONG CIVIL WAR in Nepal (1996–2006) claimed more than thirteen thousand lives. The devastating economic consequences destroyed hundreds of thousands more lives in one of the poorest countries in the world.

In the remote regions of the country, the Maoist rebels, who had taken up arms against the king, used intimidation and murder to control villages. They abducted children, forcing them to join the rebel army in the fight against the royal government.

Child traffickers, preying on villagers' fears of Maoist abductions, deceived families by promising to take their children to the safety of the Kathmandu Valley, one of the few regions left in Nepal that was still free from Maoist control. For this "service," they collected vast sums from impoverished families. The traffickers then abandoned the children in Kathmandu, hundreds of miles from their mountain villages. These children, who could be as young as three years old, effectively became orphans.

There are tens of thousands of children still missing in Nepal.

Prologue

December 20, 2006

I T WAS WELL AFTER nightfall when I realized we had gone the wrong way. The village I had been looking for was somewhere up the mountain. In my condition, it would be several hours' walk up a rocky trail, if we could even find the trail in the pitch-dark. My two porters and I had been walking for thirteen hours straight. Winter at night in the mountains of northwestern Nepal is bitterly cold, and we had no shelter. Two of our three flashlights had burned out. Worse, we were deep in a Maoist rebel stronghold, not far from where a colleague had been kidnapped almost exactly one year before. I would have shared this fact with my porters, but we were unable to communicate; I spoke only a few words of the local dialect.

Exhausted, I slumped down beside them. I zipped up my jacket and knotted my arms tightly around my chest to keep out the cold. Six days had passed since I split from my team. I had sent them home, back to their villages, promising them that I would be okay. My guide, Rinjin, tried to stay with me. Just to make sure the helicopter comes, he had said. I assured him everything would be fine and pushed him to leave with the others. The trek back to their villages would take the men several days, and they had been away from their families for almost three weeks. Rinjin had taken a last look at the empty sky, shaken his head at my stubbornness, and clasped my hand in farewell. Then he hurried to catch up with the others already descending the trail.

I reached into my bag, looking for food. I pushed aside the weather-beaten folder, crammed with my handwritten notes and photos of young children, children who had been taken from these mountains years before. The notes had been my only clues to finding their families in remote villages accessible only by foot.

Behind a crumpled, rain-stained map, my hand touched two tanger-ines—the last of our food. I passed them to the two porters.

I wondered how things would have been different if I hadn't gotten hurt. Or if I hadn't split from my team, or if I hadn't decided to wait on that moun-tain for a helicopter that never came. It didn't matter now. What did matter was figuring out how we would get through the night.

Part I

THE LITTLE PRINCES

November 2004–January 2005

One

THE BROCHURES FOR VOLUNTEERING in Nepal had said *civil war*. Being an American, I assumed the writers of the brochure were doing what I did all the time—exaggerating. No organization was going to send volunteers into a conflict zone.

Still, I made sure to point out that particular line to everybody I knew. "An orphanage in Nepal, for two months," I would tell women I'd met in bars. "Sure, there's a civil war going on. And yes, it might be dangerous. But I can't think about that," I would shout over the noise of the bar, trying to appear misty-eyed. "I have to think about the children."

Now, as I left the Kathmandu airport in a beat-up old taxi, I couldn't help but notice that the gate was guarded by men in camouflage. They peered in at me as we slowed to pass them, the barrels of their machine guns a few inches from my window. Outside the gate, sandbagged bunkers lined the airport perimeter, where young men in fatigues aimed heavy weapons at passing cars. Government buildings were wrapped in barbed wire. Gas stations were protected by armored vehicles; soldiers inspected each car in the mile-long line for gas.

In the backseat of the taxi, I dug the brochure out of my backpack and quickly flipped to the Nepal section. *Civil war,* it said again, in the same breezy font used to describe the country's fauna. Couldn't they have added exclamation points? Maybe put it in huge red letters, and followed it with "No lie!" or "Not your kind of thing!" How was I supposed to know they were telling the truth?

As we bounced along the potholed road, I turned longingly to the other opportunities in the volunteering brochure, ones that offered a six-week tour of duty in some Australian coastal paradise, petting baby koalas that were stricken—stricken!—with loneliness. I never could have gotten away with that. I needed this volunteering stint to sound as challenging as possible to my friends and family back home. In that, at least, I had succeeded: I would be taking care of orphans in one of the poorest countries in the world. It was the perfect way to begin my year-long adventure.

Nepal was merely the first stop in a one-year, solo round-the-world trip. I had spent the previous eight years working for the EastWest Institute, an international public policy think tank, out of their Prague office, and, later, the Brussels office. It had been my first and only job out of college, and I loved it. Eight years later, though, I was bored and desperately needed some kind of radical change.

Luckily, for the first time in my life, I had some real savings. I was raised in a thrifty Irish-American household; living in inexpensive Prague for six years allowed me to save much of my income. Moreover, I was single, had no mortgage or plans to get married or have kids any time in the next several decades. So I decided—rather quickly and rashly—to spend my entire net worth on a trip around the world. I couldn't get much more radical than that. I wasted no time in telling my friends about my plan, confident that it would impress them.

I soon discovered that such a trip, while sounding extremely cool, also sounded unrepentantly self-indulgent. Even my most party-hardened friends, on whom I had counted to support this adventure, hinted that this might not be the wisest life decision. They used words I hadn't heard from them before, like "retirement savings" and "your children's college fund" (I had to look that last one up—it turned out to be a real thing). More disapproval was bound to follow.

But there was something about volunteering in a Third World orphanage at the outset of my trip that would squash any potential criticism. Who would dare begrudge me my year of fun after doing something like that? If I caught any flak for my decision to travel, I would have a devastating comeback ready, like: "Well frankly Mom, I didn't peg you for somebody who hates orphans," and I would make sure to say the word *orphans* really loudly so everybody within earshot knew how selfless I was.

I looked out the dirty taxi window. Through the swarm of motorcycles and overcrowded buses, I saw a small park that had been converted into a base for military vehicles. Some children had gotten through the barbed wire fence and were playing soccer. The soldiers merely watched them, hands resting on their weapons. I took a last look at the photo of the lonely koalas, sighed, and put the brochure away. In two and a half months I would be far away from here, preferably on a conflict-free beach.

After a half hour of driving through choking traffic over a pockmarked slab of highway known as the Kathmandu Ring Road, then through a maze of smaller streets, I noticed the scene outside had changed. Moments earlier it had been a chaotic mass of poverty and pollution; this new neighborhood was almost peaceful in comparison. There were very few cars, save the occasional taxi. The shops had changed from selling household necessities like tools and plastic buckets and rice to selling more expensive, tourist-oriented things like carpets, prayer wheels, and mandalas, the beautifully detailed paintings of Buddhist and Hindu origin used by monks as a way of focusing their spiritual attention. Vendors leaned in the window as my taxi edged its way through them, offering carvings of elephants or wooden flutes or apples perched precariously on round trays. Bob Marley blared out of tinny speakers.

The biggest change was that the pedestrians were now overwhelmingly white. They fell into two broad categories: hippies in loose clothing, with beaded, kinky hair, or sunburned climbers in North Face trekking pants and boots heavy enough to kick through cinder blocks. There were no soldiers to be seen. We had arrived in the famed Thamel district.

There are really two Kathmandus: the district of Thamel and the rest. In the general madness of Nepal's capital, Thamel is a six-block embassy compound for those who want to drink beer and eat pizza and meat that they pretend is beef but is almost certainly yak or water buffalo. Backpackers and climbers set up camp here before touring the local temples or hiking into the mountains for a trek or white-water rafting. It is safe and comfortable, with the only real danger being that the street vendors may well drive you to lunacy. It was like the Nepal that you might find at Epcot Center at Disney World. I finally felt at ease. I would spend my first hours in the Thamel district, and by God I was going to enjoy it.

Orientation for the volunteer program began the next day, held at the office of the nonprofit organization known as CERV Nepal. I sat with the other dozen volunteers, mostly Americans and Canadians, and tried to focus on the presentation. The presenter was speaking in slowly enunciated detail about Nepalese culture and history. The presentation was frightfully boring. I found it impossible to keep my attention focused on the speaker, even when I concentrated and dug my nails into the palms of my hands. By the second hour, I would hear phrases like "Remember, this is Nepal, so whatever you do, try not to—" and then notice a leaf flittering past the window and get distracted again.

That changed about an hour and a half into the presentation when the entire group visibly perked up at the mention of the word *toilet*.

Travel to the developing world and you will quickly learn that toilets in the United States are the exception rather than the rule. I readily admit to my own cultural bias, but to me, toilets in America are the Bentleys of toilets, at the cutting edge of toilet technology and comfort, standing head and shoulders above what appeared to be the relatively primitive toilets of South Asia. Unfortunately, those toilets are often first discovered at terribly inopportune moments, sometimes at a full run after eating something less than sanitary, bursting through a restroom door to discover a contraption that you do not quite recognize. If there is ever a moment for panic, that is the moment.

So when I heard Deepak say "You may have noticed toilets here are different" my ears twitched. Deepak then took a deep breath and said, "Hari will now demonstrate how to use the squat toilet."

I wondered if I had heard that correctly.

Hari walked to the middle of the circle of suddenly alert volunteers. Jen, a girl from Toronto sitting a few feet away, summed up what everybody must have been thinking with a panicked whisper: "Is he gonna crap in the room?"

Hari reached for his belt. I heard somebody shout "Oh no!" but I couldn't take my eyes off the nightmare unfolding in front of me.

But wait—he was only miming undoing his belt. He then mimed lowering his trousers, mimed squatting down, mimed whistling for a few seconds, then mimed using an invisible water bucket to clean the areas that shall not be named. He stood up and gave a little "voilà!" flourish, then quickly left the circle and walked past Deepak out the door, his face bright red.

Clearly Deepak outranked Hari.

I wanted to applaud. It was the first truly practical thing we'd learned. For months afterward, I often thought of Hari at those precise moments, and I silently thanked him every time I watched a hapless tourist step into a bathroom and saw their brow furrow as the door closed behind them.

The in-office orientation lasted just one day, and then we piled into the backs of old 4x4s and drove south out of Kathmandu toward the village of Bistachhap, where we would continue our week-long orientation. We would be placed with families, one volunteer per home, to get acclimated to village life in Nepal.

Bistachhap is a tiny village on the floor of a valley surrounded by what I would have called mountains back in the United States, rising about two thousand feet above the village. With the Himalaya in the background, though, they looked like good-sized hills. These hills formed the southern wall of the Kathmandu Valley. The valley floor was covered with rice paddies and terraced mustard fields, blooming in bright yellow. Bistachhap itself was little more than a small collection of about twenty-five homes, mostly mud but some concrete, a dirt path connecting them like the wire on a set of Christmas lights. The houses sat on the north side of the floor of the valley, each one providing a view of the rice paddies on the other side of the path. I was assigned to a concrete yellow house, which looked pretty snazzy sitting next to the mud ones, though inside revealed a simple structure. I had my own bedroom, a simple affair with a single bed on a mattress of straw and a swatch of handmade carpet spread out on the floor. It was clear that some-body else in the house had vacated their room for me.

After dropping my backpack in the room, I went to formally introduce myself to my host mother, proud to be able to use one of the three expressions I had learned in Nepali: "Mero naam Conor ho." My host mother, in the middle of her workday, was caught off guard by my apparent comprehension of her language. She dropped her water bucket and raised her hands over her head in excitement and launched into a monologue about God knows what. I took a step back and held up my hands, saying "Whoa whoa whoa whoa!" for the entire time she spoke. In Nepali that must mean "Continue! I completely understand you, and I enjoy this conversation!" because damn if she didn't go on for several minutes, getting more and more excited, until her daughter, a little girl of perhaps six or seven, took my hand and dragged me away.

The daughter, whose name I would learn was Susmita, walked me out to the front porch and plopped down on a straw mat, inviting me to do the same. She pointed to the mat and said a word in Nepali, waiting for me to repeat it. I did so. Then she repeated this with the house, the door, the garden, and anything else she could think of. I repeated each word and let her correct me until I had nailed it. Her face lit up. She was going to teach me Nepali, and I was going to learn. She disappeared, returning a few moments later with her homework, wherein she drew a single character in Sanskrit over and over, as one might practice a capital *B*, pointing to each one for my benefit until her mother fetched her to help with dinner preparation.

Unsure of what to do, as I could see no other volunteers anywhere, I took a walk through the village. I called out "Namaste!" to every villager I passed, and usually received a "Namaste" in return, though they seemed oddly reluctant.

This turned out to be, not surprisingly, my own fault. I had thought "Namaste" was like "Hey there!" or "What's up?" but I would later learn that it was a far more formal greeting than this. Yoga enthusiasts will recognize it and may even know the translation, which is along the lines of "I salute the God within you." Heavy stuff. Yet I yelled it to everybody, the same way you might yell "Dude!" or "My man!" to your buddies. I accompanied it with a big friendly wave. I said it to children. I said it to people I'd just seen four minutes earlier. I saw a stray dog and bent down to give him a scratch behind the ears and saluted the God within him. I saluted the God within a mother carrying a baby, then saluted the God within the baby.

Down the path, I saw my host mother outside looking around for me. She recognized me from a distance and waved me in. I was late for dinner. I followed her into what I supposed was the kitchen. There was a mud floor, an open fire in the corner, and two boys of perhaps nine years old sitting Indian style on the floor next to Susmita, who sat next to their father. The boys patted the ground next to them happily, pleased that I was joining them. The mother, meanwhile, had squatted next to the large pot. She picked up a metal plate and dumped what looked like several pounds of rice onto it for the family, and placed it in front of me. I was about to take some and pass it along, when I saw her preparing an even bigger mountain of rice and placing it in front of the father.

After placing similar plates in front of her children, she took a ladle out of the other pot and poured steaming hot lentil soup over the rice on our plates: *daal bhat,* literally, "lentils with rice." Daal bhat is eaten by about 90 percent of Nepalese people, twice a day. The mother added some curried vegetables to my plate, at the same time shooing away a stray chicken.

When everyone was served, the mother put her hand to her mouth, indicating that I should eat. I nodded in thanks, then looked around for some kind of utensil. There was no utensil. I watched the rest of the family stick their hands into the hot goo, mash it up, and begin shoveling it into their mouths.

After maybe half a minute watching my host family eat, my jaw hanging slack near my collarbone, I noticed that they had stopped eating, one by one, and were staring at me, wondering why I wasn't eating. I came to my senses. I had been with my host family for all of ten minutes and was on the verge of causing some irrevocable offense. I forced a smile, took a chunk of rice and daal and a smidge of some kind of pickled vegetable, and placed it gently into my mouth.

It was spicy. Spicy in the way that your eyes instantly flood with tears and your sinuses feel like the last flight of the *Hindenburg,* as if somebody inside my skull had ordered a full evacuation. The children started giggling. Even the chicken stopped pecking to watch what would happen next.

What happened next was that I opened my mouth to breathe, but the back draft only fanned the flames in my throat. I grasped for the tin cup of water next to me, oblivious to the shouts of the father, mother, and three children, and realized, too late, that my hand was burning because the water in the tin cup was still boiling.

I opened my mouth and let out a kind of "Mwaaaaaaa" sound, very loudly, and used my hands, so recently used as eating utensils, to fan myself, spraying a light mist of rice and lentils into my face and hair. I opened my eyes to see the family trying to decide if I needed assistance, and if so, what that assistance might look like.

You can't go through that experience with a family and not become closer. The older of the two boys, whose name I learned was Govardhan, had a Nepali-English phrasebook with him, and we had the most basic of conversations, the one where you say Nepal is beautiful, then, because this is a phrase that I apparently got right, they began asking if the house was beautiful, if the mountains were beautiful, if the chicken was beautiful, if their mother's hair was beautiful, and so on until everybody had finished their pile of rice.

I had eaten as fast as I could through all this; my stomach felt like I'd swallowed a bag of sand. I looked down to see that I had made it through just over a third of my food. I pointed at the rice and told the mother that the rice was truly beautiful, but that my stomach (I pointed at my belly button) was not beautiful. She laughed and with a wave of her hand excused me. I waved a good night "Namaste!" and headed up to my room.

I walked outside later to brush my teeth from the water bucket, as there was no running water. I was careful not to swallow any. I brushed slowly under the thick coat of stars. The quiet was absolute. The neighbors' homes were lit by candles, with an occasional lightbulb shining in the windows of the wealthier houses. I could just make out another volunteer two houses down, also brushing his teeth using an old water bucket, also staring straight up at the stars, and maybe also wondering if he was really here, if he was really standing on the opposite side of the planet from his home. This was one of those moments I wanted to capture, to hold on to and to stare into like a snow globe. This world was already completely different from anything I had ever experienced—and this was just day one.

The immersion week was useful in getting us at least partially accustomed to this strange new culture. The most valuable part of it was practicing Nepali with Susmita. She made sounds slowly, pointing at pictures, and I repeated them. When I tried to show off my knowledge of animal names for the rest of the family on my final night in Bistachhap, they frowned and consulted each other, trying to work out what I was saying.

Finally I took Govardhan out behind the house, next to the outhouse, and pointed at the goat. I said my word, which sounded like "Faalllaaaagh." He shook his head: "Hoina, hoina," he said, which I knew meant "no." He pointed at the goat. "Kasi," he said.

Kasi? That sounded nothing like *faalllaaaagh*. Had I gotten the wrong animal?

"Who say?" Govardhan asked in English. It was the first English he had spoken.

I told him Susmita, his little sister, had told me. His eyes popped wide, and he literally doubled over laughing and ran in to tell his family. I discovered later that Susmita, my lovely little teacher, was deaf.

◇

HARI, OF TOILET-MIMING FAME, picked me up from Bistachhap in the jeep and threw my backpack in the back. He pointed across the valley.

"That is Godawari," he said, pronouncing it go-DOW-ry. "That is where you will be volunteer. I will see you very often there—I work there also. I am part-time house manager for the orphanage where you go."

I had seen the house from a distance during a trek up one of the large hills, but I knew little about it. The orphanage was called the Little Princes Children's Home, named after the French novella by Antoine de Saint-Exupéry, *Le Petit Prince*. It had been started by a French woman in her late twenties.

I nodded and made a vague comment about how excited I was to get started. But my mind was elsewhere. It would be two weeks before I would actually show up for orphan duty; before that, I would be fulfilling my dream of trekking to Everest Base Camp. I had been moved by Jon Krakauer's harrowing account of climbing Mt. Everest in a storm in 1996, on a day when eight climbers perished. The summit of the world's tallest mountain is just shy of thirty thousand feet—the cruising altitude of a Boeing 747. I would never in my life have the strength to climb the mountain, but I was dying to see it. When I learned that Everest was in Nepal (a country that I had previously confused with Tibet), I decided it was the perfect country to volunteer in—I could combine my volunteering experience with a trek to Base Camp. I was in good physical condition, so it wasn't as if I was going to keel over from altitude sickness. I couldn't wait to get started.

◇

WHEN I WASN'T LYING on the side of the trail, winded and dry-heaving from altitude sickness, I managed to take a lot of photos. There was no shortage of things to photograph: the trek up to Base Camp was spectacular. Every step is a step skyward, through simple Buddhist villages that seem to be glued to the sides of impossibly tall mountains. The Sherpa people are native to that region, having come over the mountains from Tibet hundreds of years earlier. They are traditionally Buddhist. In every village you could see carved oversized Sanskrit prayers chiseled into boulders and blackened, like tattoos.

Trekkers were expected to walk to the left of these Mani Stones, clockwise, to respect the faith of the local community.

With the extraordinary Himalayas taking up most of the sky, it was difficult to keep an eye on the trail. Yet keeping an eye on the trail was essential to survival. Enormous, shaggy yaks, laden with hundreds of pounds of climbing gear, would come barreling down the trail, seeming not to notice humans at all. The first few I saw were a novelty, but after that we loathed them as dangerous pains in the ass.

But there were bigger dangers. In the village of Lukla, the start and end point of the Everest Base Camp trek, a few dozen soldiers manned an outpost. Everest National Park (known in Nepal as Sagarmatha National Park) was one of the few regions left in Nepal over which the royal government claimed control, but even that was under constant threat by Maoist rebels who controlled the surrounding area. As I waited for a small plane to take me back to Kathmandu, sirens blared and soldiers ran past the door of the tea shop, automatic weapons in hand. There was no fighting, and I got the impression that it may have all been a drill. But when I got back to Kathmandu, I decided I had seen just about enough of the rest of this country. The Kathmandu Valley was safe from rebel attack; I wouldn't leave again for the duration of my three-month stay in Nepal.

◇

I HAD ONE FULL day to relax in the Thamel district of Kathmandu. But there was no more putting it off. I reported for duty the next day at the CERV office.

"We're ready to go—are you excited?" Hari asked.

"I sure am!" I practically shouted, because I believed that to be the only answer I could give without sounding like I was having second thoughts about this whole orphanage thing.

We drove to the village of Godawari. It was only six miles south of Kathmandu, but it felt like a different world. Inside Kathmandu's Ring Road, people, buildings, buses, and soldiers were all crammed into a small space.

There was almost nothing peaceful about the city. But outside the Ring Road, the world opened up. Suddenly there were fields everywhere. The roads disappeared, save for the single road that led south to Godawari, which ended at the base of the hills that surround the Kathmandu Valley. The air was cleaner, people walked slower, and I started to see many homes made of hardened mud.

When the paved road ended, we turned onto a small dirt road and took it a short distance. Hari stopped in front of a brick wall. There was a single blue metal gate leading into the compound. He lifted my backpack out of the back, and held it while I put it on, strapping the waist buckle. With a hearty handshake, he bade me farewell, wished me luck, and climbed back into the jeep. He backed out the way we had come in.

I watched Hari drive away, then turned back to the blue metal gate that led into the Little Princes Children's Home.

I hadn't realized until that moment how much I did not want to walk through that gate. What I wanted was to *tell* people I had volunteered in an orphanage. Now that I was actually here, the whole idea of my volunteering in this country seemed ludicrous. This had not been lost on my friends back home, a number of whom had gently suggested that caring for orphans might not be exactly what God had in mind for me. They were right, of course. I stood there and tried to come up with even a single skill that I possessed that would be applicable to working with kids, other than the ability to pick up objects from the floor. I couldn't recall ever spending time around kids, let alone looking after them.

I took a deep breath and pushed open the gate, wondering what I was supposed to do once I was inside.

As it turns out, wondering what you're supposed to do in an orphanage is like wondering what you're supposed to do at the running of the bulls in Spain—you work it out pretty quickly. I carefully closed the gate behind me, turned, and stared for the first time at a sea of wide-eyed Nepali children staring right back at me. A moment passed as we stared at one another, then I opened my mouth to introduce myself.

Before I could utter a word I was set upon—charged at, leaped on, over-run—by a herd of laughing kids, like bulls in Pamplona.

◇

THE LITTLE PRINCES CHILDREN'S Home was a well-constructed building by Nepalese standards: it was concrete, had several rooms, an indoor toilet (huzzah!), running water—though not potable—and electricity. The house was surrounded by a six-foot-high brick wall that enclosed a small garden, maybe fifty feet long by thirty feet wide. Inside the walls, half the garden was used for planting vegetables and the other half was, at least in the dry season, a hard dirt patch where the children played marbles and other games that I would come to refer to as "Rubber Band Ball Hacky Sack" and "I Kick You."

All games ceased immediately when I stepped through the gate. Soon I was lugging not only my backpack but also several small people hanging off me. Any chance of making a graceful first impression evaporated as I took slow, heavy steps toward the house. One especially small boy of about four years old hung from my neck so that his face was about three inches from my face and kept yelling "Namaste, Brother!" over and over, eyes squeezed shut to generate more decibels. In the background I saw two volunteers standing on the porch, chuckling happily as I struggled toward them.

"Hello!" cried the older one, a French woman in her late twenties who I knew to be Sandra, the founder of Little Princes. "Welcome! That boy hanging on your face is Raju."

"He's calling me 'brother.'"

"It is Nepalese custom to call men 'brother' and women 'sister.' Didn't they teach you that at the orientation?"

I had no idea if they had or not. "I should have put down my backpack before coming in," I called back, panting. "I don't know if I can make it to the house."

"Yes, they are really getting big, these children," she said thoughtfully, which was less helpful than "Children, get off the nice man." One boy was hanging by my wrist, calling up to me, "Brother, you can swing your arms, maybe?"

I collapsed onto the concrete porch with the children, which initiated a pileup. I could see only glimmers of light through various arms and legs. It was like being in a mining accident.

"Are they always this excited?" I asked when I had managed to squirm free.

"Yes, always," said Sandra. "Come inside, we're about to have daal bhat."

I went upstairs to put my stuff down in the volunteers' room, trailed by several children. We were five volunteers in total. Jenny was an American girl, a college student, who had arrived a month earlier. Chris, a German volunteer, would arrive a week later. Farid was a young French guy, thin build and my height, twenty-one years old, with long black dreadlocks. I first assumed Farid was shy, since he was not speaking much to the others, but soon realized that he was only shy about his English.

I was the last to arrive for daal bhat. I entered the dining area, a stone-floored room with two windows and no furniture save a few low bamboo stools reserved for the volunteers. The children sat on the floor with their backs against the wall, Indian style. They were arranged from youngest to oldest, right to left against three walls of the room. As they waited patiently for their food to be served, I got my first good look at them.

I counted eighteen children in total, sixteen boys and two girls. Each child seemed to be wearing every stitch of clothing he or she owned, including woolen hats. I had not worn a hat to dinner and was already regretting it. The house had no indoor heating and I could practically see my breath. Most of their jackets and sweaters had French logos on them, as the clothes were mostly donations from France. I studied their faces. The girls were easy to identify, as there were only two of them, but the boys would be more difficult to distinguish. A few really stood out—the six-year-old boy with the missing front teeth, the boy with the Tibetan facial features, the bright smile of another older boy, the diminutive size of the two youngest boys in the house. But otherwise, the only identifying features to my untrained eye would be their clothes.

Before daal bhat was served, Sandra asked the children to stand and introduce themselves, beginning with the youngest boy, Raju. He was far more shy
now than when he had been clinging to my face. The other boys whispered
loud encouragements to him to get up, and his tiny neighbor, Nuraj, dug an
elbow into his ribs. Finally he popped up, clapped his hands together as if in
prayer, the traditional greeting in Nepal, said "Namaste-my-name-is-Raju"
and collapsed back into a seated position flashing a proud grin to the others.
The rest of the kids followed suit, until it had come full circle back to me.

I stood up and imitated what they had done and sat back down. They
erupted in chatter.

"I do not think they understood your name," Sandra whispered to me.

"Oh, sorry—it's Conor," I said, speaking slowly. I could hear a volley of
versions of my name lobbed back and forth across the room as the children
corrected one another.

"Kundar?"

"*Hoina*! Krondor *ho*! Yes, Brother? Your name Krondor, yes?"

"No, no, it's *Conor*," I clarified, louder this time.

"Krondor!" they shouted in unison.

"Conor!" I repeated, shouting it.

"Krondor!"

One of the older boys spoke up helpfully: "Yes, Brother, you are saying
Krondor!"

Trust me—I wasn't saying "Krondor." The children were staring ear-
nestly at my lips and trying to repeat it exactly.

"No, boys—everybody—it's *Conor*!" This time I shouted it with a growl,
hoping to change the intonation to a least get them off Krondor, which made
me sound like a Vulcan.

There was a surprised pause. Then the children went nuts. "*Conor*!!"
they growled, imitating the comical bicep flex I had performed (instinctively,
I'm sorry to say) when I shouted my name.

"Exactly!" I said, pleased with myself.

Sandra looked around and nodded in approval. "I think you will get along with these children very well," she predicted. "Okay, children, you may begin," she said, and the children attacked their food as if they hadn't eaten in days. They spent the rest of dinner with mouths full of rice and lentils, looking at each other and growling "*Conor*!!!" flashing their muscles like tiny professional wrestlers.

There was no way to keep up the blistering pace set by the kids when they ate. They had literally licked their plates clean when I was maybe half finished. I would have to concentrate in the future. No talking, no thinking, just eating. There was far too much food on my plate, albeit mostly rice. The worst part about it was that I couldn't give the rest of mine away, since once you touched your food with your hands it was considered *juto,* or unclean, to others. The very idea of throwing away food here was unthinkable, especially with eighteen children watching you, waiting for you to finish. I force-fed myself every last grain as fast as I could, guiltily replaying scenes from my life of dumping half-full plates of food into the trash.

When I had finished, Sandra made a few announcements in English. The children understood English quite well after spending time with volunteers, and the little ones who didn't understand as well had it translated by the older children sitting near them.

The big announcement of that particular evening was the introduction of three new garbage cans that had been placed out front, one marked "Plastic and Glass," one "Paper," and one "Other." Sandra explained their fairly straightforward functions. She was rewarded with eighteen blank stares. Trash in Nepal, like all Third World countries, is a constant problem. Littering is the norm, and environmental protection falls very low on the government's priority list, well below the challenges of keeping the citizens alive with food and basic health care. Farid took a stab at explaining the concept of protecting Mother Earth, but the children still struggled to understand why anybody would categorize garbage.

"Maybe we should demonstrate it?" I suggested.

Sandra smiled. "That is a great idea. Go ahead, Conor."

This was a big moment. I had never interacted with children before in this way; I had no nieces, no nephews, no close friends with children, no baby cousins. I steeled myself for this interaction. Fact: I knew I could talk to people. Fact: Children were little people. Little, scary people. I took solace in the fact that if this demonstration went horribly wrong, I could probably outrun them.

"Okay, kids!" I declared, psyching myself up. I rubbed my hands together to let them know that fun was on the way. "Time for a demonstration!"

I picked up a piece of paper leaning against my stool and crumpled it up. I walked over to Hriteek, one of the five-year-old boys, and handed it to him.

"Okay, Hriteek, now I want you to take this and throw it in the proper garbage can!" I spoke loudly, theatrically.

Hriteek took the paper in his little hand and held it for a few seconds, looking at the three green bins lined up with their labels visible. Then he started to cry. I hadn't expected that. But I knew that kids sometimes cried—I had seen it on TV. This was no time to quit.

"C'mon, buddy," I urged him. "It's not tough—throw the trash in the right bin," I said, nodding toward the "Paper" bin.

No luck. Finally I took it from him, giving him an understanding pat on the shoulder, and walked over to throw it in the proper bin.

"Brother!" called out Anish, one of the older kids sitting opposite us. "Brother—wait, no throw, he make for you! Picture!"

I uncrumpled the paper to discover a crude but colorful picture of a large pointy mountain and a man—me, judging by the white crayon he used for skin tone—holding hands with a cow. On the bottom it was signed in large red letters: HRITEEK. *Uh-oh.*

"Hriteek! Yes! Great picture! Not trash, Hriteek! Not trash!" I said quickly. He cried louder.

Sandra leaned over to me. "It's no problem, Conor," she said, and took Hriteek's hand. "Hriteek, you do not need to cry. Conor Brother is still learning. He doesn't understand much yet. You will have to teach him." This brought a laugh from the children, and Hriteek, despite himself, started giggling.

"Sorry, Hriteek!" I said over Sandra's shoulder. "My bad, Hriteek! Your picture was very beautiful, I'm keeping it!" I smoothed it out against my chest as Hriteek eyed me suspiciously.

"Okay, everybody," Sandra said, clapping her hands. "Bedtime!"

The children leaped up, brought their plates to the kitchen, cleaned up, and marched up to bed. Anish, the eight-year-old who had informed me of my traumatic error, lingered in the kitchen to help wash the pots at the outdoor tap. By the time he finished helping clean up, the rest of the children had already gone up to their rooms. He lifted his arms to me to be carried upstairs. "We are very happy you are here, Conor Brother!" he said happily.

"I am very happy to be here, too," I replied, stretching the truth to its breaking point. I was relieved, at least, to have the first day over with. I lifted Anish and carried him up the stairs.

That night, huddled in my sleeping bag wearing three layers of clothing plus a hat, I slept more soundly than I had in a long time. I was more exhausted than I'd been after trekking to the foot of Everest, and I'd only spent two hours with the children.

◇

I WOKE THE NEXT day to the general mayhem of children sprinting through the house, half-crazed with happiness. I dove deeper into my sleeping bag and wondered what in human biology caused children around the world to take such pleasure in running as fast as they could moments after they had woken up. Unable to fall back to sleep, I nosed just far enough out of my bag to peek through the thin curtains. The sun had not yet risen above the tall hills behind the orphanage. The only source of heat in the village was direct sunlight, so I waited. At exactly 7:38 A.M. the sun flashed into the window. I got up and wandered downstairs.

Farid was sipping milk tea outside in the sun, his breath steaming in the morning chill. As I sat down next to him, a woman entered the gate, straining under the weight of an enormous pot, filled to the brim with what looked to be milk.

"Namaste, *didi*!" he called to her, lifting his tea in greeting. "She is our neighbor," he explained. He had a thick French accent that took me a minute to get used to. "She brings milk every day from her cow for the children to put in their tea."

"What did you call her? Dee-dee?"

"*Didi*. It means—do you speak French?"

"A little. Not very well I'm afraid," I apologized.

"It is okay—I must improve my English, I know it is very bad," he said. "So I saying? Ah yes—*didi*. It means 'older sister,' it is a polite way to greet a woman, as we might say *madame* or *mademoiselle*. The children call you 'brother,' yes?"

"Yeah."

"In Nepali, they call older men *dai*—it means 'older brother,' but it is a sign of respect, like *didi*. We taught them the English word *brother,* so they use that." He took a sip of his tea. "You know, it is quite useful, saying *brother*. It means you do not have to remember everybody's name."

That *was* useful, and prophetic. One of the boys came outside at that moment and plopped himself down on my lap.

"You remember my name, Brother?" he asked with a grin.

"Of course he remembers your name, Nishal!" Farid said. "Go get ready—we're going to the temple soon for washing."

I liked Farid immediately.

Going to the temple was, I learned, a Saturday tradition. Weekends in Nepal were one day only and the children savored them. Each Saturday they would begin the morning by cleaning the house together. The bigger boys would drag the carpets outside and the little boys would sweep with brooms made of thin branches tied together with twine. Then another group would finish by mopping the floor, which made the concrete at least wet if not exactly clean. Sandra told me that it was the act of the chores themselves that was valuable. If these children had been with their families, they would be tending to their homes and fields many hours per day.

With the house marginally less dirty, we walked to a nearby Hindu temple, a fifteen-minute stroll through the royal botanical gardens that happened to be just down the path from the orphanage, past the mud homes that made up the village of Godawari.

The temple was housed in a walled courtyard a little larger than a basketball court. Taking up half of that space was a shallow pool about three feet deep, constantly refilled by five spouts carved into the stone wall. Several villagers were already there, all men, leaning over to wash themselves under the spouts. (Washing at public taps, naked except for underwear, was the most common way of bathing. In Bistachhap, I had washed myself wearing only a pair of shorts at the single public tap in full view of the village, while local women waited patiently with a basket of laundry, giggling to one another and pointing at my pale skin.) Once finished, the men would dry off and go through a small gate in the back of the courtyard, where there was a grotto that housed the Hindu shrine. They would reemerge with a red tikka—rice with sticky red dye—on their forehead, then ring a large bell before leaving the temple.

The children obviously loved this place. They stripped down to their underwear, except for the two girls, Yangani and Priya, who watched from the sidelines. The boys dove in, splashing around and trying to dunk one another. One by one they would pop out and run to Farid, who would dole out a dollop of liquid soap to the older boys. The younger ones would wait patiently while Farid scrubbed them down himself. When they had completed that stage successfully, they ran to me, the Keeper of the Shampoo. Raju was the first to reach me. I squeezed a dose of shampoo the size of a quarter into his palm. His eyes grew wide at the apparently enormous pool of shampoo in his hand. I realized my mistake and started to take some back, but he sprinted back to the pool, yelling to his little friend Nuraj.

Farid noticed. "I think maybe a little less, Conor," he said, thumb and index finger indicating a tiny amount. "I learned this lesson my first time also. You will see."

Raju had rubbed the shampoo into such a thick lather that he looked like he was wearing a white afro wig. The others went bananas when they saw this, scrambling out of the pool and begging me for shampoo.

"I see what you mean," I called over to Farid.

Farid shook his head, marveling at Raju. "They are very resourceful, these children," he called back. "You will find they do very much with very little."

After twenty minutes or so, the children began to exit the pool. One of the boys—maybe seven years old, with what I thought of as Tibetan facial features—approached me.

"Brother, where you put my towel?" he said, putting his hand on my knee and twisting his torso to scan the courtyard.

To identify the children, I had memorized the outfits of a few of them. They wore the exact same thing every day, as they only had two sets of clothes each. But now, this little brown body in front of me, clad only in his underwear, looked exactly like the other seventeen children.

"Uh . . . are you sure I had your towel, Brother?" I said slowly, buying time, hoping he might accidentally yelp out his own name. The word *brother* was going to save my life here.

The boy spun back to me and his hands went to his head. "Brother, you had one minute before! You say you take before I swim!"

Time for a stab in the dark. "Oh . . . right! Sorry, Nishal, I forgot, I put your towel over—"

"Nishal?! Ahhhh! I no Nishal, Brother!"

"I never said you were, Brother!"

"You say 'Nishal'!"

"No, no, I said 'towel.'" Didn't you hear me say 'towel'?" This blew his mind.

Farid walked up just at that moment. "Come on, Krish—we'll find your towel," he said, turning him around by his shoulders and leading him away. He turned back and gave me an empathetic little shake of the head, not to worry.

I sat down near the edge of the pool, trying to blend into the stone and praying no other children would come up to me. I felt a tap on my shoulder. Anish was standing there. I recognized Anish because his skin was slightly lighter than the others, he was quite tall for an eight-year-old, and he had a distinctively round face with a smile that curved sharply up at the edges, almost cartoonish.

"Brother, you no remember names," he said. It was an observation rather than a question.

"Yes I do!" My protest was both instinctive and absurd, like a schoolboy in trouble.

Anish sat down next to me, facing the shallow pool where the boys were splashing around. He pointed at one of the boys.

"That is Hriteek. You know because he is always climbing," he said. Sure enough, Hriteek, whose picture I had crumpled up the day before, was trying to climb the entrance gate. Anish pointed at another boy. "That is Nishal, looking like he will cry right now. With the towel is Raju, he is most small boy here. That is Santosh, the tall boy. . . ."

This lesson continued for the next ten minutes, Anish slowly drying on the flagstones in the hot sun, me beside him in the shade so I wouldn't burn. When he had named all the boys and the two girls twice, he quizzed me on a few of them, all of whom I got wrong except for when he asked, slightly exasperated, if I knew *his* name.

"Yes! Anish!" I said proudly.

He smiled. "Okay, Brother. You pass," he said, and went to get his clothes.

Soon everybody was out of the pool. Then it was laundry time for all the clothes that needed washing. The children had stuffed their clothes that needed washing in small plastic bags that they had found discarded around the village. When the plastic bags tore, the children would find tape and repair them. I thought of my local grocery store double-bagging a can of soda and felt another stab of guilt over my wastefulness.

The children carried their clothes across the path to where the water flowed out of the pool and down a two-foot-wide shallow canal to a stream. Working together, they used soap to scrub their pants and shirts. The youngest boys, Raju and Nuraj, didn't have the arm strength to tackle such a project, so they concentrated on their little socks, laying them on the concrete and scraping them with a small chunk of soap. The orphanage had a woman who washed the boys' clothes for them (a washing *didi*), but this was another way of teaching the children to take responsibility for themselves, of keeping them in as normal a life as possible considering they had been robbed of their families.

Back at the orphanage, the children hung their clothes to dry, then resumed their yelling and bouncing off each other. They had boundless energy. My own energy level was not nearly so high. But as luck would have it, the most popular game at Little Princes was a board game called carrom— or carrom board, as the children called it. The children (indeed, all of Nepal) were obsessed with this game. It is played on a square board with holes in the four corners. The object of the game is to flick a blue disc across the board at the black-and-white discs in an attempt to knock the discs into the holes. It's like a cross between billiards and shuffleboard.

Every child in the house not only wanted to play this game, but they wanted to play it against me. I was first taught the rules by Santosh, who at nine years old was one of the older boys in the house.

"Look, Brother, you hit with your finger, yes, like this. See, I score, so is my turn again. And I hit again . . . and I score again, so my turn again And I score again, so my turn—"

"I get it, Santosh," I interrupted.

"You try now, Brother!"

I flicked one of the discs, which ricocheted off the board. Santosh watched it fly past him and slide under the couch. Then he looked back at the board.

"Okay, Brother, you miss, so my turn again. . . . And I score, so my turn again."

He beat me in six minutes flat; I had put up about as much fight as a loaf of bread. The children were eager to play me, not to see if they could win— they all won—but to time one another to see how quickly they could shut me out. The fact that I was trying as hard as I could to just score a single point was a severe blow to my ego. Nuraj was hardly even paying attention, and that little four-year-old ran the board on me.

I came closest to beating Raju. After initially refusing to play him a third time, citing a broken hand—it was the first excuse that came to mind—I finally played him only after he agreed to let me have the first fifteen shots in a row. I scored twice before Raju's turn. He promptly scored continuously until all his discs had disappeared down the holes. The children gathered around for that match, jabbering away in Nepali. Anish leaned over to me.

"Brother," Anish said in a loud, hoarse whisper that was louder than his normal speaking voice. "Everybody saying they never have seen Raju win this game before, Brother."

"Thanks for that translation, Anish—that's very helpful."

"You are welcome, Conor Brother," he whisper-yelled.

This loss was still fresh in my mind when Raju and Nuraj asked me to play Farmyard Snap. I felt like this was my chance to redeem myself. I smiled to myself when they challenged me, and told Raju to bring it on.

"What means 'bring it on,' Brother?"

"It means we can play."

"Brother, remember I give you many many hits and I win you in carrom board, Brother? Very funny, yes, Brother?"

"Just get the cards, Raju."

Farmyard Snap, as you may recognize from the name, is the same game as Patience, Memory, or Concentration. You turn the cards facedown, mix them up, and try to match the pairs. In this case, the pictures on the other side were of barnyard animals. It was a well-worn deck of cards, clearly used by other volunteers to help the children learn the English words for the various animals. English was an excellent skill for them to learn, and furthering the education of the children was one of the main reasons for being here. And as we laid out the cards, I tried to remind myself of that. Truly I did. But all I could think about was how badly I was going to crush these kids in Farmyard Snap.

I won the first game handily. To my slight disappointment, they both just laughed every time I uncovered a match, clapping for me as if they were letting me win. They even cheered for me when I won; Nuraj went out to tell some of the other boys like a proud father. When he returned I challenged them to a rematch to show my victory was no fluke.

"What means 'rematch,' Brother?"

"We play again—if you don't mind me winning."

"Yayyyyy!" they cried together.

Games two, three, and four didn't go as planned.

Raju and Nuraj held a quick tête-à-tête following their loss in game one and decided they would play as a single team. I consented. Their game-time chatter sounded innocuous enough. It was unclear if they were even talking about the game at all, as I noted during one particularly animated debate between them, which ended when Nuraj put his entire fist in his mouth and Raju sullenly conceded some point. Still, I couldn't trust them, and I was soon proven right. The cards were bent from extensive use, and they were able to push their little faces against the floor to see what was on the other side. Since they never actually touched the cards, I wasn't able to penalize them, nor could I get my huge head low enough to see the other side myself—though I did try, which was a source of much amusement for them. They also pointed out to each other where the other donkey was, or where they remembered seeing the ducks. When it was my turn, they tried to distract me by loudly singing Nepali songs or climbing on my back and tugging on my hair. There was nothing in the Farmyard Snap rules against this per se, but it put me at a disadvantage that I was unable to overcome.

"Remash! Remash!" they chanted after the sixth game.

"I can't— remember my broken hand?" I reminded them.

"Brother, I no think hand broken," Nuraj said, poking at my hand.

"Let's go find the other boys outside," I suggested.

"Yayyyyy!"

The rest of the boys were playing soccer next to a nearby wheat field, and I sent the two little cheaters off to join them. Then I sneaked back to my bedroom and lay down, hoping for an early-afternoon rest. I leaned over to see my travel clock. It was only 10:30 A.M. I groaned and collapsed back on the bed.

◇

I HAD FIRST ARRIVED at Little Princes when the children had a few days off from school. They returned to school only on Wednesday, four days later. That Wednesday will forever rank as one of the most peaceful days in my entire life. I took a walk through the village for the first time, along the single-track paths that led through the rice paddies and mustard fields, past the women working the fields, the men weaving baskets out of dried grass on their mud-hardened porches, the mothers carrying babies in slings as they washed their clothes at the public water tap. Everywhere I walked, people would stop what they were doing and watch me pass by. There was always time to stop what you were doing in Nepal—nobody punched a clock or tried to impress anybody else by working through lunch. They woke up, they worked until they had to prepare the fire to cook rice for dinner, then everybody came inside and ate before going to sleep. You wouldn't find a soul outside after dark.

A week after I arrived, I walked into the children's bedroom, expecting to help them get ready for school. Because they wore identical blue and gray school uniforms, the young ones needed some extra help in sorting out which pants belonged to whom. They also had trouble with their buttons and clipping on their little ties. The room was empty, so I went straight to the small cardboard box that said RAJU on the side of it to get a head start looking for his gray socks. The last two school days he had been unable to locate the pair; he was forced to wear one red sock and one gray sock, an event traumatic enough to leave him in tears. His sister, Priya, all of two years older than him but always dressed before anybody else, was by his side in an instant, holding his head as his tears stained her button-down shirt.

"It is okay, Brother, I talk to him," she said, gently waving me away.

I had found one gray sock when a boy came flying down the stairs from the rooftop terrace and raced past the door. There was a screech of bare feet against the hard floor, and Anish poked his head into the room.

"What you look for, Brother?" he asked, puzzled.

"Raju's socks . . . where is everybody?"

"No school today, Brother!" said Anish. "Today is *bandha*!"

"What's a bandha?"

"No school, Brother! Come, we play on the roof! Come!" he took my hand and leaned his body weight toward the stairs for leverage.

I learned from Farid that a bandha was a Maoist-instigated strike. The Maoist rebels had been locked in a civil war against the monarchy in their bid to establish a People's Republic of Nepal, to be founded on Communist principles. Bandhas were a common tactic used by the rebels, intended to bring the entire country to a standstill. They were extremely effective. When the Maoists called a bandha, everything was forced to close: schools, shops, and most offices. No buses, taxis, or cars were allowed on the street, so the only way around was on foot or bicycle. Strikes could go on for days, and came with virtually no warning.

Bandhas were known to turn violent if the prohibition was not respected. Buses and cars were overturned and set ablaze in the middle of the streets during the strikes. A few taxis did still operate, despite the risk. In a country as impoverished as Nepal, the extra money they could make during a bandha was too valuable to pass up. These daredevils covered their license plates with paper so as not to be identified and drove as fast as possible, stopping only to pick up and drop off passengers. Those who were caught were often physically assaulted or had their cars smashed by Maoist sympathizers. Our village, Godawari, was thirty minutes from the Ring Road of Kathmandu; thankfully, we saw very little of that violence.

The frequent bandhas led to shortages of food and kerosene. The food shortages were difficult for us, as prices for vegetables could quickly double during these times. For families barely surviving, though, it was far worse. Finding kerosene was impossible at any price, so our twenty-two-year-old cooking *didi,* Bagwati, who lived in the house with us and helped care for the children, would cook the morning and evening daal bhat on an open fire in the garden, helped by the children. Cooking rice and lentils for more than twenty people on an open fire takes several hours.

For the children at Little Princes, the biggest effect of the bandhas was that school was closed. School closings were not the euphoric celebrations they were in America, where children pray for crippling snowstorms. Children in Nepal, while they would certainly rather be playing, actually enjoyed school. I attributed that to the fact that going to school was not the inevitable daily event that it was back in the States.

Even when there was no bandha, classes were frequently canceled at the public schools like the one the children attended. The school looked, from the outside, like an abandoned single-floor building, a long mud hut painted white on the outside with a tin roof and a broken slide outside. Teachers were paid almost nothing by the government, and thus had little incentive to even come to school. Chris, the German volunteer, worked in the public school two days a week, and was often asked to stand in for teachers who didn't show up. If there were no volunteers and the teacher for the five-year-olds' class was absent, one of the seven-year-olds was sent in to teach.

With frequent school closings, we had a responsibility to keep up the children's education at the orphanage. This was probably a good thing. I saw one of Anish's English homework assignments, where he had answered questions about pictures in a book, and the teacher had marked each question correct with a green checkmark, including one picture that showed a man realizing he had forgotten his umbrella at home. Anish's sentence read: "Man housed umbrella." I was pretty sure that was wrong.

Chris, Jenny, Sandra, Farid, and I split the children into groups by age, and we each took a room. The children would rotate through our rooms and we would give them a thirty-minute class in a particular subject. Sandra would teach them basic French, Chris and Jenny would help them with reading, and Farid was going to help them not only with their writing skills but with their computer skills as well, using the ancient laptop in the office, one with a huge tracking ball that you rolled around to move the cursor.

I had no idea what to teach them. But everybody else had chosen something and they were looking at me expectantly, and I heard myself blurting out that I would teach them science. Immediately after I said it, I regretted it. Science! My God, if there is something I know less about than science, I wouldn't be able to name it.

Thankfully, my first group was the youngest boys: Raju and Nuraj. That, at least, was easy. We played Farmyard Snap again. The first card they flipped over was a goat, and I got them to repeat the word. In the village there was real relevance in learning the English word for goat.

"We no learn science, Conor Brother?" asked Raju.

"Goats are science, Raju."

I saw Nuraj turn to him to ask for a translation, and Raju translated for him that goats were science. Nuraj nodded, and we got back to the game.

Those thirty minutes passed far too quickly, and then a far bigger challenge presented itself. The bigger kids came in. This was trouble—they knew what science was. I once tried to help Bikash, the eldest boy, with his biology homework; he had asked me to explain the male and female parts of a flower.

"Flowers don't have male and female parts, Brother—that's just animals," I informed him.

He looked confused. "Oh . . . but Conor Brother, it says in my textbook that they have . . ." and he opened his textbook to a photo showing the anatomy of a flower, with male and female parts clearly labeled by authors who likely understood a thing or two about the subject.

The boys came in saying "Bonjour, mon frère!" which they had learned from Sandra. Dawa, without preamble, read out loud the story he'd written in Farid's class.

"There was tiger in jungle and he eat Nishal's goat. Finish." He looked up at me expectantly. "You like, Brother?"

"Yes I do, Dawa. Thank you for sharing that," I said. I waited, hoping somebody else might have something to kill some more time. Nobody had any more stories—apparently they had collaborated on the story about the tiger eating Nishal's goat.

Unsure what to do, I asked them to sit down in a semicircle. I rearranged them thoughtfully, buying myself time as I thought frantically about something scientific I could tell them about. What did I know? I could tell them that rocket ships went to the Moon, provided they had no follow-up questions. That would take up about sixty seconds.

"Okay, boys, so, you know how—" I began slowly, drawing out my words. Then, miraculously, I was interrupted by Santosh.

"I teach, Brother!" he said, leaping to his feet.

"Yes! You teach, Santosh!" I shouted, my arms shooting skyward in jubilation. "What would you like to teach?"

"I teach water, Brother!"

"Yes! Yes! Water! This is excellent, Santosh! Water is science! You are doing very well! Go!"

I did not care what Santosh did at that point. He could have eaten paper and I would have cried "Behold! Science!" All that mattered was that all eyes were focused on him, not me, and that the clock was ticking.

Santosh was incredibly bright. I had seen him invent toys for the other kids to play using only the bamboo shoots in the garden. When I needed to fix something in the house that was broken, I would ask Santosh how to do it. Even knowing that, I was blown away when he started talking. He taught the group about the water cycle, from start to finish, about the importance of evaporation and what causes dew, and how pollution affects the cycle. I was listening along with everybody else, thinking *Really? I had no idea!*

The thirty minutes sped by, and I dismissed the class to general applause. The next group came in, the middle kids, the seven- and eight-year-olds.

I waited for Santosh and the others to leave. Then I closed the door and again arranged the children in a semicircle.

"Okay, everybody, today we're going to learn about the water cycle!"

The children cheered, and I silently thanked Santosh.

◇

THE CHILDREN WERE OFTEN surprisingly independent. Bedtime, however, was not one of those times. In one bedroom, the six youngest boys slept together in one king-sized bed on a thin straw mattress, just like the one I used. Getting each of the six children into bed presented its own challenge. Raju would recount his entire day in painstaking detail, oblivious to your efforts to get him to raise his arms so you could get his T-shirt off. Nuraj would stand completely still, head and eyelids drooping, and allow you to undress him and outfit him in a full teddy-bear suit. After struggling to get his legs and arms into the appropriate holes and triumphantly zipping it up from ankle to neck, his eyes would pop open like an android snapping to life and he'd yell "*Toilet!!*" and he'd start thrashing around like Houdini in a straitjacket while you picked him up and raced him to the bathroom.

Evenings were a difficult time for Nishal, who was often sulking, if not outright wailing, about some injustice. Volunteers took turns comforting him, but I soon began taking care of Nishal every night. Sulking and wailing at bedtime was one of my defining traits when I was Nishal's age. I needed constant attention, and I figured the quickest way to achieve it was by sulking. Now I struggled, as my parents must have, to find the right balance between being loving and being strict. It was strangely healing for me; I had never quite gotten over a sense of guilt for my childhood temper tantrums. My mother must have had the patience of . . . well, of a mom, I guess. Making sure Nishal went to bed, absorbing that energy from him, did wonders for both my patience and peace of mind.

One by one we would round up the rest of the children and plop them into bed. When they were all lying down, covered with a large blanket with their little heads lined up in a row like a rack of bowling balls, we would give them all little hugs good night and turn off the lights, then head over to the bigger kids' room.

There were ten boys in the other room, two kids per double bed. (The two girls, Yangani and Priya, slept downstairs in a room with Bagwati, our live-in cooking *didi*.) I would come in to find Farid moving from bed to bed, getting one pair to lie down as the pair across the room popped up, a life-sized version of Whac-A-Mole. When the children saw me walk in they would leap up and yell "*Conor!!*" in the roar I had taught them on the first day, and I would assist Farid with the take-downs. Eventually the pairs of children would huddle together under the blanket for warmth; lights went out at 8:00 P.M. I heard them whisper for a few minutes before sleep took them. The house would fall silent for the first time all day. Then, each night, volunteers would gather in the living room, relax and drink tea, and tell stories about what the kids had done that day.

I recalled times when I had listened to parents speak about their own children, laughing hysterically about seemingly inconsequential things their child had done. I was beginning to understand that sentiment. We took enormous pleasure in recounting something a particular child had done, at how predictable they were and yet how they could continue to surprise us. It made each day completely different, and, at the same time, exactly the same.

◇

I WAS WOKEN UP one night in early December by a loud groaning. It was coming from the boys' room. I put on my head torch, which I kept near my bed, turned on the powerful beam, and ran into the boys' room. I scanned the ten beds. I heard the groan again. I moved closer, stopping again to listen for the next sound, like a game of Marco Polo. It was coming from Dawa's bed. I pulled back the covers to find Dawa drenched in sweat.

"Dawa—what is it? What's wrong?" I whispered frantically, my face just inches from his.

"Eyes, Brother!" he pleaded, blinking.

"Your eyes? What's wrong with your eyes?"

"Your light, Conor Brother!"

I was shining my high beam directly into his face. I turned it off and swept him up. He was shaking. I carried him to a spare bed in the volunteers' room. As I put him down, more groans came from across the room. A moment later I saw Sandra dart into the room, straight for Santosh's bed. She scooped up the groaning boy, who was clutching at his stomach, and carried him to another spare bed in the volunteers' room. There was no way to go to a doctor at that time of night, not out here in the village. We sat up with them and soothed them until they finally fell back to sleep a couple of hours later.

The next morning Farid and I took both boys to Patan Hospital in Kathmandu, a forty-five-minute bus ride from Godawari. Inside, we navigated the dense crowd. I kept my head up, looking helplessly at the signs in Sanskrit hoping for a clue as to where to go. I found the admissions desk, and told the woman on duty that we had two boys who needed to see a doctor. She called over a colleague who knew a few words of English, and we struggled to understand each other while an impatient line grew behind us.

The hospital itself was a terrible place. It felt more like an abandoned bus station than a medical facility. Everywhere patients sat or lay down with wounds covered in dirty bandages. We were shuttled between various doctors and made to wait for several hours over the course of the morning. Farid had taken Dawa to another wing to get him checked out, while Santosh and I sat together. Other patients stared openly at us, looking back and forth from me to Santosh, back and forth, until slowly making the connection, and then smiled kindly at me.

We were directed to yet another room, where we were told to take a number and wait our turn. The number on the screen was six. I looked at the number on my piece of paper. Seventy-nine. Ten minutes later, the number on the screen changed to an eight.

After having waited five hours just to get a number, I'd had about all I could take. I sat Santosh down in the recently vacated wooden chair. The doctor glanced up at me and did not ask to see my number. He set to work examining Santosh.

After six hours in the hospital, nobody could find anything wrong with him, and he was released. We found Farid and Dawa waiting outside, holding a small bag of antibiotics for Dawa's fever, and together we walked back to the bus that would take us the forty-five minutes back to Godawari.

◇

THE MORE TIME I spent with the children, the more I got a sense of how I was going to survive these two months. The key to sanity, I discovered, was understanding that the children did not need to be supervised every second of every day. If Hriteek climbed the small tree in the garden and was hanging by his knees, for example, I told myself that he had probably been doing that before I got there, and that he still had all his teeth and limbs. When we went to the botanical gardens, the lovely enormous park next door, the kids climbed all kinds of trees, fished in the stream, and had sword fights with fallen branches. It was like hanging out with eighteen little Huckleberry Finns.

Even around the house, the children at Little Princes could entertain themselves far more efficiently than I ever could. I made a mistake early on of buying them toy cars during one of my trips to Kathmandu—eighteen little cars, one for each of them. They loved them so much they literally jumped for joy. I felt like a Vanderbilt, presenting gifts to the less fortunate. The longest-surviving car of the eighteen lasted just under twenty-four hours. I found little tires and car doors scattered around the house and garden. Nishal and Hriteek, the pair of six-year-olds, shared the last car between them, sliding the wheel-less chassis back and forth across the concrete front porch a few times before running out to play soccer with a ball they had made out of an old sock stuffed with newspaper.

Though they would never admit it, the kids had far more fun with the toys they made themselves. One boy, usually Santosh, would take a plastic bottle from the trash discarded throughout the village. To this bottle he strapped two short pieces of wood, binding them with some old string. He collected four plastic bottle caps and some rusty nails and pounded them into the wood with a flat rock. And voilà! he had built a toy car. When it wobbled too much going down the hill, he discovered that he could stabilize it by filling the bottle with water. Soon it was racing down shallow hills and crashing into trees. Because he had constructed it, he was also able to fix it. By the end of the day, all the children had built their own cars.

I never bought them anything after that. Instead, I helped them search for old bottles or flip-flops they could use, or saved for them the toothpaste boxes. Those boxes were so popular that we had to set an order in which each child would receive his discarded box. They didn't really do anything with them except keep them, to have something to call their own. The cars they made, or the bow and arrows they made out of bamboo, or the little Frisbees they made out of old flip-flop plastic—those things were all individual possessions. They happily shared them with others in Little Princes, but at the end of the day the toy or the piece of prized rubbish would go into their individual cardboard containers that were large enough to hold their two sets of clothes and everything else they owned in the world.

◇

A MAN WAS LEAVING the orphanage.

I was a good distance away, walking back to the house after a hike into the hills, but I could see him well enough to know that I didn't recognize him. That was unusual; we restricted the number of people who could enter the house for the protection of the children. As safe as the village felt, and as protective as the neighbors were of the children, we could not forget the civil war. We were situated on the southern border of the Kathmandu Valley. Just over the hills were villages under Maoist control. When soldiers in single file patrols came through the village searching houses for weapons, our neighbors convinced them to skip Little Princes Children's Home so as not to disturb the children. To their credit, they always respected this.

Now, a strange man in the house made me nervous. I ran the rest of the way. Inside, I found Sandra and Farid speaking with Hari, the part-time house manager, who had just arrived from his other job over at CERV Nepal. They stopped when I came in, reading my concern. Sandra waved me to sit down with them.

"That man who just left," she said, nodding out the door. "His name is Golkka."

"Who is he? I thought we didn't let strangers visit the children," I said.

"He's not a stranger. The children know him," she said. Farid snorted derisively. Hari said nothing. I waited.

Sandra continued, "The children know him because he is the man who took the children from their villages. He is a child trafficker."

Then, for the first time, I learned the story of how the children at Little Princes had arrived in the small village of Godawari.

Golkka, like the children, was from Humla, a district in the far northwest corner of Nepal, on the border of Tibet—the most remote part of an already remote country. It is completely mountainous, with no roads leading in or out. Most villages there have no electricity or phone service. There is a single airport; from there, the entire region is accessible only on foot or by helicopter. Many children growing up there have never seen a wheeled vehicle. It was in Humla, impoverished and vulnerable, that the Maoist rebels had created one of their first strongholds.

Golkka found that there was opportunity in such a place: he could have access to cheap child labor. He rounded up children orphaned by the civil conflict, a conflict that had thus far resulted in the deaths of more than ten thousand soldiers, rebels, and civilians. He forced the children to walk many days along narrow trails through the hills and mountains—trails that must have resembled the challenging paths up to Everest Base Camp. They walked until they reached a road, where they could catch a bus to Kathmandu. Once there, he kept them in a dilapidated mud house, offering them up for labor. If they wanted to eat, they were forced to beg on the streets.

When tourists discovered the children, they came to the house and asked what they could do to help. Golkka realized he had something much more lucrative on his hands than a mere workforce. He began bringing in volunteers to visit and care for the children. When they bought mattresses so the children would no longer have to sleep on the cold mud floors, Golkka thanked them, and then promptly sold the mattresses as soon as the volunteers left the country. Clothes brought for the children were similarly worn until volunteers left, then taken from the children and given to the trafficker's family.

Sandra met these children while volunteering. She vowed to break the cycle of corruption. She raised money from France and offered to take the children off his hands. Golkka sensed another opportunity. He demanded payment, about three hundred dollars per child. This would be a small fortune in a country where the average annual salary was around two hundred and fifty dollars. Sandra refused to pay, but continued working with the government and other nonprofit organizations to secure the children's release.

Eventually, pressure from the Child Welfare Board and other organizations grew too much for him, and he let them go with her. Those eighteen children became the Little Princes.

Three months after the rescue, neighbors reported that Golkka's crumbling home was filled again. He had gone back to Humla and gotten more orphaned children.

"Why wasn't he arrested? Didn't the Child Welfare Board know what he was doing?" I asked.

"They know. But Nepal's laws are weak. He was the legal guardian of the children—he had found family members to sign custody to him. He could do almost anything he wanted with them," said Sandra.

"So we can do . . . what, nothing?"

"You have to understand, Conor, this is very serious," Sandra said, leaning forward. "We had a volunteer here four months ago. She tried to build a case against him with UNICEF and the Child Welfare Board. Golkka found out, and he came to the home and threatened physical violence against her and the children if she continued. She had to leave the country, for her safety and for the children's safety."

I didn't say anything. I was out of my depth. I was only here for another month; this wasn't my battle. But I found it difficult to control my anger against this man who seemed to be getting away with this, making a profit off the lives of the children. It wasn't my fight, maybe, but I wanted to join it anyway. I read in Farid's face a similar sentiment.

"What will happen to the children?" I asked.

"We keep them here, we raise them, and we educate them. They have no family to return to, or at least no family that we know of, except maybe distant relatives who may have signed them away, I suppose," Sandra said sadly. "Many people—many family members—have been killed in this war."

"But this guy, we have to let him in when he comes?"

"He's not just any man," Hari said, before Sandra could speak. "I know him well. His connections are powerful. He was arrested once, months ago, and he got out of jail after three days because his uncle is a politician. I do not want him here, but we cannot prevent him. He can take the children away from us." He added, his voice apologetic, "It is Nepal. It is difficult."

I went to see the children, up in their bedrooms. I was concerned that the visit from a man who had kept them as veritable slaves for two years had traumatized them. Incredibly, they were playing cards and jumping on their beds as if nothing had happened. These were the same kids who cried if they couldn't find a flip-flop. It was my first glimpse into just how resilient these kids really were. Beneath the showing off, the sulking, the hilarity, there must be an imprint of the terrors they had lived through in Humla—the killings, the child abductions by the rebel army, the starvation. I imagined a steel lockbox at the center of each of them, inside of which they quarantined these memories so that they could live seminormal lives.

It suddenly became very important to me to tell them how much I cared about them. That if they ever needed anything, they could count on me—on us—no matter what. I was going to be a better parent to them, I told myself. That started with opening up to them.

That evening, I went into the bedroom where the older boys were about to go to sleep. I cleared my throat nervously, not sure how to say what I wanted to say.

"Hey boys—listen, you guys should know that I—that all of us—all the volunteers, we really care so much—"

"Conor Brother! What you eat in your country?" Santosh shouted. I had evidently walked into a debate. "You eat meat, yes? You eat animals?"

"Uh, yeah, I guess," I said, working to regain my train of thought. "You know, chicken, pig, that kind of stuff."

"Goat?"

"Well, not really goat, no . . . more like sheep, cow—"

"Cow?!" Santosh sat up. He translated this for those who had missed it, eliciting gasps and one full shriek from Anish. It dawned on me that this might not be the kind of information I should be sharing with a room full of Hindu children.

"You *eat* cow?"

"Well, sometimes. You know, now that I think about it, it's really more my *friends* who eat—"

"You eat God, Brother?" came an incredulous voice from the other side of the room.

"No, of course not, no, I would never . . . I mean, it's not *our* God, you know, so—"

"Cow not God?!"

Yikes! "No, cow God! Cow God! It's just that in America and Europe, we—"

"Why you eat?" demanded Santosh.

I was getting desperate. "Look, it's not really God God, not in the way you're thinking, not where I'm from, and you have never tried it so you have no idea how it tastes, it's really popular, probably the most popular meat to—"

There was a thump as somebody's jaw hit the floor, then silence. I took this as my chance.

"Okay, good night, boys! Sleep well!" I called, backpedaling quickly out the door, reaching my arm back inside to slap blindly at the wall until the lights went out, then closing the door behind me.

That could have gone better, I thought. I gave up on the idea of telling the kids anything. What they needed from me was to screw up as little as possible. They needed me to not tell them, right before they went to sleep, that my favorite food was their God on a bun. They needed me, for three months, to just make sure they were okay, fed, clothed, and bandaged up when need be. I was just a caretaker, but I needed to do that well. That would be a high enough bar for me without trying to change their world.

◇

I NEVER STAYED AWAY from the orphanage long. On occasion I would head into Kathmandu to meet up with other volunteers from my orientation program, have a beer, a yak steak and fries, and exchange stories from our volunteering gigs. I would tell them about village life; they would talk about life in the city. We tried to outdo one another with crazy stories. My favorite was the time my friend Alex Tattersall, an English guy from Manchester, volunteering in an orphanage in Kathmandu for troubled kids, had his camera stolen by one of the children. By the time he found out who it was, the boy had traded it for a chicken, which he had already killed, cooked, and eaten. The camera had cost five hundred dollars. Alex took a day to cool off, then he came right back to the orphanage, forgave the child, and continued taking care of the kids.

Other times, when the children were at school, I would go into Kathmandu to visit a simple, run-down artificial climbing wall, where one could practice rock climbing right in the city. The commute to the outdoor climbing wall took three hours, round-trip. There are no destinations written on the front of the local Kathmandu buses. One learns the route from the ten-year-old boy leaning out the open side door as the bus speeds along, looking for passengers, barking the final destination. Often the bus does not even come to a full stop. You are meant to run alongside it, grab a metal bar, swing onboard, then quickly cram your way into the horde of humanity already aboard. If it's too crowded, you simply cling to the outside and hope cars don't pass too closely. Sometimes an old lady would be waiting by the side of the road, as there are few official bus stops, and the boy would pound the side to indicate that the driver should slow enough to give the woman a fighting chance to swing herself aboard with the help of the boy.

I came to enjoy the commute. It was hypnotic, watching life on the Ring Road. It's different in many ways from the center of Kathmandu, which is dominated by random alleyways lined with tiny shops just large enough for a man and his wares—carpets or plastic buckets or wool. The narrow streets expand into plazas built around Hindu temples, Buddhist stupas, and towering pagodas, giving pedestrians a breath of (relatively) fresh air, not to mention the opportunity to stand still for more than three seconds without getting hit by a bicycle.

The Ring Road is different. It's not the claustrophobic labyrinth of Kathmandu but a postapocalyptic, tattered circle of pavement where buildings often sit forty or fifty feet back from the road, choked with vehicle exhaust.

The faded yellow line dividing traffic is more of a suggested boundary; cars and motorcycles pull into the path of overladen trucks without hesitation, forcing oncoming traffic onto the dirt shoulder that could have been an extension of the road itself were it not for the clusters of pedestrians, cows, goats, stands selling plastic watch bands, and other stands selling bananas, and everything coated in dust and tinged with carbon monoxide.

Men and animals, side by side, rifle through large piles of garbage at the edge of the road. The people at this end of the economic scale are often dark-skinned. Complexion is important to social hierarchy in Nepal; it is not uncommon for a light-skinned Nepali to add a "Complexion" line to their résumé. It is a global phenomenon, this judgment of others by skin color, of course. But in Nepal, these men rummaging through the trash next to the Ring Road are undone by much more than just their skin tone. Their fate had been cemented at birth when they were born into the lowest caste of Nepalese society.

The caste system so dramatically displayed on the Ring Road is the formalized division of social stratification on the subcontinent. Even in Godawari, I often saw manifestations of the caste system. The larger, well-built mud homes typically belonged to the higher-caste residents, the Brahmins. Those belonging to other high-ranking castes often mentioned it without the slightest self-consciousness.

Even the local English-language newspaper adhered to the rigidity of the caste system. In place of weekend personal ads, they had what they called "matrimonials." As the name suggested, men, and occasionally women, sought spouses. Men were seeking, invariably, an olive-skinned, "homely" woman from a good family. In the same way personal ads in America might be divided between men seeking women and men seeking men, matrimonial ads in Nepal are broken down by caste.

The Dalits are the lowest caste. From the window of my bus, I saw Dalits living on the side of the polluted Ring Road. They are unofficially banned from places we took for granted—barber shops, tea shops, and restaurants. So they set up a small mirror on the trunk of a tree, place a wooden stool next to it, and this serves as a barber shop. I watched other men come around selling them glasses of *dud chyiaa* (milk tea) from a makeshift cup-holder. They created their own parallel lives, outside, among their own. It had been this way for their fathers and their fathers before that. But to me, it was infuriatingly unjust. I tried to accept Nepal exactly as it was; I told myself that cultures should be treated equally, that my own culture is terribly flawed and would appear even more so, I imagined, to outsiders. But I grew to despise the caste system during those long bus rides around the Ring Road, and that feeling has never left me.

◇

ONE EVENING, AFTER THE children had gone to bed, Sandra told us that she would be leaving for a while. She was heading out of the Kathmandu Valley to go trekking near Rara Lake in a region called Mugu.

"Which is where, exactly?" asked Chris.

"Western Nepal. Rara Lake—it's a trekking route, but nobody goes anymore because it is far from tourist routes, and because of the Maoists. But I found a guide who will take me!" She was giddy with excitement. Sandra was an avid hiker and mountain climber—this sounded like exactly her kind of adventure.

"And you're not worried?" I asked.

"About what?"

"I don't know—Maoists?"

I didn't know much about the civil war, but what I did know worried me. In early 1996, the Maoist Party—an extreme Communist wing—had launched an insurgency. Their objective was to end the 250-year "feudal" rule of the monarchy. For the first several years, the uprising was considered a police matter—a series of scuffles in remote villages. But the rebel army expanded its ranks, first with men, then women, then children.

With their growing numbers and no effective counterforce, the rebel army grew stronger. Villages, then districts, then entire regions fell under Maoist control. In 2002 the Maoists dragged the Royal Nepalese Army into the conflict overnight with the bombing of an army barracks in western

Nepal. Soon the Maoists controlled virtually the entire country, save the largest urban centers and the Kathmandu Valley. We were told again and again that it was simply not safe to travel in Maoist-controlled territory. Sandra's destination, Rara Lake, was in Maoist territory.

"It will be fine," she assured me. "I will be careful. But there is more to it than just trekking. I am going to see if I can get some news of the children."

This got our attention.

Mugu borders the region of Humla, where the children came from. Sandra believed that there was a chance she could visit the villages of one or two of the children to see if they had any surviving family members.

"I should be back in three weeks," she said. "Farid knows everything about how to run things here; if you have any questions you can ask him."

"The children will miss you," said Chris.

"The children, as always, will be fine," she said with a smile.

◇

ONE WEEK AFTER SANDRA left, I was in the nearby field playing soccer with the older boys when I saw Farid approaching, past the mud huts and down the path that bordered the wheat field until he reached the edge of our makeshift pitch. It was unusual for him to come out to the soccer games. He preferred to hang out with the kids in the house.

"Santosh—I have to go for a minute," I called to my teammate.

"No, Brother! You go, they score!"

"One minute, Santosh."

I went over and sat next to Farid, who was squatting down and picking apart a long straw of wheat. We sat in silence while Farid watched the game.

"They are improving, I think," he said by way of greeting.

"They've been practicing. We set up the match between Little Princes and the other orphanage, the one in Matatirtha. They're really looking forward to it," I told him.

We watched the match for a few minutes. I knew he hadn't come to talk about the children's soccer skills.

"I just heard from Sandra," he said finally, not taking his eyes off Nishal, who was yelling about some foul committed against him. "She will be home tonight."

"I thought she was coming back in three weeks?"

Farid shook his head. "I think something is wrong—she said she would tell us about it tonight."

The children were thrilled to have Sandra home. They leaped on her before she could even take off her backpack. It reminded me of what I must have looked like to the other volunteers when I first arrived more than two months earlier, back when that swarm of children had terrified me. Sandra waved to us but spent the afternoon playing with the kids, ignoring our questioning looks.

It was only after daal bhat that night, after the children went to bed and mugs of tea warmed our hands, that she told us the story of what had happened.

Sandra and Narda, her guide and a native of Mugu, had set out toward Rara Lake. It was a three-day trek from where the bus had dropped them off, where the road had ended. They walked for two full days, stopping occasionally in villages to get water and make sure they were heading in the right direction.

On the third day, two men walked toward them from up the trail. Even from a distance, their gait was different from the village farmers they were used to. They walked quickly, with purpose. Narda stood and quickly put on his backpack. He motioned to Sandra to do the same. The men were armed.

The men stopped several yards from Narda and Sandra and leveled their guns. Sandra understood enough to know that they were being asked where they were going, and why they were there. Narda explained that they were trekking, heading for Rara Lake. They asked about Sandra. Narda called back that she was a French citizen, in the country helping children. The men grew angry at this response, as if Narda had insulted them. They yelled now. They demanded to know how they had known about the meeting. Narda said nothing, but translated in a low voice for Sandra. The men yelled again, repeating themselves. Narda called back, calmly, that they knew nothing of any meeting. They were looking for Rara Lake. They were very sorry if they had interrupted something, and they would be happy to go on their way.

The men had no intention of letting them leave. Narda and Sandra were taken to a rebel-controlled village, put into a room, and made to wait several hours. Another man came in, a rebel who appeared to be of a higher rank than the other men, and interrogated Sandra. He told Narda that Sandra was tricking Narda, that she was a spy, using him. Narda could leave, the soldier said. He was a local, he could be trusted. Sandra would have to stay, they needed answers from her.

Narda didn't leave. They were left locked in the room for two days. Sandra would not admit to being a spy. The commander offered to let her buy her way out for two thousand dollars. It was an absurd sum. Sandra had only perhaps twenty dollars with her. That was unfortunate, they told her, and they left her alone again.

Narda, who was allowed to come and go, spent his time speaking with the Maoists in the encampment for hours on end, explaining the situation over and over, why they came to this particular area, who Sandra was and what she was doing to help children. He was an annoyance to them, and was ordered to go back to his village. He refused to leave without her.

After the third day, the rebels gave up. They had searched everything she had. They found no money and no evidence that she was a spy. Resources were scarce in this part of the country; Sandra and Narda had become two more people the rebels would have to feed and shelter. So they took anything they deemed valuable from her bag and sent the pair back into the forest, ill-equipped to continue their trek. They survived the difficult trip back to Kathmandu.

"It was stupid to go," she said, taking a final sip of her tea. None of us said a word. "This war, these Maoists—they are real. It is too easy to forget that."

She put down her cup and walked up the stairs to her bedroom, looking more tired than I had ever seen her.

◇

SANTOSH WAS SICK AGAIN. I had never heard him cry before, and it scared me. The sobs of Nishal and Raju and the other young boys were common; their cries were for attention as much as anything else, and needed to be investigated only on the off chance that they were seriously hurt. They never were. But Santosh's cries came from his bedroom, a place where he had hoped to stay undiscovered. Farid heard it first, and went upstairs to find Santosh in genuine pain. Sandra and I followed a few minutes later. We gave him some medicine from the first aid kit. When thirty minutes had passed with no change, we had a decision to make: Do we take him to the hospital? It was 6:00 P.M., and the last minibus to Kathmandu for the evening would leave soon. After that, there was no way into the city; soldiers began patrolling the Ring Road after nightfall to guard the capital against Maoist incursion. With the permanent curfew, very little could get in or out after the last bus had left Godawari.

Santosh wasn't getting any better. We quickly packed a small bag for him, threw in a few warm clothes for ourselves, and caught the last bus to Kathmandu's Patan Hospital.

The hospital was eerily quiet at 7:00 P.M. It was much different from my first trip there with Santosh, one month before. With the nationwide curfew, there were few visits after dark. We walked the empty hallways, looking for a doctor.

I suddenly remembered when, as a small boy, I had contracted pneumonia and was severely ill. My father had to take me to the hospital in the middle of the night. I'd held his hand tightly as I walked through the quiet halls. I remembered how scared I was, and how completely I relied on my father that night to make everything better.

As nervous as I felt now, in this strange Third World hospital, I realized that this was not the time for me to be afraid. I was the parent now. I saw how scared Santosh was; he walked slowly and slouched over, wincing in pain. I gently lifted him up and carried him in my arms toward the pediatric ward.

"You need to lose weight, Santosh. You're getting very fat," I whispered to the stick-thin boy in my arms.

He smiled. "No, Brother—you are weak, like a girl," he whispered back.

A few minutes later, we found a doctor coming out of his office. He did a quick examination of Santosh, pressing on the boy's chest, and determined there was indeed something wrong. He led us to the Constant Observation Room, where I laid Santosh on the last available bed. The other four were taken by mothers and their young children. Lying flat, Santosh's feet touched the rusting metal at the foot of the bed.

The doctor returned to take a blood sample. He struggled to find a vein in the poorly lit room, so I took out my flashlight and shone it on Santosh's arm. A minute later, sample secured, he told us we could relax for the rest of the evening. The tests would be done the following day. Sandra and I would stay overnight with him, because the pediatric ward was hopelessly under-staffed and they were unable to care for all the patients.

The only sources of heat were three portable heaters, and the nurses had commandeered all three on the other side of the glass in the Constant Obser-vation Room. Santosh was covered only by a thin blanket, so we dressed him in all the clothes we had brought for him, including his gloves and a jacket, and Sandra managed to find one more blanket. I put on two fleeces and still I was shivering.

When Santosh was finally asleep, we pulled two wooden stools up to the bed, one on each side, and laid our heads on opposite sides of the foot of the bed. The relative height of the stool to the bed plus the bitter cold conspired to make sleeping a near impossibility. When a baby began wailing a few min-utes later, Sandra raised her head, clearly exhausted.

"Listen," she whispered. "You try to find some blankets and a free bed somewhere. I will get into bed with Santosh."

"You must be joking—that bed barely fits him."

"I've slept in much worse, believe me."

After her story of being taken by the Maoists, it was easy to believe.

I knocked on the window to ask the nurse about extra blankets. After a few tired denials that such blankets existed, I asked if I might, then, borrow just one of their heaters to bring into the room to help keep Santosh warm.

She rolled her eyes, stepped over the row of three heaters, and motioned for me to follow her to a storeroom.

"All we have is here," she said. "Take what you want. Do not tell doctor I let you here."

The storeroom was almost bare. I took the only useful items I could find—a plastic hospital pillow and two tablecloths—and walked back to our bed. Sandra, sure enough, had managed to contort herself in beside Santosh.

"Okay, I'm off," I whispered.

"Good—where?"

"Uhh, not exactly sure—down the hall, I guess?"

I didn't tell her I had not yet found an extra bed. The nurse had given her reluctant permission to sleep in any spare bed I could find, provided I was up early and that nobody in the room noticed me. That was as good a deal as I was going to get that night. I wandered down the hall of the pediatric ward, my footsteps echoing. Every room was the same: overcrowded, unclean, without sinks or trash cans or any indication that it was being monitored by anybody but the patients inside.

In a wing far, far away, I poked my head into a brightly lit room. There was a bed that had been recently vacated, judging by the fact that the sheets were unmade. Inside, several tired-looking Nepali women were breast-feeding babies. I stepped back out and looked at the sign on the door. I couldn't read the Sanskrit, but the English translation below it gave me pause, even in my exhausted state. It read: MATERNITY WARD. I steeled myself, then strode in.

The women's eyes followed me as I made my way through the ward. Babies stopped nursing. The air was thick as water; time slowed down. I considered what these poor mothers who had just endured the trauma of childbirth must have been thinking, a young pale man marching in at 2:00 A.M. carrying two tablecloths and a hospital pillow, heading toward the only free bed in the room. But I was horribly cold and had no other options.

Then, a stroke of luck: there was a sheet on the bed. It was bunched up and appeared to have been used, but it would provide one more layer against the cold. I took it by the corners and whipped it to straighten it out, as if I was laying a picnic blanket. As it settled back down, I saw the vast wet blood stain in the middle of the sheet. I gasped and flung the sheet away from me.

I took a long moment to compose myself, then I put my backpack down, lay on the bed, draped the two tablecloths over me, and curled up to sleep in that bright, cold room. The room erupted in chatter. I had never been so grateful not to understand Nepali.

◇

I WOULD LEAVE NEPAL two days later. My three months were almost up, and I had a plane ticket to Thailand. I said good-bye to Santosh the following morning. Farid had taken over and would stay with him. I would learn later that they never found out what had been wrong with him, but they had kept Santosh in the hospital for two more weeks as a precaution. Farid had lived there with him while Sandra returned to the orphanage to look after the children.

That evening, I went into the boys' bedroom to say good night to them for the last time. They had stopped bouncing around. They sat propped up, attentive, two to a bed, in the oversized second- and thirdhand T-shirts that served as their pajamas.

"When you come back, Conor Brother?" asked Anish, a question that seemed to vacuum all other sound out of the room. They wanted to hear my reply.

I was expecting that. We had been strongly advised by the CERV staff to be vague and conservative in our answers to this inevitable question. Few volunteers ever returned to Nepal; it was too far away and required too much time. Volunteering in an orphanage was a one-off, an experience that you would never forget and never repeat. The staff at CERV had learned it was better not to give the children false hope that volunteers would return, as it tended to deteriorate the trust given by the children to the next group of volunteers. The children were looked after by a constantly rotating set of parents, and they were becoming accustomed to it. The system was terribly flawed, but there were few alternatives.

"I'm not sure, Anish, but I'll definitely try to get back!" I said, upbeat. This provoked no response from the boys.

"When, Brother?" Anish asked after an awkward silence.

"Well, definitely not for at least a year," I told him. "Remember I told you guys that I'm going on that big trip? I showed you on the globe?"

"So after that, maybe, Brother?"

"Maybe!" I said. They had heard this before. Some of the boys looked away, others lay down in their beds. Anish alone remained sitting on the edge of his bed. He asked the question again in a different way, then again. He asked more specifically what I planned to do at the end of the year, and whether I needed to return home, and whether I liked Godawari. I finally cut him off. "I'm not really sure, Anish. But I'll see you in the morning, okay, boys?"

"Okay, Brother," came the chorus. Anish lay down. I switched off the light.

In my room, I pulled my backpack out from under my bed, and took a pile of T-shirts off a shelf, laying them flat in my bag. And I broke down. The emotion caught me off guard. I hadn't cried in years, and I was really sobbing. I was happy in Godawari. But there's nothing here, I told myself through jerking breaths. You eat rice every day. You never go out. You never meet any women. You have not seen a movie or TV in months. You have to take care of eighteen children. You are constantly dirty and always cold.

I imagined my mom at the airport, saying good-bye to me each time I returned to Prague after spending Christmas in America. She would cry into my shoulder, sobbing like I was right now. I had always wondered where that sadness came from; leaving had never seemed like a big deal to me. And now here it was, that same desperate sadness, filling this very room.

If walking into the responsibility of caring for eighteen children was difficult, walking out on that responsibility was almost impossible. The children had become a constant presence, little spinning tops that splattered joy on everyone they bumped into. I would miss that, of course. But the deeper sadness, the deluge of emotion, came from admitting that I was walking out on them. The children, as always, will be fine, Sandra had said. She could have said the same thing to my mom at the airport. I knew she was right. But I could not leave this house unsure whether or not I would ever return. I just wasn't going to do it. Despite myself, I had become a parent to these kids—not because I was qualified, but because I had showed up.

I went back into the big boys' room. They were talking quietly in the dark.

"Conor Brother!" I recognized Anish's hoarse whisper. Dark shapes popped up in bed and whispered my name.

"Boys—I'll come back in one year, okay?" I whispered.

"Okay, Brother!"

"Good night, boys."

"Good night, Conor Brother!"

I left Little Princes with a traditional Nepali leaving ceremony. Farid had come back from the hospital for a few hours to see me off with the other volunteers. The children, one by one, placed a red tikka on my forehead, gave me flowers, and bade me a safe journey. As each of the eighteen children approached, each asked if it was true that I was coming back next year. I confirmed it again and again. Some of the volunteers looked skeptical. Farid only smiled.

I meant it. I would be back for them.

Part II

AROUND THE WORLD AND BACK

January 2005–January 2006

Two

I ARRIVED IN BANGKOK on a warm night in mid-January 2005. My flight was almost empty of tourists. Just three weeks earlier, the tsunami watched around the world had shredded the west coast of Thailand, wiping hotels off picturesque beaches at the height of tourist season. I would be meeting up with Glenn Spicker, a close friend from my years living in Prague. (His nickname, Little Glenn, came from the fact he is only about five foot eight, though he packs more energy per square inch than a white dwarf star.) When the news broke about the tsunami's devastation, we contemplated canceling our trip, but decided that the best thing we could do for the country would be to visit and spend money there.

I knocked on the door of Glenn's hotel room. There was a scurry of activity from within, the door flew open, and there was Little Glenn, freshly showered, dressed in shorts and a black button-down, holding a can of Thai beer in each fist.

"Dude!" He put the beers down, gave me a bear hug, then picked them back up and handed me one. "Put your stuff down—we're going out. Time to spend some money on this town—they need it bad. We're in Bangkok, man!

Can you believe that shi— Oh, and there's a change of plan. We're gonna buy mountain bikes and bike across South East Asia. Way cooler, and it'll impress the hell out of chicks. I thought of that on the plane—it's genius, right? You down with that?"

I dropped my stuff on one of the beds and took a long swig of beer, letting it seep through me.

"Bikes. Yes, that is definitely genius. We could . . . wait—are you serious?" I said, trying to remember the last time I had even ridden a bike.

"I never lie to you. Okay, this is awesome. Bikes it is—I'm serious. Are you ready? To go out? You need to brush your teeth or anything? The ladies are waiting, man! The real ladies, not the boys who dress up like ladies. I got your back, don't worry. I know you've been out of the game for a while, that's cool. You were saving orphans in Tibet. How was that? The orphanage? Was that crazy stuff, or what?"

"It was Nepal. And yeah, 'crazy' just about describes it," I said, nodding.

"Crazy good or crazy bad?"

"Crazy good. Strange, huh?"

"I knew you had that in you. Awesome!" We stepped out and he went to lock his door. "But no more orphans now, right? We're hanging out? We're biking? We're drinking and meeting women? This is your year, buddy. It begins now. Right, let's rock this town . . . wait, my key. I gotta find my hotel key. Here, hold my beer."

Glenn was serious about both the biking and the drinking. Two days later we purchased mountain bikes, jettisoned most of our stuff, and set off riding across Thailand. We rode several hours per day. It took us two or three days to get to towns that took most backpackers a few hours on a bus, but when we did get there we were rewarded with impressed stares from women when we told them how we had gotten there.

"I told you, man—I *told* you!" Glenn would shout across the bar at me.

We rode until we reached the northern border between Thailand and Myanmar (Burma), then turned right and rode until we got to Laos. That's where the road ended.

"There's no road? Anywhere around here?" Glenn was asking the woman in the tourist office. He was studying the map behind her head.

"No, sir, I am very sorry—the only road is back where you came, back into Thailand," she said with an apologetic smile.

"Wait—what's this? Is this a road?" He was pointing at a long purple line that bisected Laos.

"That is a river, sir. The Mekong."

"Well . . . you got boats?"

Four hours later, our bicycles were strapped to the roof of a boat. We floated down the Mekong for two days until we reached the former capital of Laos, Luang Prabang, with its fading colonial homes and buzzing night markets. The road reappeared in Luang Prabang, and we took off again.

We pedaled our way up twelve-mile ascents, stopping to rest in jungle villages. Children ran to greet us and held on to us, our bikes, our legs, our saddlebags, studying us like fireflies they had caught in a jar. I would get off my bike and lie down in the grass and let the little ones pile on top of me, grabbing my face and touching my hair and untying my shoes. The older boys, those who reminded me of Anish and Santosh and the others, would sit a few feet away with wide grins, enjoying the scene but tinged by just enough self-consciousness not to join the pileup. I would sit with them too, unable to communicate. Glenn, having found some water in the village, would join us, talking to the kids as if they were old friends of his from Prague. The kids couldn't stop giggling at him.

◇

I TRAVELED TO SIXTEEN countries over the next nine months. After six weeks of biking with Glenn, I convinced Alex, my friend from Kathmandu who famously had his camera stolen and traded for a chicken, to catch up with me. He too was going around the world. When I told him what I was doing, he bought a mountain bike and met me in Cambodia. Three days later, we were biking south, sixty miles into a headwind, to the Cambodian coast. From there it was over the border into Vietnam and Ho Chi Minh City

(Saigon), which, according to the guidebook, had two million motorcycles ricocheting through its streets. I believed it. It felt like a dam had burst above a Kawasaki factory and we were caught in the floodwaters. But we escaped after a few days and some very late and drunken nights with our fellow backpackers, then it was north through the rice paddies and along the coast until we reached Hanoi.

I thought I would sell my bike when I returned to Bangkok, but it gave me such a sense of empowerment, not to mention detox after the nights of drinking, that I was unable to part with it. So when it was time to say goodbye to Alex and move on to Sri Lanka by myself, I packed up my bike and brought it with me. For three weeks I rode alone through the jungles of Sri Lanka, another country almost empty of tourists after the tsunami. After that, I cycled for a few days in Indonesia before giving up, throwing my bike onto a train, and coasting all the way to Bali, where I learned to surf from the young local boys giving lessons on the beach.

I finally gave up my bike in South America, where I hiked the Inca Trail with not just my old college buddies—Charlie, Steve, and Kelly—and their wives, but also with my brother and my mom. I flew into northern Peru and floated twelve hundred miles down the Amazon in a local boat, lying in a hammock packed in among the natives, eating the piranha they served twice a day plus (thank God) some granola bars, and watching the jungle pass by through sheets of rain.

I spent many days alone, but most of the time I was with other backpackers. In every country, backpackers were in vacation mode, travel mode, drinking mode, anything-goes mode. I bungee-jumped in Peru, became a licensed paragliding pilot in Bolivia, learned to windsurf in Vietnam, and rock-climbed in Thailand. I thwarted gangs attempting to mug me twice in the same day in Ecuador, got my camera snatched right out of my hand in Indonesia, got stitches in my calf in Vietnam, had X-rays taken of my knee in Singapore, and saw some of the world's magnificent sights.

I found I had developed new feelings toward the children I saw begging on the street. Street children are common to every poor city, and I had always gone well out of my way to avoid them. I knew that they were working for somebody, that the begging was a scam. But since my experience in Nepal, for the first time, I saw them as normal children. Given a safe home, an opportunity to go to school, and people who could look out for them, they would be no different from the children at Little Princes. It made me miss Nepal and Little Princes all the more.

On a warm day in late October 2005, I walked off the plane at JFK Airport in New York, having completed my year-long round-the-world adventure. With almost no savings left, I stayed with my father and stepmother, both professors at Vassar College in New York, who had rented a beach house for the winter on Long Beach Island, a peaceful New Jersey coastal community, during their sabbatical. I needed a break after twelve months of nonstop travel, living out of a backpack. But within a couple of weeks, I found myself missing Nepal. In January 2006, almost exactly a year after I'd left Nepal, I landed back in Kathmandu for another three-month stint. I had just about run through my entire savings. It would be a nice way to officially end my travels before rejoining the working world.

◇

THE BUS FROM KATHMANDU to the village was crammed with the familiar smells of dust and sweat and spice. I was returning to a country that afforded me no personal space, that gave no thought to hygiene, that offered no decent food. My throat tightened as the minibus pulled into Godawari. I walked slowly down the path, past the wheat fields and mud houses where buffalo were staked to front porches, squeezing past the women coming back from the rice paddies, single file, eyes cast downward, carrying planet-sized loads of grass on their backs. What was I trying to prove? I had accomplished what I had set out to do the year before. I passed the last mud house on the right, where the path dipped and Little Princes Children's Home came into view.

From a distance I saw the children playing on the rooftop terrace. One small figure stopped what he was doing and stared in my direction. Then, like a sailor spotting a whale, he pointed at me and waved his arms at the others, desperate to get their attention. Suddenly a mass of children were pointing at me, waving. From across the fields the wind carried *"Conorrrrr!"* in waves.

Wading through a sea of children once again—I remembered to take off my backpack this time—I discovered the only person above four feet tall was Farid. He had been here for the entire year.

"Welcome, Conor!" he called to me. "I think the children are very happy to see you!"

A wide smile spread across my face. I was happy to see them, too.

◇

EVERYONE HAD CHANGED IN the year I was gone. Sandra had returned to France. The other volunteers were long gone. Farid had buzzed off his long dreadlocks, and his English had improved, which was good because my French had not. Santosh, who had sprouted a full two inches since I'd last seen him, took my bag and carried it up to my room, commenting all the way how weak I looked and how thankful I must be that I had such a strong man to carry my stuff. I tipped him with an empty gum wrapper when he held out his hand with mock expectation.

But the place itself was just as I had left it. I sat down on my old bed, on the same thin straw mattress, my sleeping bag rolled up under the bed, right where I had left it. Even the weather was the same. I knew exactly what would happen when I walked out the door. I knew these eighteen children like I knew my own brothers. I relaxed. Godawari was home.

My first full day back in Nepal coincided with a Hindu festival. The festivals were a reminder that just when you thought you were as far from your normal life as possible, there is always a little bit farther you could go. I had experienced Hindu festivals before, more or less by accident. In the small town of Pushkar, India, I collided with a celebration for some unknown holiday. My memory of it was little more than a blaze of colors and flowers and music. I had been pulled into a group of large, middle-aged sari-clad ladies who begged me to dance with them, right there on the street, a crowd gathering around us.

That morning in Godawari, I woke in a haze of jetlag. Through blurred vision, I saw an eye peeking through the inch-wide opening at my door. I raised my head slowly off the pillow, and the eye disappeared, quickly replaced by a small mouth, lips pushing their way through the crack.

"Brother! Brother!" yelled the lips. "Festival today, Brother!" It was Raju's voice.

For a moment I couldn't even figure out where I was or why somebody was yelling at me.

Raju repeated himself at full-throated yell until I was fully awake.

"Okay, Raju . . . okay, I'm up. What festival?"

He paused, and the bemused sliver of his face showed that the question had caught him off guard. He disappeared for a second and I heard him whispering with somebody, and heard the reply, which could only be Nuraj—his distinctively gruff voice made him sound like he had a perpetual cold. Raju's lips reappeared in the crack.

"I don't know, Brother!" he shouted.

None of the kids knew. It was simply "Festival!" and that meant extra food. I had been looking forward to my first daal bhat, but instead found some kind of pale brown vegetable-ish object on my plate. I took a sniff. It was almost completely odorless, which made me trust it even less. I watched as the semicircle of children gobbled theirs up. I glanced at Farid.

"What is this?"

"I do not know. I do not want to know," he declared, pushing it farther away from him.

"Hey, guys," I said loudly to the sixteen boys and two girls sitting around me. Everybody froze. I forgot that meal times were a time to focus on getting food from the plate into one's mouth, not a time for talking. The children stared, waiting for whatever urgent news I was about to deliver.

"What is this thing? This food you're eating?" I asked.

My question set off a flurry of discussion among them. They knew the name in their own language, but had no idea what it was called in English. The big boys were discussing possible translations, but one by one they fell completely silent. They all looked to Santosh. Santosh's eyes searched the ceiling for an answer. Everyone held their breath in anticipation.

Suddenly Santosh leaped to his feet, sending his plate skidding across the floor, and he jabbed an index finger skyward in a Eureka-type gesture.

"Kind of *potato,* Brother!"

Euphoric cries filled the room. "Yes! Yes! Potato!" shouted Anish. Hriteek's hands shot out toward me, imploringly. "Potato, Brother! Kind of potato!" he cried.

I looked down at my plate. I've seen potatoes. I'm half Irish—I've eaten hundreds of potatoes in my life. My friends, this was no potato. This was not even a kind of potato, as the children were suggesting. It may have been some kind of root vegetable, based on how ugly it was; like those animals that live on the ocean floor, where it's so dark that looks don't matter. But it didn't belong on my plate, and it sure as hell wasn't going in my mouth.

I put the kind of potato to one side and picked up the other object on the plate, which looked like a ball of dried dung covered in sesame seeds. This, according to the children, was a "treat." Nepali treats are to be feared. I learned that the previous year when I purchased, at the urging of the children, a drink box called Drinking Jelly. (Drinking Jelly is not a treat, for the curious among you. Drinking Jelly tastes like you are drinking jelly.) The sesame dung was a step down on the horrendous scale. It was sticky on the outside and tasted as what I imagine sugar-free soy chocolate might taste like if it had fallen in tar, fossilized, and been dug up millions of years later by hungry scientists.

After our morning visit to the temple, we returned to the house to find Bagwati, our cooking *didi,* standing on the front porch, wielding a jar of cooking oil. Something about this made me nervous. I kept several feet back as the children marched past me. I asked her what she was planning on doing with the cooking oil.

"Cooking oil, Brother!" she said, pouring some in her hands.

"Yes, oil . . . I know, I was wondering why you have it—" I didn't finish my sentence. She had snagged Raju like a bear snatching a salmon, and was pulling off his T-shirt in one practiced motion. Suddenly she was rubbing him all over with cooking oil, all over his skin and scrubbing it in his hair like it was conditioner. The other children, squeaky clean from washing in the temple, were merrily stripping down to their skivvies and dousing each other with the oil from the jar, rubbing it on one another's backs and arms.

Nishal ran toward me, glistening like an oil slick, hands cupped with oil. I saw him too late. I tried to run but slipped on a stray flip-flop. Nishal grabbed my arm and slathered me with oil.

"Nishal!"

"For festival, Brother!"

When one is not able to shower every day, one has, at best, mixed feelings about getting smothered in cooking oil. But a festival was a festival.

◇

I FELL BACK INTO village life. I became closer with the children. The older boys stayed up later than they had the previous year, and they wanted to hear about life in America, and to share their memories from their home region of Humla. They asked me about things they had learned in school: airplanes, Michael Jordan, American football, the fastest cars, Australia, whales, World War II, electricity, and so on. They never believed me about the Moon, that men had walked on it, or about the size of the ocean. One afternoon I took them up to the roof terrace, from where you could see for several miles.

"Now imagine water as far as you can see, and as deep as the tops of the Himalaya, there in the distance," I told the boys.

In unison: "Waaaaow!" For days afterward, they asked me to confirm it.

"Water would go from Godawari to Kathmandu, yes, Brother?" Anish would ask.

"No, it farther, yes, Brother?" Santosh would say. "You say many many farther!"

"Here to Kathmandu is only ten kilometers, right, Anish?"

"I don't know, Brother."

"It is, trust me. So the ocean, the biggest one, is called the Pacific, and it would be like going to Kathmandu and back here one thousand times."

"Waaaaaow!"

I loved the children at Little Princes. I hadn't realized how very much I had missed them for the last twelve months until that day.

I watched Farid with the children. He had spent almost twelve months with them, alone for much of that time, though Sandra had visited twice during that year. With only one volunteer, as opposed to the four they had had the previous year, the children had grown more independent. I watched Nishal chase Hriteek across the roof terrace, then trip and tumble head over heels. Miraculously, he leaped up again and continued the chase. A year ago, Nishal would have sat there crying until a volunteer came to pick him up. Anish, who had often helped with washing pots, above and beyond his nightly chores, now spent more time with Nanu, our washing *didi,* helping her with the laundry, as they beat the clothes against the concrete and wrung them out, one twisting in one direction, the other twisting in the other. Priya, Raju's seven-year-old sister, was learning to cook together with Bagwati, watching her make daal bhat, helping pour in the spices.

Farid didn't coddle the children. He treated them as his own brothers and sisters. Like a good brother, he had practiced carrom board enough to beat the older boys. There was not much else to do in the village. Most volunteers would let the children win at whatever they played. Not Farid. He played in earnest and called them out when they broke the rules.

"No, Dawa!" he would cry. "You are a cheating boy! I see you cheating!"

The boys loved playing with Farid. He understood them better than anyone. They also knew Farid hated spiders, really hated them, so every time the boys saw one in the woods, the enormous green ones that live in the trees in Nepal, they would call Farid over to them, pretending they had a secret to tell him.

"I am not falling for that trick with the spider, Santosh. I am not stupid, you know!" He pronounced it stu-*peed.*

"Just come, Farid Brother!"

"If I come there I am going to make you eat that spider—you know that, Santosh? You know that you will have to eat that spider, yes?" The boys would fall over laughing at that. Though I never admitted it to Farid, I would encourage the children at every opportunity to try to get Farid to touch a spider. It was endlessly entertaining.

◇

THE CIVIL WAR IN Nepal had gotten worse during the year I was away. Just after I left for the first time in early 2005, King Gyanendra had seized absolute power over the country, dissolving the parliament. The move, intended to crush the Maoist rebellion once and for all, was initially popular with the people, proving just how desperate Nepalis were for an end to the fighting. The Nepali royal family was not, after all, known for its stability.

Four years earlier, in an incident that made international headlines, King Gyanendra's predecessor, King Birendra, was murdered, along with the queen and most of the royal family, by his own son, Crown Prince Dipendra. The prince, apparently displeased with his father's refusal to approve the prince's intended future bride, opened fire with an automatic weapon at the dinner table, ultimately killing nine members of the royal family and injuring five before turning the gun on himself. But his suicide attempt failed, and he lapsed into a coma caused by his severe head wound.

Then, in what can only be described as an astonishingly rigid adherence to the succession of power, Prince Dipendra, mass murderer and now in a vegetative state thanks to his failed suicide, was crowned king of Nepal.

The prince died three days later, never waking from his coma. Gyanendra, uncle to Dipendra, third in line for the monarchy, ascended to the throne. Along with divine authority to rule, the new king inherited the civil war.

But the war looked to be ending in the fall of 2005, when the Maoists declared a ceasefire. It happened as I was getting ready to return to Nepal.

"See? Totally safe!" I think were my words, flapping the newspaper triumphantly for my parents.

What I did not point out to them was that King Gyanendra rejected the ceasefire almost immediately. He wanted unconditional surrender, despite the fact that the citizens of Nepal were desperate for an end to the war. The king ordered the Royal Nepalese Army to increase its attacks on the rebels. In response, the Maoists began attacking targets in the Kathmandu Valley, home to the country's capital, and the village of Godawari, where Little Princes was located.

The war would continue.

◇

WE FELT THE EFFECTS of the conflict in Godawari, though the bombings never got closer than five miles away. On my trips from the village to Kathmandu, I was now forced to clear a military checkpoint in both directions. The minibus would be stopped, and I and the rest of the passengers were forced to disembark and submit to a search by soldiers. The minibus itself would then also be searched for bombs. The road from Godawari, from the southern point of the Kathmandu Valley, was a potential entry point for the rebels, and bombings had become more frequent. At the intersection where the village road met Kathmandu's Ring Road, a tank guarded the southern entrance to the capital.

The older boys at Little Princes now sat with the newspaper every morning, reading news of the increased killings around the country. There were more every day; soldiers killing rebels, rebels killing police, rebels killing civilians, rebels destroying homes, and so on. Punishment for breaking the strikes was becoming more severe. We read of taxi drivers caught driving during the bandha who were executed in their cars.

Virtually all western governments urged travelers to defer all nonessential travel to Nepal due to the instability. Farid and I had been expecting a new French volunteer named Cecile to join us in January. We assured her that Godawari was safe, but advised that she had to follow her instincts. Just three days after Farid had written her an e-mail, eighty-five children were abducted from a school in western Nepal. The Maoist rebels simply walked into the school, murdered the teachers, and walked out with seven dozen new conscripts for their army. Farid read this article aloud to me, translating from a French newswire. He concluded and looked back up at me.

"I think Cecile will not come," he said, shaking his head. "And I cannot blame her."

Cecile canceled her trip three days later.

Even in the face of increasing carnage inflicted on that beautiful country, Farid and I had felt that the children were safest there in Godawari at the Little Princes orphanage. There were no military or other strategic targets in Godawari, after all, and there had never been an abduction inside the Kathmandu Valley. Besides, nobody even knew Little Princes existed.

Or so we thought.

◇

"HOW CERTAIN ARE YOU, Hari? It's a rumor, or you know it for sure?"

Farid and I were sitting on the roof. The sun had only just risen over the hills—most of Godawari was still in the shade, covered by a frosty dew. Hari, our house manager, had come over early, saying he needed to speak to us urgently.

He ran his finger nervously around the rim of his metal tea cup. "It is only what I hear, Conor Brother. Maybe it is rumor. But it is possible that the Maoists have found us here. I am sorry, I cannot say for certain," he said.

Hari's message was serious. The children at Little Princes were potential Maoist recruits. He had met the brother of Golkka, the child trafficker, who had recently come from Humla. The brother said that the Maoists had learned of his scheme to take children from Humla, and that the rebels were furious. Each family was expected to give one child to the rebel army to join the fight against the king. They had found Golkka's brother and given him a message to pass on to anybody protecting Humli children in Kathmandu: the children were to be returned to Humla. Immediately.

The rumor was even more alarming. Hari had heard that the Maoists knew of Little Princes. They knew where it was and how many children were there. And the Maoists wanted them.

Farid and I did not look at each other. We could hear the children down-stairs, getting ready for school.

"What do you think?" I asked Farid, breaking the silence.

"I do not know," Farid said. He looked at Hari. "What is your opinion, Hari? Is there something we should do? You think it is true? They know where we are?"

Hari hesitated, clearing his throat a couple of times before speaking. "Farid Brother, I think you and Conor Brother maybe think about leaving Nepal. It is not very safe here. If Maoists come, you can do nothing anyway—they have guns, they take the children. Maybe better you are with your own families. We can take care of children here, me, Bagwati, Nanu—we have done it before, it is okay, no problem for us," he said. He did not make eye contact with us.

"No, Hari. Thank you, I understand why you're saying that, but we will stay here as long as we can," I said, looking to Farid, who was nodding his head. "But what do *you* think, Hari—your own opinion. There is no right or wrong. Do you think they would come for the children?"

Hari waited a long time before answering. He usually tried to give the answers he thought we wanted to hear. I saw him wrestling with this instinct now. "Conor Brother, I tell you my opinion. It is only my opinion, I do not know," he said slowly. "In my opinion, we are safe here. Maoists will never take risk here in Kathmandu Valley—too much risk for them, too much easy opportunity outside Kathmandu."

Farid turned to me. "I believe this also, Conor. I think the children are safe here."

I trusted their instincts. "Okay, then," I said, getting up. "Let's get the kids ready for school—they're running a bit late, no?"

◆

WITH THE INCREASING FREQUENCY of the bandhas, the children often stayed home from school. Farid and I rarely left the orphanage. That meant a lot of time on the roof. Godawari was at a slightly higher altitude than the capital, but even in February it was still warm during the day, provided you stayed in direct sunlight. The winter in Kathmandu, lasting from December to February, brought temperatures ranging from forty to fifty degrees Fahrenheit during the day. After that it got progressively warmer until August, when temperatures reached into the seventies before gradually cooling. With virtually no artificial heating or air-conditioning indoors, one was sensitive to even slight changes in temperature.

The flat roofs that topped every home in Nepal served an important purpose for precisely that reason. Families spent more time on their roofs than inside their homes, at least during the day. Clothes were laid flat to dry on roofs; wheat was stacked and stored there. Little Princes was no different, except that a low wall ran the perimeter of the roof terrace to prevent falls. With the exception of the rainy season, which blasted Nepal from early June to late September, the children practically lived on the roof.

The broad roof of the orphanage provided us with an ideal lookout post. We could keep an eye on the children with us, see down into the garden, and even over to the nearby field where the children played soccer, dodging and weaving between grazing cows. We leaned against the railing and drank milk tea and spoke, mostly, about Nepal, undistracted by Nuraj and Raju using us as a kind of jungle gym. When we weren't talking about Nepal, we were talking about food. Farid missed French food like a prisoner misses sunlight, though he had never in his life been anything but skinny. He could hold forth on the different types of *saucisson,* dried sausage, for literally an entire hour—the best regions for it, the best ingredients, the kind of bread that should accompany it (*un boule*) and the one meal he would have if he could have anything at that precise moment (*saucission, boule,* and as many French fries as would fit in the room).

Farid spoke little about himself and his life in France before Nepal. But I knew that he was a foster child. I knew that he did not know his own father, an Algerian who had returned to his own country. I knew that he hoped, one day, to find him. He spoke of these things only in passing, as if he was protecting himself from thinking on it too deeply, from putting too much significance in the fact that he, a young man who had been given up as a child, had spent the last year of his life taking care of eighteen orphans on the other side of the world. So we stood on the roof, watching the village and describing, in dizzying detail, our favorite meals.

◇

FROM A DISTANCE, THERE was nothing unique about the woman walking toward the orphanage.

Farid and I were on the roof. We all were; it was a Saturday afternoon, the floors inside were freshly mopped and would take an hour to dry properly. The children had used chalk to draw a hopscotch board and were lined up, each clutching a small stone. I saw her first, approaching from the path leading from the single paved road that connected Godawari to the rest of the world. That was strange. There was a bandha that day—no minibuses had been on the road. Wherever she had come from, she had walked.

She came closer. There was something else strange about her. Women in the village often walked with their heads down, because either they were carrying a heavy load or they were intent on getting home. Not this woman. She walked slowly, her eyes fixed on the orphanage. I worried that she would trip on the uneven trail. As she got closer, I realized she was staring at the children. Stranger still, I saw that the children had stopped their game and were staring right back at her.

She stopped outside the gate of the orphanage, not knocking, just standing calmly, waiting.

Farid was in the middle of describing a dish his mother made for his birthday one year, when he realized I was staring past him. He turned to see what I was looking at.

"Who is that wom—" he started, and stopped. He stared at her, then said, "Conor, I think I know who this woman is."

I saw what he saw. Unmistakably, in her distinctively angular features, her wide face, her Tibetan eyes, was a face that we had somehow seen before. On one of the Little Princes.

This woman was Nuraj's mother.

Nuraj was frozen to the railing, hands gripping it tightly. Krish, his brother, had pushed through the other boys and put his arm around his little brother, but said nothing. Farid said nothing to the boys, but ran to the stairs leading down. I followed him, stopping only to pull Santosh aside.

"Santosh, I want you and Bikash to keep the boys on the roof—you understand?"

"I understand, Conor Brother," he said. I hurried downstairs after Farid.

Farid was already outside when I reached him. He had opened the gate and was facing the woman. She did not enter, but only murmured "Namaste," putting the palms of her hands together. We returned the greeting, and continued to stare at the woman. Farid asked her, in Nepali, if she was here to see the children.

Her head wobbled back and forth on her head. In the United States it was a gesture that signified uncertainty. In Nepal, it was an emphatic *yes*. I could not understand what she was saying to Farid, but two words needed no translation: "Nuraj" and "Krish."

We invited the woman inside and offered her tea; it was custom in Nepal to offer tea to any guest who crossed your threshold. I went to look for Hari, and found him in our small office downstairs, going over our weekly food budget.

"Hari—we need you in the other room to translate for us. A woman just arrived—the mother of Nuraj and Krish. She's here," I said.

Hari put down his pencil. "I do not think so, Conor Brother—their mother is dead."

"I know, but . . . you have to see this woman."

He pushed back his chair and followed me into the living room. Farid sat on a small stool, the mother sat on the floor, her legs tucked beneath her.

Hari was right. This woman should be dead. We had been told as much by the children themselves. But there was no mistaking this woman. I saw it on Hari's face as well when he greeted her; this was the boys' mother. Hari pulled up a stool next to her and spoke quietly to her for a few minutes. Then he looked back at us.

"Farid Brother, Conor Brother, this is the mother of Nuraj," he said simply. "I can translate for you if you tell me what you would like to know.

"Everything, Hari," said Farid, leaning toward the mother. She would not meet his eyes. "We want to know everything."

That's how we learned the full story of the children at Little Princes.

Two years earlier, Nuraj's mother, like so many mothers during Nepal's civil war, feared for the lives of her children. Humla, all but cut off from the world, was fertile ground for the brutal Maoist takeover. Far from the reach of any police force or law, the Maoist rebels exiled the locally elected officials, promising a better life for the community under their rule. The impoverished villagers were left with little choice. Certainly they had no means of fighting back. Many even held out hope that the Maoists would keep their promise. The monarch was the root of their misery, they were told by the rebels, not the drought or isolation or severe underdevelopment. Everything would change now.

But the Maoists had an army to build. They had to stay strong to protect the village from the royal oppressor, they said. They destroyed the bridges, making it all but impossible for the Royal Nepalese Army, recently mobilized against the rebel threat, to enter the villages of southern Humla. The Maoists preached the tenets of communism. They put in place a law that said families had to provide food to the rebel army. Subsistence farmers gave freely at first, hoping their contribution from their scant reserves would suffice. But the army grew quickly, and with it the demand for food. Men were unable to feed their families, as everything was going to the Maoists. They asked the rebel leaders to leave them with enough for their children. Still the Maoists demanded more, but now at gunpoint. When they were refused, persuasion turned to threats that turned to beatings.

And then just food was not enough. The Maoist rebels wanted more power, a bigger army. They asked for volunteers. Some joined out of belief for the cause, but many more joined out of fear and desperation. The rebels had already taken their food; it would be better to be on the strong side and at least be able to feed their families. When the pool of volunteers dried up, the Maoists made another law: each family would give one child to the rebel army. Maoist soldiers conscripted children as young as five years old to become fighters, cooks, porters, or messengers depending on the child's age and ability. There was nowhere to hide. Children were taken from their mothers, disappearing into the rebellion.

Then, one day, as if delivered by God, a man came to the village. The man was the brother of a former district leader, a powerful man in the region before the rebels took over. He could protect the children. He would take them far away from Humla to the last refuge in Nepal, the Kathmandu Valley. He would put them in boarding schools, where they would learn to read and write for the first time in their lives. The children would be fed and cared for. Most importantly, they could never be abducted by the rebel army. This man was Golkka.

Nuraj's mother and father begged him to take their children. It would be expensive, they understood, but they would pay anything. To raise the money, they sold their home and moved into single-room huts with their neighbors. They sold their land, their livestock. They borrowed from distant relatives. They would be going into debt for the rest of their lives, putting the rest of their family at risk, but it was worth every rupee to save their boys from the Maoist army. In villages throughout Humla, other parents were taking the same drastic steps to save their children.

Nuraj's mother packed a small bag for her sons with the few possessions they had—a small shirt, some dried rice. She comforted Nuraj and Krish as she sent them away with a stranger. They were going on an adventure, she told them. They would be safe. This man was going to take care of them, so they must be good boys and do what the man said. She would talk to both of them very soon.

A few months passed, and Nuraj's mother heard no news of her children. She asked the other villagers who had sent their children. None of them had heard from the man. Nuraj's father took the phone number given to him by the man and walked for several days until he reached Simikot, the largest village in Humla, where there was a phone.

Nuraj's father listened to the empty ringing on the other end. He hung up, and checked the number again. Yes, he had dialed the right number. The man had even written his name next to the number: Golkka. He dialed again, but it made no difference. Nobody ever answered. He had been given a false number. His child was gone, lost in the chaos of Kathmandu, hundreds of miles away. He hung up the phone, and started the days-long walk back to his village. He would have to tell his wife, the boy's mother, that their sons were gone.

Farid and I listened to Nuraj's mother, speechless. The Little Princes Children's Home was not an orphanage at all. These children had parents who were alive. And by some miracle, one of them had found us.

Nuraj's mother had come that day from the Ring Road around Kathmandu, where she lived. They had lost almost everything in Humla, thanks to the child trafficker; they had little choice but to seek work in Kathmandu. When she described where she lived, I knew the place exactly; it was only a few minutes walk from the climbing wall that I frequented. It was a terribly impoverished area, a neighborhood that I would pass on the bus and wonder who could survive in such a place. She had moved into a shack there, leased to her by a woman with some neighboring land. She tended the land in exchange for the shelter. Her husband had gone to Nepalganj, Nepal's second largest city in the south of the country, to find work. She lived alone with her youngest son, a disabled boy of two years old, the younger brother that Nuraj and Krish did not even know they had.

Their mother had learned about the Little Princes when an international aid worker had come to her shack; he had been told of the family by a neighbor who saw the mother living in destitution. The doctor had offered to take the son to the hospital for a check-up. When the aid worker heard her story about her journey from Humla, he told her about an orphanage he had heard about in the village of Godawari. He suggested they might know something about her two missing sons. She left her youngest with a neighbor, and set off walking to Godawari, along the empty roads, cleared out by the bandha. It had taken her all day. She had not asked directions. When she saw the path leading down to the orphanage, she said, she knew it was the right way. When she saw the yellow house in the distance, she knew her sons were there.

She had waited long enough. I went upstairs and brought down Krish and Nuraj. I walked into the room, and Nuraj clutched the arm of his older brother. Krish was only seven, but was a great protector of his little brother. I stood back, expecting a joyous reunion.

The boys, though, stayed at the edge of the room. They would barely even look at their mother. Farid walked to them and squatted down, trying to get them to speak to her. They said nothing, and continued to stare at the floor. The mother walked slowly to them and sat in front of them, on the floor, taking their hands in her hands and speaking softly to them. Still the boys did not react.

After a few moments, the mother got up slowly and approached Hari. She said something that I could not hear. Then she turned to Farid and me, clasping her hands together in prayer-like fashion and saying *dhanyabhad,* thank you, and she walked back out the way she had come in.

"Wait . . . what did she say, Hari? Why is she leaving?"

"She say she understand reaction of her sons. She say she will come back. She say thank you to me and to you and to Farid Brother."

The two boys never looked up. Farid asked me to take Nuraj back upstairs with the other boys, and then he put his arm around Krish and led him out into the front garden. This would be a sensitive conversation. The children trusted Farid above all others, and Krish was a bright young boy.

I ignored the flurry of interest from the other boys up on the roof. Raju was part of the group, too, but his questions, shouted above the other questions, were not about the strange woman and what had happened, but whether Nuraj wanted to play carrom board. I left Nuraj with him and brought the rest of the kids to the far corner of the roof, leaving them with strict instructions not to bother Nuraj. An hour later, Farid and Krish came back inside, and he sent Krish back to the roof to play with the other boys.

"What was that all about?" I asked him as we went back out to the garden to talk.

"You would not believe it," Farid said, cursing under his breath in French.

The children had been instructed by Golkka to tell anyone who asked that their parents were dead. It was more effective in getting donations from tourists, and would also help explain to local authorities why one man had so many children under his guardianship.

"If a child made a mistake and told of his parents being alive, Golkka beat him. Can you imagine?" Farid said. "Krish saw his mother coming— his own mother, after this long—and all he could think was that they were in trouble. He warned his brother to pretend not to recognize her. He was scared that if he said anything, we would beat Nuraj."

It was unbelievable. "So they know her?"

"Of course they know her. She is their mother," he said. "Conor, I did not tell you, but I have seen this woman before. In this village. I suspected she might be their mother, but I could not believe it. I ran out to find her, but it was too late, she was gone, unable to find her children. She must have come back, to look again."

"How did you not tell me this before?" I asked, confused.

He shook his head. "It did not seem possible that it was her. I thought I must have imagined the entire thing. Today, I can see that it was. This is their mother."

We spent a lot of time with Nuraj and Krish over the next few days, and using Hari as a translator to make sure there were no misunderstandings, we told them that their mother coming was a very good thing, that this was cause for celebration. They had an opportunity that none of the other children had—to spend time with their mother for the first time in years. We repeated this message like a mantra, not just to the two boys, but to all eighteen children. We promised Krish and Nuraj that as soon as the strike ended, we would take them into Kathmandu to see their mother on a regular basis, to reestablish a relationship between them.

The children saw that Farid and I, unlike the child trafficker, were not punishing Nuraj and Krish for speaking about their mother. They saw that, on the contrary, we were celebrating the fact that their mother was alive.

They could trust us—really trust us—in a way that had not been possible for them since they had left their villages. It brought us even closer to the children. We watched layers of fear that we had not even known existed peeling away from them.

They began to speak about their families for the first time in years, at least what they remembered of them. The children were more animated than I had ever seen them. In the evenings they spoke at length about Humla and their brothers and sisters and parents, and their villages came alive before me. But there was sadness, too. For the first time, I heard bigger boys crying at night, when they thought everybody was asleep. We had opened caged memories, but we had no solution for the children. There was still a war. Humla was still inaccessible. Their parents had no idea where they were. The children remembered, but with those memories was the realization that their mothers and fathers might as well have been on the other side of the moon. They were still alone. Nothing had changed.

◇

THE STRIKE ENDED A few days later. Once again minibuses were running to Kathmandu. While I stayed at Little Princes, Farid took Krish and Nuraj to see their mother and their little brother. They returned several hours later, glowing. The children gathered around them and soaked up every last detail of what it had been like to spend an afternoon with their mother. What had she said? What had they talked about? What did they do together?

Every few days Farid and I would take them on the long bus ride to see their mother. The change in the boys was visible. They were still our boys, still part of the house, but the two brothers spent more time together. They spent more time studying. They spent more time alone, talking. Mostly, they looked forward to these visits with their mother.

But as the security situation worsened, traveling to and from Kathmandu became more and more difficult. The country was now caught between the Maoist rebels on one side and a dictator in King Gyanendra on the other.

Journalists bold enough to criticize the monarchy were thrown in prison. Democratically elected opposition leaders were placed under house arrest. And that was only the beginning.

The king, declaring a return to democracy, had called for municipal elections in February 2006. But there was a catch: The elected leaders would be operating as puppets under the king's absolute authority. The election was boycotted by every political party in Nepal and condemned by the international community. Protests ignited on the streets of Kathmandu. The police, under the king's orders, donned bulletproof vests and carried automatic weapons, and set about arresting and beating the protesters, killing one.

Citizens took to the streets. The king tried to contain them. Ahead of a widely publicized prodemocracy rally, the government cut off all mobile phone service and kept it off for a month. Still, word managed to get out. So the royal government called a curfew for the entire day of the scheduled rally. Those brave enough to show up were beaten. Government agents began arresting student leaders, simply walking into their classrooms and taking them away.

To add to the misery of the population, the Maoists called for a nationwide bandha, or strike, prohibiting all travel on the day of the election. Anyone caught going to a polling station would be attacked by Maoist sympathizers.

Then things really got strange.

The royal government was unable to convince citizens to risk life and limb to violate the bandha in order to vote in the farcical election. So the king took a different approach. If the citizens would not violate the bandha on their own free will, then he would force them to violate it.

Overnight, the police impounded five hundred random cars in Kathmandu. An announcement was released to the news stations: owners of the vehicles must pick up their cars from the police compound on the first day of the bandha and drive them home. If they did not, they would forfeit their car forever. These unlucky citizens would be forced to put their lives and their vehicles—which represented a significant portion of their net worth—at risk.

The announcement went on to imply that the government was not insensitive to the potential risks; they would offer insurance on all the vehicles in the (highly likely) event of damage to the car. The government also announced, as was quoted in the newspaper: "In case of death of driver, co-driver, or helper of vehicle plying during the strike, the government will give an additional percent amount besides insurance compensation."

The February elections were, by any measure, a complete failure. Public turnout measured about 2 percent. Most polling stations had more soldiers than voters. There were not even enough candidates to fill the positions; only about two thousand candidates offered their names for about four thousand seats. Maoists had threatened to murder candidates, and they succeeded in at least one case. A candidate was gunned down in the street; others had their houses bombed. The government, in response, offered free life insurance to anybody willing to run for office.

The king declared the election a victory for democracy.

◇

KRISH AND NURAJ CAME back from visiting their mother one afternoon especially animated. The two boys ran down the path and through the blue gate, blowing past me and running straight to a group of the older boys. The children gathered around and listened to their story of what had happened that day. Farid, who had taken them, arrived a couple of minutes later. He asked me to join him on the roof. The sun was low in the sky, so I put on a hat and an extra fleece and went upstairs.

The roof was empty except for Farid, sitting on the railing, looking out toward the mountains. On clear afternoons like this, the Himalaya were visible across the Kathmandu Valley, lit up with a dull pink by the setting sun. Even from this distance, they dwarfed everything else in sight.

"There are more children there, Conor," he said.

"More children where?"

"With the mother. There are seven, living with her in that tiny shack. Humli children."

Farid told me what he had understood from the mother. Golkka was still trafficking children. The worse the war got, the more families were willing to pay him to take children from the villages. He was dumping them with orphanages run by international organizations, organizations that were concerned only about the safety of the children and often bought his story that the children were true orphans. But word spread in Kathmandu of his practices. Organizations had to make a hard choice. They stopped taking children from him, even knowing that some children might have been in danger. But there was no other way to stem the flow of his trafficking.

The business was too lucrative for Golkka to give it up that easily. Then, he found Nuraj's mother. He recognized her from Humla, and knew that her husband was away. He knew he could take advantage of her. A poor, uneducated woman from a remote village simply did not stand up to a man like Golkka. He brought her seven children and told her to keep them. Then he vanished again.

"How does she support them? I thought she could barely feed her own son," I said.

"This is the problem—she cannot support them. They are starving. I have seen it. They could die, these children," he said. Farid was having difficulty controlling his anger. "We have to do something about this, Conor. We must."

I agreed completely. Not just for the seven, but also for the mother. She was barely surviving herself. Golkka had added seven more people to a sinking lifeboat.

Two days later, when the children were in school, Farid and I took the bus to the mother's shack. We stopped in a local shop on the way. It was a typical shop, a small hut with one wall open to the street where you could buy rice and vegetables by the kilo from old cloth sacks. We bought as much as we could carry and lugged it to the mother's home. We entered a gate into a small compound.

Three children peered out the open door of a one-room brick shack, loosely covered by a sheet of corrugated tin. Another small face appeared out of the dark room and stared at us. I had become accustomed to the gregarious Little Princes, the way they would leap at strangers like mad little alligator wrestlers, hanging on for dear life and machine-gunning questions at their new friend. These children, shadowy figures peering out the door lit by an overcast sky, were silent. They were not afraid, but their curiosity and suspicion seemed to keep them in a perfect balance of wanting to come closer and wanting to disappear back inside. Approaching the doorway, I counted seven children. They were filthy. Their skin was dried and cracked, their clothes dusty and torn, their hair chopped unevenly. Most of them were barefoot.

Farid and I carried the food inside. We greeted Nuraj's mother, who stood up with her two-year-old son, whose deformed back was exposed. I cringed, despite myself. The mother smiled apologetically and pulled a shirt over the boy. I felt like a complete jerk.

The eldest of the seven, a lanky boy of maybe twelve named Navin, sat inside on one of the two beds. The only light came in from the narrow doorway. There were no windows, and any holes in the brick had been stuffed with old newspaper to keep out the cold. In the dark, I could see that he had something wrapped around his hand that he held tightly. Farid took him gently by the elbow and led him outside. Wrapped around his finger was an old rag that he must have found on the street. Farid carefully unwrapped it. His head recoiled, and he wrapped it back up and whispered something to the boy. The boy said something back. Farid nodded and hurried over to me.

"You can stay with the children?" he asked me. "I must take Navin to hospital—his finger was caught in a gate, the . . . this part," he pointed to the tip of his own index finger, "this part is almost off."

I told him I would stay, and he took Navin down to the Ring Road where they immediately caught one of the ubiquitous old hatchback taxis and sped off.

This appeared to be more excitement than the children had seen in some time. They were now all outside, staring at me, perhaps wondering if I too might grab one of them and fling them into a taxi and speed off to God knows where. That could explain why they kept their distance. I sat on the ground and took them in. There were six of them now. The eldest of the remaining boys bore a resemblance to Navin; I wondered if they might be related. He turned away and walked back inside the shack. The others remained, plopping themselves down, one by one, in the dirt, waiting to see what I would do next. They ranged in age from perhaps five years old to about nine. The youngest was a tiny thing, even smaller than Raju, and he wore a permanent grimace. They all did, now that I got a better look at them.

There was only one girl in the group, a girl I would come to know as Amita. She had long, straggly black hair and Tibetan facial features, narrow eyes and wide cheekbones. It was a common look in Humla and in the north of the country, when her ancestors had come over the mountains from Tibet and the surrounding region more than four hundred years earlier. The ratio—one girl to six boys—was in keeping with the approximate proportion of girls to boys brought out of Humla. When parents sent their children with child traffickers, they sent boys most of the time. They believed that the boys were at greater risk of abduction, but they also believed that a boy would do better in school and would be able to return to Humla as a grown man to take care of his family.

For now, though, Amita seemed to be one of the leaders of this little group. She was whispering something to the skinny young boy next to her, a boy whose name, I would learn, was Dirgha. Dirgha, whose notable front teeth reminded me of Bugs Bunny, was despondent and stared at the dirt, drawing small shapes with a stick.

We sat and stared at one another for maybe twenty minutes. There was not much else to do. I had learned a kind of patience in Nepal that did not come naturally to me. There is less stimulation, fewer pressures to get things done, and the people in Nepal have a peaceful way about them that allows them to sit, quietly, for long periods of time, staring out at fields, or at their livestock, or at their infant children playing on the porch.

Wanting to interact with the children but not wanting to scare them off, I took a walk in the field beside the shack. The wheat field was small—about half the size of a football field—and bare. The mother had been stacking hay. As I suspected, the children followed me, though at a safe distance. When I turned around, they stopped their low chatter and froze, like a game I used to play as a child that we called Red Light, Green Light. I would start walking again, and each time turn around more quickly. After a few times they realized we were playing a game. Amita cracked a smile. It was hugely rewarding, despite the fact that the moment Dirgha saw that he was meant to be having fun, he returned to the shack, picked up his stick, and once again began drawing in the dirt.

Farid came back two hours later with Navin. The boy's finger was now in a clean, tightly wound white bandage. We said good-bye to Krish and Nuraj's mother and waved to the children. Only Amita waved back. We caught one of the buses on the Ring Road, leaping on as it slowed down enough for us to catch it, and made the ninety-minute commute back to Godawari.

Every few days we brought food to Krish and Nuraj's mother and the seven children. The children warmed to us. On our third visit they ran to greet us. Dirgha still stayed behind in the shack. He kept his hands jammed in the pockets of his ragged pants as if to prove his point, dragging his bare feet through the dirt and rarely looking up.

I had brought along my small digital camera on the third trip. After leaving a sack of vegetables near the doorway, I took a few dozen photos of the children as they clowned around. I didn't tell them what I was doing; they had never seen a camera before, and it was easier to get candid shots. In contrast, when the kids at Little Princes saw the camera come out, they would race to press their faces against the lens, ensuring that the majority of my photos were of Hriteek's cheek or Nishal's hairline. But eventually the seven became curious. They stood on their tiptoes and tried to see what I was looking at on the tiny screen.

On our fourth visit, I took out my camera again. The children were playing on a small haystack in the field. Dirgha, as usual, was sitting on a small pile of bricks at the side of the house, tying long blades of grass together, end to end, and holding them up, like a prayer flag strung between his two tiny arms. I walked over to him. He looked up at me and looked back down, defiant, concentrating on his task. I pointed the camera at his face, two feet away. His face filled the screen. I took the close-up. Then I turned the camera around, a few feet away from him, so he could see the mysterious little screen.

He couldn't resist. He stood up and walked toward me, still sullen lest I think he was enjoying himself. He peered down at the screen. And his eyes widened. From behind me I heard excited shouts and the patter of bare feet across the dirt. The mystery was being revealed. The others plowed into me like a freeway pileup, cramming their heads together to see the screen. A second of silence as they took it in, then shouts. Those shouts became shrieks of glee. Amita was shaking Dirgha with breathless excitement, telling him what he did not yet understand. The picture on the screen was him—this was what he looked like.

It had not occurred to me that the boy had likely never seen his own face. He had come from a village with no mirrors, no glass, no reflective surfaces at all. As the others howled with delight and begged to have their own photos taken, Dirgha gripped the camera tightly and gazed at himself. For the first time, a toothy smile spread across his face.

Dirgha was never shy again. He was still defiant, but in small, almost adorable ways. When Amita, little tomboy that she was, found an old plastic ball, she decided we would play catch. She took a long running start and skidded to a stop three feet away from me and threw the ball with every ounce of strength she possessed. Dirgha, standing near me and evidently eager to impress his fellow seven-year-old, leaped to intercept the ball, presumably just to show that he was still in charge. It sailed through his hands and into mine. He turned to me, furious in his frustration, and stamped his foot. He sat down, arms crossed. Another boy to remind me of my younger self. I went to throw the ball back to Amita but pretended to drop it, right next to Dirgha. He pounced dramatically, as if athletic prowess alone had allowed him to steal the ball. He leaped up and was all smiles again. He even threw it back to me, a sympathetic toss so that I would still feel included. I gave him a grateful nod.

I looked forward to my visits with the seven children. The children at Little Princes were like brothers and sisters; going back to them felt like going home to family. But for the seven children, there were no volunteers. They had been abandoned. Nobody was looking out for them, sending them to school, collecting donations for them, reading them bedtime stories. They were not protected by any organization. These seven were off the radar, and in this country that meant they were at risk of not surviving.

So we still had reason to worry. Nepal's political situation was getting worse. The Maoists were speaking openly of an uprising, of bringing the monarchy to an end no matter what the cost. Revolution was brewing. If there was a prolonged bandha, as rumors said, we would be unable to get food to the children. We needed a permanent solution if the children were going to survive.

With the country deteriorating around us, Farid and I worked with an urgency we had not had before. We looked for children's homes to take the seven children to, but found none. We had underestimated how awful the situation was for trafficked and displaced children; every organization was already overcrowded. I was sympathetic—we had just taken in two more children at Little Princes, and only because they were the younger brothers of two of our boys (Santosh's younger brother and the little brother of a boy named Mahendra). We were now at maximum capacity, twenty children; taking in any more would put us in violation of children's home codes that limited the number of children per square meter of space. We could not take the risk. We needed another solution, fast.

◇

MY RETURN PLANE TICKET was for April 4, 2006. I could not have known it when I chose that date, but that would be the day that foreign nationals would be clamoring at the airport to get on any plane leaving the country. The Maoists had called for a large-scale bandha to run from April 5 to 9, with the threat that it would continue indefinitely until the king was ousted. It was now the end of March, and we were running out of time. Through

my friend Devendra, a young Nepali guy who worked at CERV Nepal, the
organization through which I had first volunteered, I set up a meeting with
the head of the Child Welfare Board, a man named Gyan Bahadur. Devendra
had cautioned me that Gyan Bahadur was quite possibly the busiest man in
Kathmandu; but if we could be at the CERV offices in Thamel at 1:00 P.M.
on Thursday, Gyan would try to meet us.

Farid and I arrived early. We were asked to wait in one of the small meeting rooms with cushions on the floor. Devendra came in thirty minutes later
with a message from Gyan. He was running late. Could we meet at 4:00 P.M.
instead? Farid and I went to a nearby local restaurant that served an excellent
tandoori chicken—one of the things we craved almost daily in Godawari. We
sat on the rooftop terrace of the restaurant and talked for the next few hours,
brainstorming about strategies for the children, trading gossip about the
political situation, and just sitting quietly, watching the river of people below,
noting how few tourists there were at what should have been the height of the
trekking season. Even the ones we spotted were getting into taxis with their
bags and heading off in the direction of the airport. The world was leaving
Nepal to its war. Soon we would be forced to do the same.

Back at CERV, Gyan Bahadur sat across from us on a cushion on the
floor. Next to him sat Devendra, who had grown up in Bistachhap, the village
near Godawari where we had had our initial orientation week. More important, he knew the situation with the seven children and wanted to help.

"Conor-ji, Farid-ji, it is my pleasure to meet you," said Gyan, using the
formal suffix to greet us. "How can I be of assistance to you?"

I told Gyan about Little Princes, about Golkka, about the seven children,
about our current dilemma. He listened intently, never interrupting, never
revealing any emotion.

"Conor sir," he said when I gave a clear indication that I was finished.
"Thank you for sharing this. I was very eager to hear your and Farid sir's
opinion. I am well aware of the activities of Golkka. As you have guessed,
there are many more children besides your twenty children and the seven
you have found near the Ring Road. I have been tracking this man for two

years now. It is my estimate that he has trafficked close to four hundred children."

He must have seen the astonishment on my face because he nodded at me as if to agree that this was the appropriate reaction.

"As you may be thinking, it is very difficult to arrest this man," he continued. "Once before, he was arrested. He has very powerful relations, they allowed him to be free after three days. Evidence is not strong against him, not for Nepal system," Gyan said with a sad smile. "But what you say gives me some hope. These children are evidence, in a way. They are evidence that he mistreats children, that he leaves them to starve, to die. Perhaps these children will be evidence enough to arrest Golkka. To stop him from taking more Humli children."

Gyan stood up. "I am very sorry, I must go," he said, looking at his watch. "You are looking for a home for these seven— I understand you correctly?"

"That's right, yes, sir. And I leave in three days," I told him.

"Then it must be done quickly, I think. You both should leave Nepal soon, before violence begins. I fear it will begin soon. And we must find protection for these seven. This is our top mission, the three of us, am I correct?" he said to Farid and me.

"It would be very good, yes," Farid answered. "Nobody can take the seven children. I have called many places. It has been very difficult for the children—they are very young." I could hear him struggling to control his emotions.

Gyan picked up his motorcycle helmet and tapped it lightly against his chin, thinking. At last he said, "Tomorrow or next day you will get a phone call. You will have a home for the seven children."

With that, he pressed his hands together to bid us farewell, shook hands with Devendra, and walked quickly out to his motorcycle, kicking it to life before taking off, weaving between pedestrians.

Two days later the phone rang. I had never heard of the Umbrella Foundation. But when I did, it sounded like some kind of divine gift to the children of Nepal. Umbrella was founded by a woman named Viva Bell, a lovely

Northern Irish woman who had been living in Kathmandu for fourteen years. Her partner, Jacky Buk, a Frenchman, with a rugged face and wild, gray, half-dreadlocked hair, ran the organization's day-to-day operations. Together, they had under their care more than 150 children in four children's homes, all next door to each other, in Kathmandu. Viva told me that Gyan had asked her to call me, that I had something to ask her.

"So then, what's all this about a favor, Conor?" she asked in a thick Irish accent that reminded me of my summers in Ireland with my father.

I told her the abbreviated version of the story of the seven children. I concluded by assuring her, "We will of course be very happy to pay all their expenses, but I wasn't sure if you might possibly have enough space for—"

Viva didn't even let me finish.

"Sure we'd love to have 'em!" she said. "Just tell us where they are, we'll round them up!"

I was unable to speak for a moment. When I did, I found my throat blocked by an enormous lump. I took a breath before saying, stupidly and instinctively, "Are you sure? Because I wouldn't want to put you out at all—"

"Now don't go gettin' all polite and American on me, Conor, you've been here too long to do that. We'll take the children, you've done very well to keep them safe this long. They'll be grand with us—sure they'll have a blast with the other kiddies!"

I stared out the window for several minutes after we had hung up. Then I found Farid on the roof, talking with some of the older kids.

"We found them a home," I said, speaking over the heads of the growing boys.

"That's good—how many can they take?" Farid asked, braced for disappointment.

"All seven."

Farid said nothing at first. Then he shook his head in amazement. "That is very, very good news, Conor."

The next day I gathered the children together to say good-bye to them.

As was the custom, they had given me flowers and tikkas to stick to my forehead to wish me a safe journey. As I expected, they asked when I would return.

"In one year, yes, Brother?" asked Anish. "Same like last time, yes?"

I told them the truth. I told them I loved Nepal, I loved spending time with them and living here in the village. But I had to go home, and I would likely not be able to make it back for a few years, when they were all much bigger. I had to start a new career. I was completely broke, and I had to buy food and rent a home.

"And get married, yes, Brother?" said Santosh, smiling.

"Uh—yeah. Well, no—not really, to be honest. I think you will be married before me, Santosh," I said, happy that the children took this as a joke.

Then the children started with a chorus of "What about me, Brother? You will be married before me?" and I had to go through the whole list of children, all the way down to assuring Raju that yes, even he would probably be married before me.

I waved good-bye to the children, not wanting to prolong it any longer. They were in good hands. We had a contingency plan in place at Little Princes for when we had no volunteers—it had happened before, a year earlier, when Farid had to return to France for a month when his visa expired. At those times, our Nepali staff would take over. Hari would stay at the house during the day, together with Bagwati and Nanu, our washing *didi* who lived next door. At night, Bagwati stayed with them. Hari, Bagwati, and Nanu had proven themselves a highly capable staff. They also had the support of the entire village, who watched out for the kids as they ran through the dirt paths and fields. The staff would take over for us when Farid left in a week. The older boys would have to take on more responsibility, getting the younger boys ready for school, for example. But, as always, I told myself, I had to trust that the children would be fine.

Farid walked me to the road to wait for the bus. He wished me a safe journey home and a nice time seeing my family, and he promised to let me know if he heard anything about the Umbrella Foundation picking up the seven children. He reassured me that they would be okay—they had survived for this long, they had enough food to last three weeks, let alone a few days. If it got bad, we could ask Hari to bring them more. All this made sense to me, I knew it was true. Still, it was good to hear it from Farid.

"I hope you can get your flight out, Farid. It is going to get ugly—I hope you get transportation," I said. He laughed.

"This is Nepal, Conor. I take what it gives me," he said.

My last view of Nepal was the Himalayan range, eye level with my window seat. I very much hoped I would see it again someday.

Part III

SEVEN NEEDLES IN A HAYSTACK

April 2006–November 2006

Three

STEPPING OFF THE PLANE in Newark, New Jersey, the first familiar face I saw was my mother's. As always, she was standing in the front row of the crowd, leaning into the railing, scanning the faces of the tired travelers emerging through the sliding doors. I saw her before she saw me; her face serious, her hands gripping the railing, eyes checking the screen to confirm that the flight from Delhi was—yes, there it was—on time. She recognized me instantly, never mind that my clothes hung off my skinny frame, that my hair had been hacked short, that I had not shaved in a month. Her eyes lit up and I knew what she would shout "Yes! Woo hoo!" startling the small Indian woman next to her. After all these years, her reaction still embarrassed me. But maybe this time it embarrassed me a little less than before.

We drove home to Jersey City, past the New York skyline. My mom first asked about the children, all of whom she knew by name from my e-mails home. Nepal was in the news, she told me. To prove it, she turned on National Public Radio. Sure enough, within fifteen minutes there was an update about Nepal. I soon realized that my mother knew far more than I did about the political situation in the country. She had absorbed every bit of information she could find. For ten minutes she gave me a rundown of everything that had happened, of the Maoist attacks and the Royal Nepalese Army's counterattacks, of journalists being thrown in prison and citizens being beaten down by both sides.

She stopped in front of our house in Jersey City, turned off the car, and we sat quietly for a moment.

"Anyway. I'm just glad you're home," she said.

My mother left the next day to go back to Florida, where she had moved permanently. She was going to put the Jersey City house on the market, but she would wait until I had found an apartment of my own.

Two days later, my friends started calling. Every night a different group of friends, friends I hadn't seen in more than a year, took me out to celebrate my homecoming. For the first time in ten years, I had come home to stay, to find a job, to settle down. We talked about what neighborhood of New York City I should live in and which women they thought I should meet. There was much talk around candidates for blind dates. They insisted on picking up the tabs in bars and restaurants across the city. "Please—you've been off saving orphans," they would say. "This is the *least* we can do."

I know I should have politely refused their generous offers. But the food . . . the food was just so beautiful. It was wonderful. It was delicious. I should have been filming commercials for TGI Friday's, the way my face flushed with ecstasy with every bite of a potato skin. I ate anything that didn't have rice. I relished drinking water straight from the tap, guzzling it without fear of parasites. Beer tasted heavenly. I ate my first piece of chocolate in four months.

And everything, everywhere, seemed squeaky clean. Everyone in the city was dressed in clothes that positively gleamed, in collared shirts, gorgeously pressed and starched. Nobody wore the same clothes even two days in a row, let alone two months in a row. No fleece for miles around—no flip-flops, either. Everywhere the sweet symphony of English, of new cars humming, of air-conditioning sweeping through rooms, of toilets flushing. Perhaps the strangest feeling of all was seeing children, so many of them with glowing white skin, that unfortunate translucent paleness that I shared. After months of rich, brown skin of a thousand shades, it looked like these children had been bleached.

During the days, I was putting together my résumé. It was hopelessly out-of-date. I had decided I would get back into public policy. It seemed like the right transition, and I knew I could get a job fairly easily, which was important after being without a salary for so long. New York was expensive, and I was broke. On my résumé I listed the work I had done for the EastWest Institute in Prague and Brussels. I hoped the year of travel wouldn't count against me. And under the final section, the one titled *Other Interests,* I wrote "Little Princes Children's Home, Nepal: Volunteer."

That was it. The entire experience, living for months with eighteen children, each one unique and crazy and swimming in my memory, boiled down to a single line that would likely never be read. And maybe that was how it should be, I thought. It was time to move on—to a real job, to dating, to starting a life near my family and friends.

But I struggled with the moving-on part. I had already written four e-mails to the Little Princes e mail address. I knew that Farid or Hari would read them to the children. I wrote to Hari to ask him to go check on the seven children when they landed at the Umbrella Foundation—when the political situation calmed down, of course—to tell them that we were thinking of them. I wanted to send them the photos I had taken of them. I found myself wanting to maintain that connection, not to be a volunteer who disappeared back into his everyday life once he had left Nepal.

As I tried to start the job hunt, I was distracted by the news from Nepal as it unfolded live on CNN. People were taking to the streets, not at the orders of the Maoists, though the rebels did all they could to support it, but at the urging of the political parties that had been kicked out of parliament when the king had seized power. Protests were organized by activists and promoted by journalists—the ones not yet thrown in jail.

Nepal had reached a boiling point. King Gyanendra, desperate to maintain his grip on power, had issued a curfew to stop the protests against his autocratic regime. When that failed, he gave the orders for the police to shoot protestors on sight. Eight people were shot dead on the street on the first day of protests.

The Maoist uprising was now a popular uprising, and it grew stronger by the hour. Farid, who had made it back to France, and I kept in close touch by e-mail. We shared any information we had, any rumors, any news from our friends and colleagues in Nepal. We marveled at the images on TV, at the faces of these peaceful, wonderful, loving people, suddenly crazed with passion, with determination, with revolution, with the spirit that drives men and women to stand on front lines and absorb bullets and batterings to win freedom for those who stand behind them.

The king had sealed his fate with the killings. It seemed the entire country had descended on the streets of Kathmandu. On April 24, 2006, the monarchy crumbled. The king, with the citizens of Nepal literally beating at the door to the royal palace, announced the reinstatement of the democratically elected parliament. This announcement, the only announcement he could make, may have saved his life. The faces of the people, the close-ups with a CNN logo hovering in the bottom right corner of the screen, told stories of relief, disbelief, jubilation, and optimism.

I turned off the TV. I felt like I had been watching for days. Nepal still had a long road ahead of it—What of the Maoists? What of the king? Who would rule Nepal?—but for now the country had untied itself from the railway tracks. I thought about those faces on TV. They were fathers and mothers, expressing a joy that came from making a difference, from making the world a better place for their children. I swelled with pride for my foster country. And I thought that maybe, just maybe, our children—the Little Princes and the seven children—had a brighter future ahead of them.

Then the e-mail came that changed everything.

◇

THE E-MAIL WAS FROM Viva Bell. With the uprising, it had taken their team three weeks to get across town to pick up the children. It had been impossible to move in Kathmandu before that; nothing could ply the roads. Once the king was overthrown, it took them just two days to organize a small van to get the children. Jacky, Viva's partner, went with two of their staff—two women, who could comfort the children when they were picked up. Jacky found the shack without any problem, the directions were perfect. He opened the gate, greeted Nuraj's mother and her young son with a smile, and walked inside the shack.

The seven children were gone.

The mother told Jacky that Golkka had gotten word that the children were going to be rescued. Golkka somehow knew my name, and he knew that I had been speaking to the government's Child Welfare Board about the children and their plight. Golkka knew exactly how to exploit the law to remain out of jail, but he recognized these seven children, their very existence, because of the conditions in which they lived, could be used as evidence against him—evidence he might not be able to refute in a criminal case.

Golkka took no chances. The moment the king was overthrown and the curfews lifted, he struck. He took the children away under the cover of a euphoric capital. He kidnapped them so they could not create problems for him. In the race for the children, he had beaten Umbrella by forty-eight hours. And just like that, they had vanished.

Haunting me were the last words I had said to the children before I left them. I told them that somebody was coming for them, somebody who they could trust. Somebody who would take them to a safe place, where there would be many children and they could go to school and be well fed and sleep in beds and have proper shoes. They didn't believe it. They had heard this before, from their mothers and fathers in their villages in Humla, right before they were taken and abandoned and left without food or proper shelter. I sat beside them and looked them in the eye and told them I understood. I promised them that this time, it was true.

Three weeks later, somebody did come for them, just as I had promised. But not to take them to a safe place. Amita and Dirgha and little Bishnu and the others—they would all know by now that I had betrayed them. That I was just like the others. The only difference, as I was all too aware, was that this time, nobody knew where they were.

I read and re-read that e-mail from Viva, sitting in the same bedroom where I had spent much of my childhood. The phone rang twice, friends calling back to tell me which bar we were meeting at that night. I let it ring. When I looked up at the clock again, I saw that I had been sitting there for more than an hour, staring at that e-mail. It was now dark out.

Next to my computer I kept a notebook of my job search. It was meticulously organized, a sign of my excitement. The prospect of rejoining this life in New York was a dream. It was a life where I had friends and money and dates and food I had been craving for the past year. And it would be in America, near my family, where everybody spoke English and where we shared a common history and cultural references.

I took one last look at those pages, of the list of institutes and companies who I thought I might work for, of the pros and cons of each, of the approximate starting salaries of each position. Then I tore those pages out. On a fresh sheet of paper, I wrote down the names of the seven children: Navin, Madan, Samir, Dirgha, Amita, Kumar, Bishnu.

I turned back to my laptop and composed an e-mail to Farid. I explained what had happened, including the entire text of Viva's e-mail. I ended my message with a single line: "I'm going back to Nepal."

He responded immediately from France: "I'm coming with you."

◇

MY INSTINCT WAS TO buy a plane ticket that day. I could borrow the money for it; I could be in Kathmandu by the end of the week. With the recent violence, flights would be empty. But what would I do when I landed? Finding the children would be a near impossibility in Kathmandu, a city of one million. Hundreds of thousands of refugees had flooded into the city during the civil war. Thousands of children had disappeared. I wouldn't know where to begin. This would take more planning than I was used to, and that frustrated me. I was not a good planner. I was good at making quick, rash decisions, of hurling myself into difficult situations, making the best of it, then squirming out of them again.

What was I supposed to do first? I took out my notebook and listed the steps. I came up with one, and it wasn't even the first step: Go to Kathmandu. After that, I was lost. I put down my pen and stewed some more. The more I stewed, the angrier I got. All I had been trying to do in Nepal was get seven children out of harm's way. To bring them across town to a children's home. That was it. I wasn't trying to be Mother Teresa. And still I had failed.

I looked at the photos from Nepal, of the jubilation in the streets after the king's resignation. That made me even angrier. Why weren't Nepalis looking for these kids? These were *their* children, not mine. But all they could do was celebrate, as if everything was all better now. Nobody cared about these vanished children. If a five-year-old boy went missing in the United States, it would be front-page news for days. Entire towns would hold vigils. Millions of dollars would be spent to find him. The governor would hold a press conference. In Kathmandu, seven children vanished into thin air and nobody even missed them. Of course they didn't—they had saps like me bringing them rice and calling everybody I knew to try to put them in a home.

Farid let me ramble until I had exhausted my bluster, then he wrote back. He told me, in his undiplomatic way, that I was being—what was the word in English?—unjust. I was being unjust toward these people. (He later added "irrational" after consulting a dictionary.) He didn't explain himself; he didn't need to. My fiery anger was dunked into Farid's pool of reason and emerged, dripping, as guilt. I had spent all my money traveling around the world. I would never struggle to get medical attention for my children, or to keep them out of the hands of armed men trying to abduct them. I would never watch my friends and neighbors waste away from starvation. I would never pray to God for rain to keep crops alive. But if I ever did experience even a fraction of one of these fears, I was certain, I had to admit, that I would not spend my time worrying about children I had never met. I would be concerned about keeping my own family alive.

I began to think more rationally. Farid and I spent entire days brainstorming. A quick move back to Kathmandu would do us no good; we had no resources. Even if by some miracle we found some of the children, how would we support them? How would we protect them? They could stay at Umbrella temporarily, but I knew in my heart that these seven children were not Umbrella's responsibility. They were mine. Umbrella had done their part to rescue them and keep them safe. They needed a home, and if we were going after them, then it was also our responsibility to give them a home. I had promised them that before I left. Until we raised enough money to give them some stability, there was little point in returning.

A plan was taking shape.

I needed to raise money. I wrote that down. It became the step before "Fly to Kathmandu." I had raised a little money in the past through my travel blog, writing about Little Princes. I needed a better structure. People would need to be convinced that this was a real venture, that there was a tax deduction in it for them. How I was going to find these people was a different story; I ignored that step for now. I needed an official nonprofit organization.

The problem was, of course, that I had no idea how to start a nonprofit organization. I asked friends and the contacts of friends, and every one of them recommended that I hire a lawyer to set it up. A lawyer? I thought, hanging up with a friend of mine who had started a nonprofit. I can barely afford to buy groceries. Unwilling to give up food, I located a law library in New York City, and started commuting in every day to do research. After two weeks, I felt like I had a grasp of how to do it myself. But that was only the beginning—it was like buying a car without knowing how to drive. There were pages and pages of legal documents required for the organization. They asked questions that should have been basic, the answers should have rolled off my tongue. What is your mission? How are you going to accomplish it? What is your strategy? How much money will you raise? Who is on your board of directors? I had no idea. I wanted to find children, but I didn't know how much that would cost. I wanted to give them a home, but I had no idea how to accomplish that.

Launching this organization in Nepal was consuming all my time. I had

no social life at all now. I tried to distract my single-mindedness by watching television in the evenings, but I only got through thirty minutes before
I went back to work. It was exhausting, never more so than when I tried to
sleep. It took ages to try to relax, to calm my mind enough to actually fall
asleep. Thoughts, ideas, people I could talk to or meet—they all careened
through my mind as if on a Roller Derby, elbowing one another in the face
to vie for my attention. But one night, I was actually awoken out of a dead
sleep by an idea. This one had serious momentum. It was soon moving with
such speed around my head that I found myself sitting bolt upright, feet on
the floor. I knew what we were going to do. I stumbled to my computer and
wrote to Farid.

I wrote without preamble:

We can find their families, the families of the children. The
families of the Little Princes, for starters, and of the seven children
if we ever find them. Think about it—there's a truce. The Royal
Nepalese Army is no longer fighting. The rebels have called a
cease-fire. Nobody is going to want to fight now that the king is
out of power. We have a window of opportunity to go to Humla.
We might be able to pass freely into the villages without getting
kidnapped or attacked, especially if the Maoists are trying to
become a legitimate political party. The future of Nepal depends on
reconnecting this lost, displaced generation with their families and
communities. We could try, right? Do you think that could work?

It must have been early morning in France, but Farid wrote back in less
than an hour:

Conor, I like this idea very much. We must try this.

Our mission statement was vague, but I knew what we meant. We
would rescue trafficked children. We would try to find their families. That

was enough for the documents, at least. I didn't specify that we were only
thinking about rescuing seven children, and that finding them, let alone their
families, might prove impossible. I was even more vague on the strategy questions and the fund-raising questions. How would we find the children? I had
no idea. Talking to the government for starters, maybe. How much money
would we need? Not sure—I estimated about twelve thousand dollars. The
only real expenses were flying to Nepal and opening a children's home, not
just for seven but for two dozen, maybe. One by one, I filled in answers—
guesses, really—to these questions. I tried to be specific enough to not attract
attention to the fact that I had no idea what I was doing.

When it was completed, I realized one line was still blank: the name of
the organization. Nothing came to mind. So I spent the evening saying potential organization names aloud to myself, introducing myself together with
those names and imagining how each would sound with a Nepali accent. I
came up with a few good names. All of them were taken. I remembered the
e-mail to Farid, about the lost generation of kids. So I settled for one where
the acronym wouldn't spell some kind of curse word. I named the organization Next Generation Nepal.

Now I was not only coming up with steps, I was actually checking some
off. I am easily inspired by measurable progress, and I worked even harder.
I would go two or three days in a row without leaving the house, planted in
front of my computer. I reconnected with some of the brightest and most
compassionate former colleagues from my eight years at the EastWest Institute and convinced them to serve on the NGN Board of Directors. I filled out
pages of IRS applications for tax-exempt status. I wrote in my blog about the
organization. I asked my immediate family members for a very early Christmas present: a donation to NGN. I asked my friends to help the orphans they
had read so much about on my blog over the last year. I asked other friends to
help me throw small fund-raisers.

The fund-raisers were the first moments I realized I was actually going
to do this. I had to stand up in front of fifty people who had given twenty dollars each and announce that NGN would be the first organization (or at least

the first one that I'd heard of, and I had done a lot of research) to not only stop trafficking in Nepal, but to try to reverse it. We would search the hills and mountains of Nepal, in some of the most remote regions in the world, until we found the families of trafficked children. People clapped. I did not add that I might be completely full of crap.

I rarely mentioned the true inspiration for starting Next Generation Nepal: the seven children. The idea of searching for families was far-fetched, I knew that. At least it was a task, though, something I could try, even if I just walked the streets of Kathmandu. But Dirgha, Amita, Bishnu, Navin . . . these were real children. I did not share their names with anybody. To do so would have been to admit responsibility for what had happened. I told myself that there was nothing I could have done, but that wasn't true. I could have squeezed them into Little Princes until we had a better solution. I could have avoided speaking to so many people about it—Golkka had many contacts, and he had learned of our interest in the children, which directly led to his retrafficking them. There was no escaping the fact that seven children were gone because of me, and it was very possible that I would never get them back. That crushed me every day. So I kept their names to myself and accepted the applause at that fund-raiser for being such a brave, selfless soul.

I was learning more about Nepal that summer, leveraging policy and international organization contacts I had built over the years at the EastWest Institute, building a contact database for when I returned to Kathmandu. But nobody I spoke to could tell me anything about Humla, the remote region where the Little Princes were from. It was a complete unknown. Until I found Anna Howe.

Anna was based in Kathmandu. She was one of the few people I had heard of who had actually been to Humla, who had actually worked on com-munity development projects there. Like Viva at Umbrella, Anna had been in Nepal for about fifteen years. She was American, I guessed in her early fif-ties, and a practicing Buddhist. She would go on to become a Buddhist nun, to shave her head and wear the gorgeous maroon robes, but when I met her she was the country director for an international organization called ISIS that helped rescue children who had been trafficked from Humla. I e-mailed her, explaining who I was and what I was trying to do. She wrote back immediately, eager to help in any way she could. Helping Humli children was a life's mission for her.

We e-mailed often. Anna knew Nepal as well as anybody. She knew the story of how children were trafficked, and she knew Golkka; he had trafficked many children besides those at Little Princes. Unfortunately, Golkka also knew Anna. A local journalist had written an article detailing the work she was doing in Kathmandu. Despite her plea to remain anonymous for personal safety reasons, the journalist published her name. Days later, Golkka called her cell phone, which he had procured through his network, and told her in no uncertain terms to immediately cease all involvement with Humla. In typical Anna style, she politely told him to go to hell. But she was also much more vigilant when she left her house.

Anna became something of a mentor to me. From my bedroom halfway around the world, we instant-messaged for hours, brainstormed about how I could search for families of trafficked children. She knew the region well. She had gone to Humla during the war, and had been captured, only briefly, by Maoists who demanded she pay a ransom to let her go.

Clearly, the rebels didn't know Anna Howe. In fluent Nepali, she shamed the young teenage rebels, asking them if they even knew anything about Mao, what they were fighting for, and if they were honestly demanding an older woman, traveling alone, on a mission to help impoverished villagers, pay them all the money she had, which would leave her stranded in Humla. They let her leave.

Over and over, she told me that I was doing the right thing, that the children needed me to do this. That encouragement helped keep my spirits up over the summer when the weight of the task ahead threatened to overwhelm me.

Farid was my full-time partner in this mission. We wrote several times per day. He understood my obsession because he shared it. He started a smaller version of NGN in France, naming it Karya. It was a much better name than Next Generation Nepal, I admitted with a sigh. *Karya* sounded like a French word, but was Nepali for "work." Karya would bring in some money and, critically, find excellent, dedicated people in France who could help, some of whom had been former volunteers at Little Princes. It was a French woman, after all, who started Little Princes to begin with. Farid and I knew that, together, we could open a children's home. We knew how to manage a children's home—we had done it with Little Princes for months. Farid had long been an expert in how many kilos of rice one child could eat per week, the price of potatoes, how much to pay for a tailor.

How to rescue children, though, was another matter. I had no answer for those who asked me how we would do it. Nor did I have an answer to the question of how I would even begin to find families of trafficked children in the remote villages of Nepal. All I could tell them was that we were going to try, but we needed their donation to do it. And bless them, many people gave. They gave in small amounts, ten dollars, twenty dollars. I received checks from people who had followed the blog for two years, who told me that they felt like they had been living at the Little Princes with me. I wrote back to each and every person who donated. I wrote gushing thank-you letters that probably embarrassed some people. To me, each donation was a touching display of blind faith that I would be able to accomplish something. Each donation showed a confidence in me that I did not share.

By August, after four months of uninterrupted begging, I reached my goal of raising five thousand dollars. I figured that would be enough money to get back to Nepal and support a children's home for a few months while I continued to fund-raise. I was practically sweating from the effort. Then I was rewarded with my first lucky break. One of my college buddies from the University of Virginia, Josh Arbaugh, had contacted the local paper in Charlottesville, Virginia, and convinced them to run a story about what I was doing. It would run the following month, in September, when I was already in Nepal. The paper promised a big article with a photo of me and the kids. The article would also detail the story of the seven children. That small, local paper in Charlottesville was going to hold me accountable.

I looked at my checklist. Seven steps had been crossed off. The next one was the very first one I had written down: Fly to Kathmandu. It happened in early September 2006.

Four

NEPAL WAS A DIFFERENT country from the one I had left in April. My trip out of the country involved weaving around burning tires on the Ring Road and pressing through the crush of the few remaining panicked tourists to make my flight. For the first time, there was not a swarm of people milling outside the airport's borders, waiting for their family or friends to arrive; they were now allowed inside to the arrivals area. The machine gun nests near the entrance sat empty. Gone were the soldiers at every intersection and the tank that guarded the southern road that led from Kathmandu to Godawari. We drove past what had been the military checkpoint, the point on this road where I was so accustomed to getting off the minibus, submitting to a search, and getting back on the bus to continue my journey. It was as if the closing bell had rung, and the entire war had just packed up and left.

One hour and seven dollars later, we were driving into Godawari, back where it all began.

I had not told the children I was coming. They were a quarter mile away from where I got out of the taxi. For all they knew, it would be several years before I returned. Halfway down the path to the children's home,

I ran into Nishal. He was sitting on the ground, cross-legged, peeling a small orange and chattering away to Hriteek, who was hanging by his knees from a branch directly above him. Nishal held up his arm to hand him the peeled fruit, and set to work peeling another. Hriteek took the orange and continued to stare into space. I happened to enter that space, from his point of view, upside down. I watched him snap out of his blank stare and try to rotate his head.

"Conor Brother!" he yelled, falling out of the tree and landing on Nishal, who shrieked first at the sight of Hriteek free-falling toward his head, then at the sight of me coming down the path. They scrambled to untangle themselves, then sprinted toward me, plowing into me like crash-test dummies. They grabbed my hands and shook them with glee, then ran ahead of me, racing to see who could break the news first.

In the few quiet moments between the time Nishal and Hriteek disappeared and the herd of children stampeded back up the path, some still holding pencils and notebooks from their study time, I took in the new landscape. It was the end of the rainy season in Nepal; I had only ever been there in the dry season. Gone were the bright cloudless days. Mist hung around the hills and mountains, catching in the trees like a *Lord of the Rings* set piece. The fields were thick and green with wheat. The garden, the dead patch of dirt and dry vegetable patch, now sprouted above the seven-foot walls surrounding the home, a thicket of bamboo obscuring part of the house. It was drizzling, the first rain I'd ever experienced in this country, and some of the children were holding enormous *Jurassic Park*–style leaves over their heads as umbrellas. Then I was overrun.

The children, in their hepped-up craziness at seeing me, actually calmed me. It was not just because this was like coming home to family, nor was it because I felt a surge of joy in seeing these twenty little Nepali tornados, an emotion I never would have thought I would feel here three years ago, when I first arrived at that blue gate. I felt something else, too: respect. For the children. Because after all the rage and revolution that had clawed at Nepal for years, after being forcibly marched through the mountains, after being taken from their parents and watching volunteers leave them just when their country was imploding, these kids were still laughing, still studying, and still showing off. They were survivors. That's how kids are in Nepal. I felt no less urgency about finding the seven children, but it gave me hope that even if I didn't find them tomorrow, that they might somehow hang on.

I had not been to church since I was ten years old, and even then it had bored me. But that night, in the thick September humidity, I lay in bed and prayed aloud. I asked God to consider this remote country and those seven children in it, seven dots of humanity. I asked only that He keep them safe, just long enough for me to find them. I admitted, silently and only because I figured that He knew it already, that this was as much for me, for making up for my own failure and assuaging my guilt, as it was for the kids.

◇

"YOU ARE MARRIED, BROTHER?" Santosh asked. I was buttoning up Nuraj's shirt. He was, as usual, the last one ready for school. The other boys were ready, shoes shined, shirts tucked in, gripping the shoulder straps of their backpacks with some cartoon French logos on them.

"No, not yet, because it's only been—"

"You have girlfriend?" This was from Bikash, the eldest.

"No. Like I said, I have been very busy with—"

"You find girlfriend soon? Nepali girl? You are getting very old, Brother!"

I could hear an alarm ringing, like when two submarines came too close together. If I gave even the slightest hint that I was open to finding a Nepali girlfriend, the children would go momentarily catatonic, then emerge with a single-minded directive: find Conor-Brother-Girlfriend-in-Godawari-How-About-Her-or-Her-or-Her. . . .

"Absolutely not. I am here for you guys, I came to see you," I declared, too emphatically perhaps. "Besides, my parents would not be here to approve her," I added.

This registered. Over 90 percent of all marriages in Nepal were arranged marriages. The idea that I may be any different, that I could simply marry any girl I wished without my parents' permission, was unthinkable. They nodded solemnly.

I watched them march off, single file, their hair pasted down with oil to look presentable for school. They looked like a line of busboys in a 1940s nightclub. Once they were all the way down the road and the house was quiet, the real work began.

While preparing for my return to Nepal, I had reached out to everybody I'd ever made contact with in Nepal—aid workers, UNICEF representatives, other volunteers, Nepali friends. I would need as broad a network as possible for what I was trying to do. I told each of them that I was searching for seven children from Humla who had disappeared after the April uprising. Many were curious, some were outright skeptical of my motives. Surely there was some other purpose? Surely these seven children were the side project to some larger agenda? Regardless of the reaction, the response was uniform: admirable but impossible, I was told in so many words. We will keep our eyes open, they said, for every one of them. But please, they implored me, do not get your hopes up.

I met Viva Bell and Jacky Buk, of the Umbrella Foundation, for the first time in person. They had their hands full; Umbrella now had five children's homes in Kathmandu. The homes were almost next door to one another, and in turn next door to their own house. Within that one area of Kathmandu, a remarkably quiet neighborhood in the northwest side of the city, they and their staff looked after more than 170 formerly trafficked children. They had worked hard, and had probably taken in more children than any other child protection organization in the country. Still, as we sipped tea in Viva's living room, all she could talk about was her deep regret that they had not reached the seven children in time. I reminded her of the military-imposed curfew and that they had missed them by only two days. She shook her head.

"No, no . . . that was our chance, Conor," she said, putting down her tea. "You haven't had to look for children in this city before. I have. It's like looking for a needle in a haystack—it simply can't be—"

She cut herself off and looked at Jacky, who only smiled at her. She continued, "Look, if you find them, any of them—they're probably not together anymore—they can stay here with us. We'll take 'em in for as long as you need until you can get your own children's home up and running. You're doing fine work."

We finished our tea, and they walked me to the door. I hated to leave. Viva had been here fourteen years, Jacky two. Both were former hippies. Viva had a teenage son. They had built a life here. My time in their living room, where I would be a lot in the future, felt safe, like a home away from home. They were equal parts encouraging and honest. They had been through these same trials with children in Nepal and I felt a deep connection with them. Farid would not be able to come to Nepal until late November, and I felt very much alone with a very large task before me.

As I walked to the door, Jacky asked me to wait. He took out his cell phone and dialed, speaking quickly to the person on the other end. Two minutes later he was off again.

"That was Gyan Bahadur, from the Child Welfare Board—*tu le connais, non?*" He spoke in a funny mix of English and French; I don't know if he was even aware of it. "You met him last year. You should go to his office *immediatement*. He can see you. If anybody can help, it is Gyan." He walked me to the front door. "*Bonne chance,* eh?"

Gyan Bahadur, the Child Welfare Board official who had helped us months earlier, would soon become one of the most important people in my world. The exact position he held was unclear due to the complexity of the Nepal bureaucracy, but he commanded authority. That much was clear from the buzz in his office, the way families gathered around him, pleading with him to help them. That he had made time for me in the middle of what appeared to be a hellacious workday was a testament to how much he respected the Umbrella Foundation.

In a country where many public officials must be viewed with suspicion, Gyan genuinely wanted to help children. His responsibility was overwhelming; his jurisdiction was the Kathmandu Valley, the epicenter for child trafficking in Nepal. Still, he never gave up, never slowed down, and maintained his calm Buddhist demeanor in every interaction. When I approached his desk that first day, he waved away a man who was raising his voice and walked over to me to shake my hand. I told him quickly what had happened to the seven children he had tried to help protect, and the reason why I had returned to Nepal. He was dismayed to learn of their fate.

"This was Golkka, we know this," he said. He paused. "I do not wish to alarm you, Conor sir, but . . . time is not on our side. It has already been many months and no one making sure children stay healthy. I will ask people if they hear of these children."

I had many more questions for him, but I knew he had to get back to work—the man who had been raising his voice was now pounding on the desk to get Gyan's attention. Gyan smiled at him, almost serenely, and politely indicated that he should take a seat. I walked outside and caught a bus back to Godawari.

◇

MY WORKDAY BEGAN WHEN the children went to school, which was just about every day now that there were no bandhas, and it ended when they came home. I continued at 8:00 P.M., after they went to bed. During the day, I spent a lot of time with Viva and Jacky. I sought out anybody who knew anything about Humla, specifically whether or not it was safe to travel there. Nobody had any definitive answers, even people from Humla itself. I also called Gyan frequently. Although he was always clearly in the middle of something urgent, he always took time to speak to me. He sensed my growing frustration.

"We must search, yes, but also be patient," Gyan said one afternoon. "We will find, but it will take time. . . . I am sorry, Conor sir—you know that I have so much work to do here." I was visiting him in his office. As usual, he had excused himself from a family to speak to me. My raincoat was dripping wet from the monsoon outside.

"We don't *have* time, Gyan—you know that."

"I will ask some more people if they have any information."

"Nobody has any information. Nobody has seen them. Or maybe nobody is telling us even if they have. How many illegal orphanages are holding these trafficked children? Two hundred?" I could hear myself getting angry.

Gyan shook his head. "There are more than two hundred."

"And our kids could be in any one of them, or they could be somewhere completely different. We are never going to find them, Gyan." It was the first time I had said this out loud, and the truth of it struck me. It made me ill. I didn't know what I was doing, and it seemed nobody could help.

Gyan stared at me for a moment, then walked back to his desk. That was my signal to leave. I wasn't even angry anymore; I just felt slightly dizzy, like walking away from a car accident. This was all a charade. Everything I had said I could do could not be done. The children were gone. That was life in Nepal. This packed room of distressed parents told that story every single day.

Gyan reached his desk and put down the papers he was holding. Then he took his jacket off a hook behind his chair, said something to his colleague, and walked back to me.

"Follow me," he said, and he walked out of his office, down the stairs, and into the heavy rain. I hurried after him and shouted over the rain.

"Where are we going? Gyan?"

Gyan kept walking until we reached his motorcycle. He climbed on, and handed me the spare helmet.

"We're going to look for your seven children," he said, kicking the motor-cycle to life. "Get on. And hold tight—roads are very slippery."

◇

THE RAIN HIT MY helmet like falling acorns. We muscled through it, down narrow alleys in areas of Kathmandu I had never seen. After thirty minutes of dodging traffic and spitting caked mud from our tires, Gyan pulled over. In front of us was the gate of a house that appeared typical of its neighborhood in every way. Gyan dismounted, took off his helmet, and walked to the gate and started pounding on it. By the time I had joined him, the gate was cracked open; a woman peeked out to see who it was. Her eyes widened as she recognized Gyan. She spoke quickly, but Gyan's voice rose and drowned her out. I had never seen him like this—threatening. She gave a weak response. Gyan glared. She reluctantly opened the gate and stepped back, eyeing me warily.

I followed Gyan through another narrow passage. We stopped in front of an old wooden door, paint peeling off it like dead bark. Gyan turned to the woman and instructed her to go back to the front gate and wait there. She protested. Gyan said nothing, he just stared at her. The woman mumbled under her breath and went back the way we had come in.

Gyan slowly pushed open the door. It was dark. A moldy smell washed over us as we stepped carefully inside. Several seconds passed as my eyes grew accustomed to the gloom. At first, it looked to be an empty room. Then shapes began to distinguish themselves. A long wooden table stood in the middle of a concrete floor, bunk beds lined the walls. The only other light came from the narrow gap between the concrete walls and the tin roof. The air was as thick as the inside of a coffin. I could hear my own breathing.

Beside me, Gyan spoke in a low, gentle voice. After a long minute, I heard rustling from the dark corners of the room. He kept speaking. Then a shape appeared, dimly lit by the light from the doorway. It was a child. He must have been seven or eight years old, but he was dangerously thin and was clutching a handful of rice. Gyan squatted next to him and spoke to him. His voice was healing, even to me. The boy whispered something. Gyan smiled and continued talking to him. Then the boy turned his head and spoke, louder this time, back into the darkness. Soon more children were coming out, boys and girls. Most were bald, their heads clumsily shaven to banish lice. They stood in a group, arms and shoulders touching. There were more than thirty of them.

"Conor sir—you see any of your children here?"

I couldn't move. The children were staring at me, unsure what I was doing here, unsure whether this was a good thing or yet another bad thing. My hand shook as I took out the photo of the seven that I had kept from nine months earlier, and looked from face to face. None of the children looked familiar.

"No, they're not here," I said.

"Okay. Then we must go," he said, putting his helmet back on his head.

"Wait, what about these—are you just going to leave these kids here? They're starving!"

Gyan took off his helmet. "I can see that, Conor sir. What would you like me to do?" he asked.

"Take them with us, put them in a home!"

"Which home, Conor sir? Your home?"

"I don't have a home yet, Gyan, you know that. I mean a government home," I said.

"We do not have a home, either, Conor sir, not one with room. Nobody has homes for these children," he said. I could see him clearly in the darkness now. He was staring at me, as if waiting for something to dawn on me. "I know this is difficult. This is not like your country. We do not have solutions as you do."

I said nothing. I just stared at the children. "So we are going to leave them here? With this woman? With so little food, living in this hole?"

"This is Nepal, Conor sir. There are thousands of children like this. But now we must continue to search for your seven children. We cannot give them up, no?"

"No, we cannot give them up."

"Then we must go. I hope I may come back for them. But this woman knows I am watching her. She will not let them expire. This visit has scared her. The children will eat better tonight, trust me."

Leaving that house was one of the most difficult things I'd ever had to do in my life.

Gyan and I sped through more alleys, visiting more of those terrible places, searching for a needle in a haystack. We saw a hundred children, at least, in the next few hours. All of them were in the same condition. In each room we stood, raincoats dripping water onto the floor, and I showed the photos over and over, thoughtlessly. I was no longer looking for the seven children—they were in front of me. The children in these rooms were the ones I hadn't found, the ones I hadn't lost. They were never even blips on the radar.

Then, in one room, excited chatter. I was holding the photo up to a group of older boys, and they pointed and spoke quickly, first among one another, then to Gyan. Gyan took the photo from me, and pointed at four of the boys, confirming. A boy wearing a long, dirty white T-shirt, torn across the back, nodded and pointed as well. I looked closer. He had pointed at Navin, Madan, Samir, and Dirgha.

"What did he say?" I asked.

Gyan questioned the boy one more time, and the boy nodded again. Gyan stood up. "These four boys were here, maybe three weeks ago. They are not here anymore," he said. Anticipating my next question, he said, "They do not know where they went. A man took them away again."

"What about the other three children? Have they seen Amita, the girl? Or Bishnu? He is the young one, the small boy—was he here?" I addressed the boy.

"Only these four, Conor sir. The others were not here."

Golkka had split the children up.

◇

I RETURNED TO LITTLE Princes. I had to work. Fund-raising, I soon learned, is an exhausting and interminable process. It involved writing to everybody I knew, keeping them updated on my progress even when there was none, asking friends and contacts to put me in touch with their friends and their contacts. Asking people for favors, again and again and again.

I had a laptop with me; we had a weak Internet connection via modem that worked on and off. I went into the small office in the home and sat down at the desk to work.

My laptop was missing.

My palms were against my forehead. I spun around, scanning the room. None of my work was possible without it. On it were all my notes, my documents, my e-mails, my database of names. I felt the panic rising in my chest, slowly sealing off my throat. It's okay, I thought, taking deep breaths through my nose. One of the children might know where it is.

I went upstairs. No children. No children in the bedroom either. I came back down, and where the living room had been silent moments earlier, it was now loud with cheers. I walked in to find twenty children gathered around my laptop, watching a terrible-quality, horribly sound-tracked, out-of-focus Bollywood movie on DVD. The cheering had erupted when the hero—a hairy, leather-clad fellow carefully bleeding from his left cheek—leaped off a roof and into a circle of villains who appeared to be taunting a distraught young woman.

"Where did you guys get this movie?" I asked the group at large.

Anish spun around, agitated to the point of almost shaking. I suddenly felt bad; I hadn't meant to get them in trouble. They just wanted to borrow the computer. Anish opened his mouth to apologize.

"Brother, no talk! Please, Brother! Hero fight! Hero fight!!" he cried breathlessly, pointing at the screen and spun back around.

On screen, the villains were laughing that odd, fake laugh that exists only in movies to show just how ridiculous it is that one man is about to fight twelve. The camera zoomed in on the hero's face, the side with the manicured gash. He tore off his sunglasses and, staring at the main villain, growled "*Yabba dabba dabba!*" (I don't speak Hindi). He flew through the air, and sank his fist, elbow-deep, into the ribs of one of the bad guys. The kids went berserk.

"Listen, guys—I'm serious, I really need my computer, so if one of you guys can unplug it—" I was cut off by another eruption from the children as the hero flew back the other way now, from right to left, foot first this time. He appeared not to need to touch the ground. The camera caught a shot of his heel entering the mouth of another bad guy, who suddenly didn't think everything was so fake-funny. The children were almost levitating in their euphoria. Nuraj leaped up and launched into a spontaneous dance.

Hari was standing on the other side of the room, arms folded, staring at the small screen.

"Hari, where did they get this?"

"Friend from school give, Brother. It is Bollywood movie, on DVD. You like?"

"I'm not sure, I just got here—how long are these things?"

Hari considered this. "I will guess this movie . . . four hour long?"

Four hours? Of this?

"When did they start it?"

"Ten minute ago, Brother," he said.

I looked at my watch. I couldn't really do much without my computer. Another squeal of delight rose from the masses. What the hell, I thought. I sat down to watch, just as the screen filled with two villain heads being knocked together by disembodied hands. The crowd went wild.

◇

AT THE END OF September, I received an e-mail that caught my attention. It came from a fellow University of Virginia graduate, albeit from the law school, whereas I had been an undergraduate there. Her name was Liz Flanagan. She had discovered NGN through the article in the Charlottesville newspaper and had written to ask me more about it. In all the e-mails I had received by people saying they hoped to one day also have the opportunity to work with impoverished children, Liz's was the first that talked about what she had already done and why she wanted to continue doing it. She was writing because she was traveling to India at Christmas to volunteer, and she wanted to know if Next Generation Nepal was perhaps affiliated with a global organization that I could recommend.

I wrote back the same day. I explained that we were an independent organization, but that I would be happy to help her if I could. I asked her where else she had volunteered.

"In Zambia, at an orphanage out there," she wrote. "It seems like you were a natural with kids from day one—I didn't have that at all! When I first showed up to the orphanage, I tried to be sensitive to their needs and show them as much affection as possible, but mostly they seemed to want me to chase them. I couldn't get them to calm down, so finally I gave up and chased them for about nine days straight. Sometimes they slowed down and I could talk to them and get to know them a bit. I also made up songs about them. . . . Come to think of it, I'm not sure what my value added was. I'm sure they're still talking about that strange white girl from America."

It was nice to know that somebody had been as clueless as I had been in those first moments with children, even if she didn't know it. I also liked that she was willing to admit how tough it had been working with children at first. I told her about the first day I walked into Little Princes.

"I had no idea what I was doing," I wrote, after describing my entry into the children's home, when I couldn't get the kids to stop jumping on me. "I think mostly I was trying to mask my fear of taking care of kids."

"Yeah, that sounds familiar. But I bet the kids loved piling up on you. Maybe sometimes that's all they need?"

In our next e-mail exchange, I learned that Liz was an attorney and had been practicing corporate law at a large New York City firm for several years. Then, two years earlier, she decided to take off with her best friend, Elena, in 2004 for three months of traveling around the world before taking a new job as the in-house counsel at a technology company. She had been struck by the same desire I'd had that very same year, when I planned my world trip: the need to see what else was out there.

On Easter morning 2004, in the small town of Hoi An, Vietnam, after another long night out with her fellow backpackers, Liz decided to take a walk. In the quiet streets, she came upon a young boy, perhaps eight years old, who was severely physically handicapped. Something about him caused her to stop and sit with him for a while, though he didn't speak a word of English. The boy, clearly enamored, took Liz's hand and led her down the street and to his home: an orphanage for handicapped children in the back alleys of Hoi An. Something was sparked in her. The next summer she volunteered in Zambia with HIV kids, and then on to South Africa. This Christmas she was going to India.

"So you're a born traveler," I observed.

"Actually, I'm the exact *opposite* of a born traveler," she wrote back. She told me that, when she was twenty-two, she moved to England with her then fiancé. She barely left her room for the first week. "The accents scared me. The buses and Underground scared me. The food scared me—it actually scared me. I couldn't figure out why they were putting sweet corn on pizza. Who does that? I made my fiancé buy only food that was readily available in the States. I hated it, I just wanted to go home. And that was *England*."

I liked Liz immediately.

◇

EARLY ONE MORNING IN October, the phone rang. It was Anna Howe. She had heard a rumor less than an hour earlier, something I needed to know immediately.

Since our long conversations over the summer, when she told me everything she knew about Humla, about her experiences, Anna and I had remained close. She was about the same age as my own mother, and she became just as protective. A few days after I arrived in Nepal, we met up at the local tea shop. It would become the first of a regular series of meetings, sitting at a café and discussing strategies for getting me safely into—and out of—Humla. We discussed the safest route, the safest time to travel, who I could meet there.

In our third meeting, Anna appeared especially excited. A Humli man named D.B., a colleague and old friend of hers, had agreed to travel to Humla on behalf of ISIS, the international organization Anna worked for in Kathmandu. ISIS was also taking care of children from Humla. Anna suggested that D.B. and I travel together, to see if we could help each other find the families of the children in those remote villages. She introduced us. That introduction, in D.B.'s living room, with Buddhist icons lining the walls, sitting Indian style on traditional Nepalese carpets, was a turning point. A mission to Humla was suddenly looking, if not easy, at least possible. D.B. and I began formulating a plan to travel to Humla together, putting our two teams together.

On that October morning, Anna said she had urgent news. She had heard that some children from Humla had recently appeared in Thangkot, a village in the western Kathmandu Valley. I knew the place—Golkka and his trafficking ring used it as a home base. I had gone two weeks earlier by myself to visit the illegal children's homes that I knew about. There were dozens of children from Humla, but none of the seven were among them. I told Anna as much.

"It is worth investigating again, Conor," she said. "Most of the new children in the village are too old to match the descriptions of the children you are looking for. But there was one that did: a little girl, with long black hair and Tibetan features, maybe seven or eight years old. Nobody had ever seen her before. You said you were looking for a girl like that, didn't you?"

I can't remember even hanging up the phone. Within minutes I was out the door and on a minibus, the first in a series of long bus rides that would take me to Thangkot. If Amita—if it was indeed her—was there, there was no telling how long she would be there. Golkka had moved her at least once, and there was no way of knowing how often he was moving the children. Time was short. Unfortunately, it was a bad time for trying to get anywhere quickly. It was Dasain.

Dasain is the most important Hindu festival of the year in Nepal. I could never quite figure out what it was all about. What I did know was that at Dasain, the Ring Road on the western side of Kathmandu was almost impassable, thanks to a massive goat market that popped up seemingly overnight. Goats played a critical role in Dasain. Per tradition, each family, even the poorest, would slaughter a goat for the festival. Before eating that goat, the family would spray its blood on their cars, motorcycles, and, yes, buses, as a *puja,* or blessing. It was a sign of my growing comfort with Nepal that as I boarded a blood-splattered bus, all I could think was how bad the traffic was going to be.

To avoid the congestion on the Ring Road, our minibus took an unusual route. We weaved our way through the mazelike back alleys of the capital that seemed designed for nothing wider than fat donkeys. At times, both sides of the bus literally scraped both walls; if we got stuck we would have to kick out

the front windshield to escape. Once back on the main road, our driver continued his practice of getting to our destination by any means necessary, first
driving on the dirt shoulder and, when that got clogged up, driving on the
shoulder of the *oncoming* traffic, honking madly at pedestrians. It was a bold
move even in Kathmandu. But it also got me to Thangkot by late morning.

It was a hot day, and I regretted not bringing water. The rainy season
had ended suddenly, almost overnight, and had left the dirt roads scarred
by dried, caked tracks, imprints left by cars in the mud that would become
permanent contours of the roads. I walked along the main path through one
of the rice paddies. It ended in a T-junction. Left led toward the hills, right
toward a cluster of mud homes. I went right.

Two hours later, sweating and tired, I was unsure what I was doing. I had
no strategy except to hope the little girl would be outside at exactly the right
moment, standing in the exact path that I was walking on, exactly on this day
on this morning, waiting for me to physically bump into her. I scanned the
rice paddies and the paths and the homes and the main road. There was a
chance she was here, and still, she was a needle in a haystack. How had I ever
thought I could just show up in Thangkot and magically find her? I would
need a platoon, knocking on every door and hoping they would give me a full
census of their home.

This was the first time I had searched—really searched—for the children on my own. If I doubted myself before, after the last two hours I felt
pathetic, like an outright fraud for even trying. I took the path leading back to
the main road and Godawari. I was going to find a way to make a difference
for the kids in Nepal. Just not this way.

Then I saw her.

The little girl stood on the path, twenty feet ahead of me, staring at me.
She wore an oversized boy's shirt; her hair was long and tangled. In each hand
she carried a beat-up two-liter plastic bottle, taken from the trash, used for
collecting drinking water at the public tap.

I didn't move. Then slowly, I reached into my back pocket. I took out the
worn, stained photo of the seven children, unfolded it, and studied it. The

girl in the photo had a mischievous smile on her face; the girl in front of me was stone-faced. I walked to her, pausing between steps. Five feet from her, I squatted down. In basic Nepali, I asked her if she remembered me. She did not move, did not change her expression. I turned the photo around so she could see it. I saw her eyes drift across the faces, and stop at her own face, on the far right. I asked her again: Did she remember me?

She nodded and tears welled up in her eyes. I took the bottles from her and laid them on the ground. I took her hand and led her up to the road. She followed without a word. We walked around and found a shop, a typical simple wood kiosk, with a telephone. I called Gyan Bahadur and told him I had found Amita.

"You *found* her, Conor sir? How? Where was she?"

"Thangkot, just on the path leading into a field," I said.

There was a pause. "Yes, that makes sense. Golkka's wife—one of his wives—lives in Thangkot. Perhaps the girl was staying with her. And the other six? You found them also?"

"No—only Amita. I didn't go into the house, I didn't even know where it was."

"Okay, Conor sir. No problem. Somebody from Umbrella will meet you at the tea shop at the intersection. I will come this afternoon with one man from my office. We see if the other children are there as well."

"That would be wonderful, Gyan—thank you."

"I am very happy for this, Conor sir."

An hour later a staff member of Umbrella came—I recognized him as one of the house managers; he recognized me because I was the only white guy for miles. I sent Amita with him in a taxi, and I waited for Gyan for the next two hours. He arrived with a younger man I had seen in his office. He swung himself off his motorcycle and walked quickly over to me and shook my hand, wearing a big smile.

"You have done very well, Conor sir. Now you take the bus, go back to Godawari. We do not want risk Golkka or his wife seeing you, maybe recognizing you. We go and look ourselves. If the children are there, we will bring them

back. Go now. Be happy," he said, patting my shoulder and calling for his assistant to join him. They walked quickly down the dirt path and into the field.

◇

BACK IN GODAWARI, I received a phone call from Gyan.

"I spoke to Viva and Jacky sir. Amita is safe with Umbrella, they take
good care of her," he said.

"And the others? You found them?"

"No—they were not in this house with the girl. But we do not give up,
Conor sir."

I had so badly wanted him to say that he had found all seven children.
But I also wanted to take that evening and relish our victory. It was the only
one I had had. The first thing I did when I got off the phone with Gyan was
to e-mail Liz. I told her what had happened. I even attached the photo I had
taken of Amita on the path the moment I found her, standing on the road
holding the two bottles, stone-faced. I told her that the little girl was now safe
and sound at the Umbrella Foundation.

Liz responded with an e-mail that read, simply, "Woooooo hoooooooo!!!!"
Then, a few minutes later, she wrote, "Okay, sorry, had to get that out. That
was an amazing photo—what a sweet, sweet little girl she is. I'm so glad she's
safe! What was it like to see her that first time?"

I told her that the little girl's appearance was so utterly unlikely that for a
split second I thought I was hallucinating, or that God had plunked her down
in front of me so that I couldn't miss her.

"I think I know what you mean," Liz wrote back. I knew what she was
referring to—Liz was a Christian. She had told me that early on in our conversations, when we were first learning about each other. This was the first
reference to it she had made in any of our subsequent e-mails. "I know this
is not how you see it, necessarily," she wrote, "but I want you to know that I
truly believe that God wants you to find these children."

It had been a long time since I had been friends with a Christian—not
since I was a boy, really. I had spent many years living in Prague and Brussels,

where my friends and acquaintences often equated American Christianity with crazy fundamentalism. But Liz and I were becoming fast friends, and I was grateful to be reminded about how absurd those fundamentalist stereotypes were. Liz's faith was simply a part of her—the central part, perhaps, but a part nonetheless. I liked that she neither tried to persuade me of its veracity, nor did she shrink from it. I found myself wanting to learn more about her every time we wrote.

◇

JUST THREE DAYS LATER, the phone rang at Little Princes. Dawa, one of the older boys, ran all the way out to the field where I was playing soccer with the kids.

"Conor Brother—there is call for you. A man says he must speak to you," he panted.

"Who is it?"

"Nepali man, Brother."

It was Gyan; he was calling to tell me he had found four of the boys. I was ecstatic. I also was beginning to believe Liz—maybe we really were going to find all the children. I decided that night I would say a prayer of thanks.

But Gyan hadn't finished. There was bad news. Two of the boys—Navin, the oldest, and Dirgha, whose photo I had taken and shown to him so long ago—had been starved half to death. They had been rushed to the hospital.

"I am very, very sorry, Conor sir," said Gyan in a soft voice, "but the younger boy, Dirgha, will likely not live through the night."

◇

THE MALNUTRITION WARD OF the Kathmandu hospital is a terrifying place for children on the verge of death. I arrived in the evening, and the doctor brought me to Dirgha. He was lying on a cot in the hallway. Navin sat at the foot of the bed, staring at the floor. He would not look up at me; or maybe he didn't have the strength to. The doctor asked me to carry Dirgha, who had not woken up since he arrived at the hospital, to the only free bed in the ward. The boy was as light as a feather. The last time I had seen him, he was stubbornly pretending not to have fun playing catch with Amita and me. Seeing him like this, carrying him, unconscious, listening to the pessimism in the doctor's voice, was almost unbearable.

Navin stumbled beside me like a sleepwalker. He was the oldest of the seven, the commander in chief of the little band. Now he could barely walk. We entered a long room with many beds, each of them occupied except for the one at the end. The fluorescent lights, many of them broken, were flickering on as the sunlight faded from the room. The doctor pointed to the last remaining bed and indicated the two boys would have to share it. Then he left us alone with the other patients.

Navin started to climb up on the bed when I pulled him back. A bloody syringe lay on the bed. I gingerly picked it up, holding it as far from Dirgha as I could, and looked around for a trash can. There was none. I dropped it on the floor and kicked it far under the bed. Then I laid Dirgha down on the unwashed sheets. Navin climbed in next to him.

In the room were perhaps twenty beds in all, each one occupied by a single child with either a mother or a father lying next to the son or daughter, talking quietly, soothing their child. I examined my two boys. Dirgha was unconscious. Navin was glassy-eyed and starting to drift off. The boys were dangerously malnourished, in agony, confused. They surely did not remember my name. I was unable to communicate with them beyond basic phrases, unable to offer even the barest comfort. Nepal had taught me that children needed very little to survive. But, in this moment, possibly on the verge of the unthinkable happening, I felt woefully, embarrassingly inadequate: I could do nothing but sit on their bed and rest my hands on their feet.

The doctor returned with instructions. I was to give the boys water mixed with dehydration salts every ten minutes when they were awake, and, if they were able to eat, a few biscuits. Waking Dirgha, though, proved difficult. I was only able to do it every few hours or so and only for a few minutes at a time. He refused the water, so I had to force him to drink. He would take a sip and immediately pass out again, his breathing shallow.

Navin, though, seemed to get a bit stronger as the night went on. Sometime in the middle of the night, he awoke asking for food. I gave him a biscuit. Moments later, he got violently ill in a bucket next to the bed. I went to empty it when I saw that he had expelled a foot-long tapeworm. I dumped it all in the toilet—a hole in the floor—and went looking for a working sink so I could at least clean his face. There were no towels, so I soaked an extra T-shirt I had brought and carefully wiped him clean. He did not protest, but only stared at me as if he would never speak again. When he finally fell asleep, I sat on a short wooden stool and laid my head at the foot of the bed to try to nap.

We passed another day and night like that. Around midafternoon, I took a break to get food. A kind mother in a bed nearby, who had been watching us with great interest for the past day, indicated with sign language that she would keep an eye on the boys. Walking back, carrying what passed for dinner—some fried food wrapped in newspaper that I had bought on the street—I couldn't seem to work out how I had ended up here. Not just in Nepal, but in this hospital, with these kids. Nepal was supposed to be just a brief stop on a world tour. Or was it? I could not think of a single thing I would have done differently over the past year, even over the past several years. Each of those things had led me to this moment   to be walking back into a hospital that, in another life, I would have avoided like a structure fire. Returning to a ward that contained not even a single bar of soap, preparing to spend another night with two young boys whose language I did not speak, about to ingest some fantastically unsanitary food for dinner. This was where I belonged. That realization brought me immense comfort.

On the second day Dirgha woke up. It was early in the morning, and I had fallen asleep at last, sitting on a wooden stool, head resting on the foot of the bed. I woke up only when the sun hit my face through the thin curtains. I felt the heat of it first, then sensed the translucent red of the back of my eyes, and opened them in a cautious squint. Dirgha was sitting upright, his back against the metal headboard of the hospital bed. His arms were skinny and hung loose at his side. He was watching me, stone-faced. But he was awake.

The worst was over; the boys had survived. I brought them to the Umbrella Foundation by taxi. Viva had told me over the phone that the staff and older children would be waiting to take care of them. Sure enough, I was met at the door of one of the Umbrella children's homes. This house had a small room that served as a nursing station, with two beds and a medicine cabinet. I was met, not by staff member, but by a singular fourteen-year-old boy named Jagrit.

Jagrit was one of the more than 170 children at the Umbrella Foundation. I got to know dozens of these children in my time there. I tried not to play favorites, and I failed. I love Jagrit. He is exceptionally bright, and his English is amazing. But mostly he is a smart aleck. I have a weakness for smart alecks.

The first time I ever visited Umbrella, I wandered into the children's home where he lived to meet the kids. There were so many of them. I just stood and watched them running around the field outside the house. Jagrit walked up to me.

"You are friend of Viva and Jacky sir, I think. I can give you a tour if you like, sir!" he said loudly. "What is your name?"

"That sounds great. But don't call me 'sir'—my name is Conor," I told him.

"Okay, Conor! I am Jagrit. And I do not charge you anything, sir. But do not worry because this is going to be a very good tour. I am very entertaining," he informed me.

Jagrit turned out to be hilarious, smart, and well respected by the younger kids. He asked many questions about America and my family. I asked him where he was from.

"I am from Humla, sir. I do not think you know Humla, not tourist place like Sagarmatha. Very few children at Umbrella from Humla. But it is very beautiful."

I told him that, as a matter of fact, I did know Humla. The kids at Little Princes were from that region, and they had told me all about it.

"You are joking I think, sir! It is a good joke. I congratulate you."

"I'm not joking, Jagrit. I know it," I said. "It's in northwest Nepal. The largest village, the district headquarters, is called Simikot."

Jagrit was speechless for all of two seconds. "Okay, now I really will not charge you. I was going to charge you many thousands of rupees at the end of the tour, but now I will not."

This was a fairly typical exchange with Jagrit. The more time I spent at the Umbrella homes, the better we got to know each other. Usually we found ways to make fun of each other.

"Today you are very fat, sir," Jagrit would say when I came to Umbrella after being away for a few days. After a couple of months on a diet of daal bhat, I was pretty sure that I was significantly underweight.

"Fat? Where are your glasses, Jagrit? Let me guess—you don't wear them because you are trying to look pretty? For the girls?"

"I use for reading! I do not need to see you so enormous! I hear you coming before I see you. I hear you ten minute before, walking down street like elephant."

When I arrived at Umbrella carrying Dirgha and walking slowly next to Navin, Jagrit was waiting at the front gate of one of the homes. Viva had told him the situation; he had been waiting for me for two hours. He said nothing, but took Navin's hand and led him to one of the small beds in the nursing station.

I followed him inside with Dirgha, laying the boy down on the other bed. Jagrit went to get water for the boys, then disappeared and returned with two boys about his age and two younger girls.

"They watch boys, sir. If they need water or biscuits, they can fetch, no problem," he said.

"Okay, great," I said, and turned to the four children who would be keeping a vigil over our boys. "Thank you—it's very kind of you," I said. The children smiled, thrilled at the idea that they were helping a grown-up.

"Conor sir, you look very tired. You go sleep in my bed—it is the top bunk in the upstairs room," he said. "It is very cozy bed, you see."

"It's all right, Jagrit—I have a bed next door."

"What are the names of these boys?" he asked. I told him. He relayed the information to the other four.

"Okay, no problem now, sir. You go. We take care," said Jagrit, and he gave me an affectionate push toward the door.

I believed him. I went next door, to a tiny room with a bunk bed on the top floor of one of the children's homes where volunteers could stay. I was asleep in minutes. Two hours later I came down to find Jagrit still there, but with four new children watching the boys. In a stack were dozens of hand-made get-well cards that the Umbrella kids had made for them. That image stayed with me: a beautiful six-year-old girl handing Dirgha a piece of paper with a clumsily painted blue flower hovering above the words "Get Well Soon," clearly taught to them by Jagrit. That's Nepal. Children take care of one another.

◇

FIVE OF THE SEVEN children were now safely at the Umbrella children's homes in Kathmandu. Two were still missing: Kumar, a boy of about nine, and Bishnu, the youngest. But there was more news. Gyan had located Kumar. I couldn't believe our luck. The information came less than a week after we had rescued the other four boys. I was anxious to pick him up.

It was too late to take the bus to Kathmandu that evening, but the next morning, I was on a minibus to the capital. I took it directly to Gyan's office; I wanted to be with him when he got Kumar. I waited for him outside his office until he had finished with the parents standing at his desk, then I squeezed between the waiting parents and children to where I could catch Gyan's eye. He said something to his assistant, then walked over to me. He took me by the arm and led me out into the dank hallway.

"There is complication, Conor sir," he told me. "Kumar is in Kathmandu, we found him in the Kalanky district. But he has been sold. He is servant."

"A servant? He's nine years old—a servant to whom?"

"That is complication."

I was accustomed to Nepalis speaking around issues. It often took extensive probing to reach the heart of the matter, especially if the topic was sensitive. I was not used to it with Gyan, though. He was trying to explain the situation in such a roundabout way that I finally interrupted him.

"Who is holding him, Gyan?" I asked.

He hesitated. "I have heard that it is a member of the local government," he said. "I do not know if it is true. I am finding out. If so, he must be persuaded to give boy voluntarily, or it will be . . . difficult."

"But you know where he is?"

"Yes, we know."

"So we can go get him. It's not legal, is it? To have a nine-year-old boy as a domestic slave? Your job is to enforce the law, isn't it, Gyan? Isn't that your job? Am I missing something?"

Gyan sighed. "Conor sir, I promise we will get this boy. You believe me?"

"Of course I believe you, it's not the point—we need to go, right now, Gyan. We can't leave him there. You saw what happened to the other two boys. You're the one who *found* them, for God's sake."

"If you believe me, then please trust, Conor sir. This is complication." He motioned that he had to go back into his office to the waiting mass of people. "Nepal is difficult, I know this. But I will get Kumar."

I stood outside his office, seething, but I could do no more at that moment. I took the bus back to Godawari, frustrated at Nepal and everybody in it.

Back at Little Princes, I ignored Hriteek's attempts to climb up my back onto my shoulders. Raju ran to show me a toy that he had made out of bottle caps, and I ignored him, too. Only the older boys sensed that something was wrong and stayed out of my way. I stomped into the office, sat down at my computer, and started composing an e-mail to Farid. We wrote frequently—I kept him up-to-date on everything. He was counting the days until he could get a visa into Nepal. He had rejoiced at my finding the five children. But now I had bad news for him. I had to tell him that I had information about Kumar, that I knew he was working as a domestic slave, that Gyan even knew where he was, and that I was unable to act on it. He would ask me—he would have to—why I could not get him right that moment, why I was sitting at my computer when a child was in danger. I wouldn't have an answer.

Sitting there, wondering what to say, I came to an unpleasant realization. My foul mood was not just out of fear for Kumar's safety. It was also from guilt. It was the thought of admitting to Farid that I had not stood up to Gyan, that I had not rescued Kumar, even after seeing the danger these children were in. That guilt made me want to bang my fists against the cement in frustration. I wanted to go back to Gyan's office, almost two hours by bus, and demand that we go get Kumar that instant.

I found myself writing down these exact sentiments, almost word for word. Not to Farid, but in an e-mail to Liz. I told her what had happened that day. I told her I felt like I had abandoned a child for reasons that made no sense to me; that I had not pushed harder because I trusted Gyan. But what if I was wrong? What if Gyan was protecting somebody and Kumar disappeared again? The boy would spend his childhood in slavery, and it would be my fault, because I did not stand up to Gyan.

I waited a long hour until Liz wrote back; it was early morning in Washington, D.C. "First of all, I am so sorry—this must be incredibly difficult," she wrote. "Do you really think Gyan is corrupt? Or are you just afraid that he is? Has he done anything so far that has made you doubt him? It sounds like he has been pretty faithful to everything he promised he would do for the children and for you."

I thought about that. "I guess I am afraid he is corrupt. And no, he's never done anything to make me doubt him," I wrote.

"I think you're doing a great thing, Conor," Liz wrote back. "I think in this case, you need to have faith, and put your trust in somebody else to get the job done. I know that's not really useful advice, since from what you said it doesn't sound like you have a lot of good options. But it sounds like Gyan is an honest guy, and if anybody can help Kumar, it's him. You did the right thing."

As soon as I read that, I realized that was what I needed—somebody to tell me I had done the right thing, even if I didn't really have much of a choice. It wasn't easy for me to be working alone. I often wondered if I was doing a thing right, or if I was making the right decision. In this case,

I had no idea if Kumar would be okay, or if someone more experienced would have done things differently. But Liz was right: Gyan had never let me down. I wrote to Farid to tell him what had happened. I told him my concerns and said I had done what I had done because Gyan had always come through for us.

Farid wrote back immediately, incredibly frustrated. I knew what he felt, but this was the right decision. I was glad he was not in the room with me; he would have seen doubt all over my face. Our conversation ended with his telling me he was confident that if I truly believed it to be right, then yes, my decision was the right call. He trusted me and asked me to keep him updated.

A week passed. I was in a perpetually foul mood. I had called Gyan every day and received the same answer every day; he told me I had to trust him. He offered no more information. It was maddening. I also wrote to Liz every day. I leaned on her for reassurance that I was doing the right thing. Any moment she would surely write back "I don't know, Conor—you're there, I'm not. I have no idea what you should do."

But she never did. She encouraged me, day after day, asking if there had been any progress, telling me that it would turn out okay. Liz's e-mails were like kindling, sparks of inspiration in a dark week.

Eight more days passed. With no news of Kumar, I wrote to Farid less. I hadn't called Gyan in four days.

There were few places to be alone in the children's home. On an early Sunday morning, I was almost alone on the roof. Raju was several feet away, pretending I wasn't there but sneaking glances at me, silently willing me to come play with him. The awkward silence was broken by footsteps pounding up the concrete stairs. Hari's head appeared, and seeing me in the far corner, he walked quickly toward me. He was trying unsuccessfully to mask a look of dismay.

"Viva calling for you, Brother," he said nervously. Hari knew what that meant. Calls from Viva were almost universally bad news. I thanked him and took my time getting to the phone. I wasn't sure how much more of this I could take.

"Conor, it's Viva, how are you?" The line was drenched in static.

"I'm fine—what is it, Viva?" I could barely hear her. I pressed my ear against the phone.

"Listen, Conor, Gyan just brought a very nice boy to us that he says is one of yours. I'm standing next to him right now—his name is Kumar. You know him?"

The air drained from my lungs as I slumped into a chair. "Yeah, I know him," I said. "I'll be right there."

I looked at my watch—there was no rush. I dashed off e-mails to Farid and Liz. Then I went upstairs to find Raju standing in the same spot, chin resting on the railing, staring out at the fields. I crept up behind him, snatched him up by the waist, tossed him over my shoulder, and carried him back downstairs. I laid him out, laughing, on the sofa in the living room. Then I deliberately turned my back on him and walked slowly away, knowing that at that very moment Raju was likely climbing up onto the back of the couch. At the top, he would yell the name of some professional wrestler—probably his current favorite, The Undertaker—at the moment he leaped, giving me just enough time to brace for—

"Undy-tekkeeeaaahhh!" I spun around in time to catch Raju belly flopping into my face.

Life was good again.

◇

BY MID-NOVEMBER 2006, I was spending most of my time in Kathmandu. Six of the seven children were at Umbrella, and I wanted to help them adjust to their new lives. The other reason I spent so much time in the capital was that I was looking for a house that would become NGN's children's home. I had continued to raise money from the United States. With six thousand dollars in our bank account, I was confident enough to put the down payment on the first four months' rent, knowing we would have enough for rent, furnishings, and support of any children we managed to rescue, starting with the six. My goal was to have the house when Farid arrived, which would be any day now. I was talking over my plan with Jacky and Viva over one of our usual afternoon teas.

"Jacky, did you tell Conor about the house?" Viva asked. I was in their living room, the warmest room in Nepal. They had a kerosene heater on at full blast and a thick wall-to-wall carpet to insulate the floor. We could have been at their home in Northern Ireland.

I looked at Jacky. "What house?"

"Yes, Conor—we have the perfect house for you. Truly, it is perfect. It is this yellow house next door to the other Umbrella houses, you know this one? It can hold maybe twenty-five children, no problem. And it has a well in the front patio—a deep well! You can have water for free, you do not have to pay this stupid truck to come give you water," he said. He took a drag from his cigarette and held out his arms toward Viva. "Kathmandu! It's madness! No water! Why there is no water here?"

"They've overbuilt in this part of the city, they have no capacity, Jacky. I've been dealing with this for years. Years. You'd better get used to it because I'm tellin' ya right now, it ain't gonna change in our lifetime. But enough of that, my love—tell him about the house, will ya?"

"*Ah oui, la maison. C'est parfait,* Conor. And it is available. I spoke to the man, he can give it for a very good price. Twelve thousands rupees per month, about 160 U.S. dollars. It is very good price, believe me."

I didn't know the house, so when I left Jacky and Viva's, I went to find Jagrit. He knew the neighborhood like the back of his hand. I found him sitting outside with some of the older boys, just inside the gate of one of the Umbrella homes.

"Jagrit," I said when I got close to him. "Come over here please, *bai*. I need your help." (*Bai* means "younger brother" and was a common term we used for the kids.)

"Yes, Conor sir! I am at your service!" he called, and he turned to the others sitting next to him and spoke to them in a mock-dramatic voice and in English, clearly for my benefit. "I am sorry, I must go. I have important work to do. Sir needs me. Without my help, he say he may even die—"

"All right, Jagrit. . . ."

"You hear his voice? It is shaking! I think he is very afraid. I must go."

When he came close enough, a big grin on his face, I got him in a headlock, which he quickly managed to escape from. We walked back out the front gate.

Jagrit knew which house Jacky meant, and I followed him. It was only four houses away, down a small path. As soon as I saw it, I knew it was our house. It had a field right outside and a small front patio, as well as a front gate with a lock. Best of all, it was right in the neighborhood, next to the other Umbrella homes, only a couple of minutes from the small primary school and Jacky and Viva's house. I negotiated a deal with the owner later that afternoon, using Jagrit as translator. We shook on it, and it was done. Next Generation Nepal officially had a children's home.

I sent Farid a photo of the house. He loved it. Liz wanted to see the photo as well, so I e-mailed it to her, too. Since I was already attaching that photo, I included other photos for her as well, of Little Princes, of the six children playing together, of Kumar smiling for the first time, the day Gyan had brought him to Umbrella. In return, Liz e-mailed me a photo, the first she had ever sent. The photo showed Liz hugging a girl to whom she had become attached, a Zambian orphan of about ten years old named Basinati. I knew of the girl; Liz had described her in detail to me. In the picture, Basinati wore a simple yellow dress and a bright smile.

But all I could think about in that photo was Liz. She was gorgeous.

I was so taken aback that I wrote to ask her, as casually as I could, "Oh, is that you in the photo?"

"Yeah, Conor, that's me, the short one in the yellow dress. No idea who the weird blond girl is hugging me," she wrote back.

Okay, I had deserved that. But I couldn't stop looking at the photo. This woman who had been my confidante, who had kept me going through difficult times and with whom I found myself building a real intimacy, was stunning. I put the photo on my desktop. If there had been a church nearby, I would have lit about four hundred candles.

◇

FARID ARRIVED IN NEPAL on November 21, cleaner than I'd ever seen him. That would change soon, I thought, noticing my own dust-infused fleece and worn-out trekking pants. With Farid back in Godawari, it was like a family reunion. The children were ecstatic, and I wasn't far behind them. It never felt quite right going through all this without him.

I waited for his arrival to break the news to the children: I was moving out of Godawari, out of Little Princes. If we were going to build a new home for trafficked children in Kathmandu, then I needed to be in Kathmandu.

The children protested. Farid and I told them about the seven children and why it was important to open this new home. We explained that they were fortunate to be in a safe environment at Little Princes. They had people looking out for them, a good home, and the chance to go to school. Many other children, children just like them, were less fortunate. They needed help, and we were going to try to help them. Besides, we said, they were getting old. They hardly needed us anymore. The bigger boys were already doing a great job taking care of the younger children, just how it would be if they were back in their own villages. The older boys smiled and looked at one another, proud of their responsibility.

Farid saved the good news for last: he would be staying in Godawari for at least the next week. The children cheered. They adored Farid and had asked about him constantly when he was still in France. He was both a father and an older brother to them.

As it was a sunny November afternoon and a school holiday, Farid and I sent the children outside. The two of us sat drinking tea as the kids kicked around a half-inflated soccer ball and threw an old Frisbee that, when flung, would go either straight into the dirt, or fly in a wild arc, often landing several hundred feet from the intended target. While we watched this with amusement, Rohan, one of the youngest boys, ran up to us.

"Brother, I take Jablo, okay?"

I looked at Farid, and back at Rohan.

"You take what?"

"Jablo, Brother! Jablo!"

"I don't think that's a word, Rohan."

He marched past us and into the house then the office, where I could see him digging through the box of secondhand toys. He came back out with two sticks attached by a small rope, and a yellow plastic thing that looked like a double-ended goblet or oversized hourglass.

"Jablo, Brother!" said Rohan, holding it up. "I take, okay?"

I had seen one before, but only at a Phish concert during college, where shaggy-haired young people stood around in clouds of marijuana smoke. I certainly didn't have the faintest clue how to use it. As it turned out, neither did Rohan. He knew that the two sticks were to be used to toss the goblet up in the air. He poked at the goblet with the sticks with all the finesse of Edward Scissorhands trying to lift a teacup. No luck. Then Nishal, who had just hurled the Frisbee into a tree, saw and came running over. He grabbed the sticks from Rohan and took center stage in front of Farid and me.

"I do, Brother! Watch!"

Nishal apparently knew how this thing worked. He rolled the yellow goblet thing back and forth until it caught the rope between the sticks, at which point he kind of slid it back and forth moving his arms, and finally tossed it up. The goblet went high in the air and sliced right through the web of this bright green spider the size of a cat, sending the eight-legged beast careening down toward us, which nobody saw except Farid and me. We shrieked and tripped over each other scrambling to get out of the way. Everyone stopped what they were doing. Nishal quietly returned the Jablo to the box, where it stayed for several months.

I would later learn that the children did not want to take it out because of us; they had decided that, for some reason they would never fully understand, foreigners were terrified of Jablo.

◇

SETTING UP THE NEXT Generation Nepal children's home would take time. There was no such thing as a one-stop shop in Kathmandu, an Ikea-type warehouse where you could order everything you needed. Farid and I, together with a Nepali friend of ours, drove through the alleys of Kathmandu collecting everything we needed. The wall-to-wall carpeting we bought was the only furnishing not made by hand. Thirty bunk beds? We visited a metal smith and negotiated a price. Mattresses? We had our choice of mattress stuffing: synthetic materials at the high end, straw-stuffed sheets at the low end, the same material we used in Little Princes. We chose the middle route: mattresses stuffed with coconut hair. It was not exactly comfortable, but it was a hell of a lot more comfortable than those hay-stuffed things we had in Godawari. Where they got the coconut hair was a mystery; I didn't recall seeing even a single coconut in the country. Free-standing shelves were made by the bamboo maker. Wooden shelving was made by the local carpenter, who, per Nepalese tradition, had shaved his head and wore only white for exactly one year to mourn the passing of his father. Purchasing sheets meant negotiating a price on meters of fabric, while buying blankets required haggling over the weight and quality of the cotton inside.

I foolishly expected the blankets to be delivered to our house in normal, blanket form. Instead, a man showed up at our house the next day, not with a blanket, but with some fabric and a bag of cotton. I thought back to the conversation with the shop owner, wondering whether there had been an additional fee for actually assembling the blankets. As it turned out, the common practice was to make the blanket right on your front porch. The blanket-maker dumped the cotton into a heap about the size of an armchair. Then he took a long, thin stick and beat the cotton until it was the proper . . . I don't know, fluffiness, maybe? He stuffed it all into the sheets that he had sewn together and voilà. A blanket was born.

Even more interesting, I learned, was what happens if, say, a year down the road, you find that the blanket has lost its fluffy factor. You simply wait for another man, who every few days patrols the neighborhood. You don't see him coming, but you hear him—he plucks an object slung over his shoulder, something that looks like a one-stringed harp. You can hear him coming from far away. Flag him down, pay him a small fee, and he takes apart your blanket, dumps the cotton back out, and uses this harp thing to twang at the cotton until its fluff factor is back up to fluffy standards. This began an e-mail debate with Liz about how this actually worked.

"So he just twangs the cotton, and that makes it all fluffy again?" Liz wrote. "What's the physics behind *that*?"

"I have no clue. Maybe it has to do with the revitalizing property of the metallic vibrations?" I offered.

"Yeah . . . I'm not a physicist or anything, but that doesn't sound right to me."

"No, me neither. But it sounded smart, right?"

"A little, I guess," she wrote. "You should have said you were quoting it from an article, like from *Scientific American. That* would have sounded smart."

"Right. Next time."

Dhaulagiri House (we named it after one of the highest mountains in the Himalaya) was finally ready. Farid and I made up the beds ourselves, eliciting giggles from the local women helping us. When the last sheets had been laid, Farid and I went outside and then walked back in, to get the full effect of the house. I walked slowly from room to room. It was beautiful. Farid had put a tremendous amount of work into it, having done most of the calculating of what we needed and most of the shopping. When it was done, there was something magical about it, as if we had managed to close our eyes and wish hard enough for a home for twenty-five children. And suddenly here it was, under our feet, surrounding us, pristine, unmarked by a single footprint or smudge on the wall. This would change soon enough. But at that moment, it was still fresh, like the perfect gift still in its original packaging. And we had created it.

Farid and I walked back outside. Farid had a wide grin on his face.

"Conor, would you mind if I went to get them?" he said. He had been looking forward to this moment for many months. The moment was here, and I felt it belonged to Farid.

"Go for it," I said.

Farid went around to the neighboring children's homes and gathered up

Kumar, Amita, Dirgha, Navin, Madan, and Samir. He brought them back to the front gate of the house where I was waiting for them. I lined them up, shoulder to shoulder, and Farid and I stood in front of them.

"You have been inside this house?" Farid asked them.

They shook their heads vigorously. "No, Brother—no, promise, Brother!" I realized, as did Farid by the look on his face, that the six children were afraid they had done something wrong. In their short life experience, that meant getting beaten.

Farid walked to the wooden front door, exquisitely carved with the story of the Buddha. He swung the door open and turned back to the children.

"This is yours. This is your new home," he said.

They didn't move. They must have thought it a game, or a test, or something else that they couldn't yet work out. Navin, back to being the man in charge after his stay in the hospital, finally pushed past the others and walked inside. The other five slowly followed him. Nobody touched anything. They peeked into the living room. They congregated near the front door, a couple of them smiling nervously. Samir, six years old, tugged on my pants and asked, in Nepali, whose house this was. The other children stared at me. Everybody was smiling now, waiting for the punch line of this little adventure.

"Brother, Farid already told you. This is your house."

"Our house?"

"Your house."

A pause.

"Our house?"

"Yes, your house."

"We sleep here?"

"Your beds are upstairs."

Another pause.

"We can see?" Kumar asked, hesitantly, worried about looking foolish.

"Yes, you can go see," I said.

Nobody wanted to be the first, but the second Navin put one foot on the first step, Kumar ran past him, up three steps, bolder. Suddenly they were racing, falling over each other to get upstairs first. Even Dirgha, his usual stubborn self, held back only for a few seconds before sprinting after them. It was gratifying to see him run like that, fully recovered from his battle in the malnutrition ward.

Farid and I wandered back outside. We could hear shrieks and squeals of delight. The children popped their heads out of windows and reappeared on balconies and called from the roof, asking if this was really their house. We called back that yes, it was really their house.

Then a blur of the six children streamed past us, running out the front door and into the Umbrella house next door where they had lived for the past few weeks. Less than five minutes later they stormed back into their new house, carrying one armful of clothing each—their only possessions—and sprinting back up the stairs.

We followed to find them setting up in the front bedroom, where the beds were made up. "You sleep here, this bed, Brother?" asked Samir, pointing to the seventh, empty bed.

Kumar answered. "No—for Bishnu, yes, Brother?"

I was surprised. I hadn't spoken to them about Bishnu. I wasn't even sure they remembered him. He had disappeared nine months earlier; that was an eternity for children their age.

"Yes, it's for Bishnu," I told them. Farid came in and said it was time for sleep. They climbed into their selected beds and we turned off the lights and went back downstairs.

◇

THE APARTMENT I WENT to see had three bedrooms and a brand-new smell to it, as distinctive as a new car. Walking down the long corridor, my footsteps echoed off the long slabs of marble. It was absurd. Not that the rent was so bad—I could afford it—but it was just so big. A Nepali family would squeeze about nine generations into that place. As was typical, there was no heating system, very limited hot water, no fridge, no oven, no microwave, and the shower was just a showerhead in the middle of the bathroom that drained out the floor.

The owner followed me down the hall. I dramatically paused halfway down the corridor to catch my breath. He laughed.

"Yes, very big, sir. Very good for sir's whole family. And very much marble," he said proudly, pointing at some marble.

"It's actually too big—I'm not married. But thank you for showing me," I told him.

He stopped in his tracks. "No wife?"

"No, no wife."

"You have girlfriend?"

"No, no girlfriend."

"You are a gay man?"

This was the obvious conclusion in Nepal, I supposed.

"Gay? No, I'm not gay—I'm just not interested in a relationship. I am very busy taking care of these children, as I mentioned earlier. I don't have so much free time, I'm afraid."

"You had girlfriend recently?"

Was this conversation really happening? "No, not really, no, not since . . . uh . . ." I thought about that, and found myself counting not weeks or months, but years. "I'm not sure. I think 2003? 2004, maybe?"

"2003? The year 2003?" he asked, incredulous.

I remembered that Nepal was on a different calendar than we were. It was something like 2066 here. "No, American 2003. Maybe three years ago."

He nodded and squinted at me. "You must find a wife and start making children very soon. You can live here. I give you good price," he said. "You need this apartment."

I laughed at that, and kept on walking through the apartment. I reached the back bedroom. It was wonderfully bright, with windows on two walls. I opened one of them and leaned out, taking in the fields. It was strange to see such fields right in the middle of Kathmandu. It would all be overrun soon enough. I was about to tell him no thanks again. I had told the children I would be over at Dhaulagiri by now.

Then I saw it, across the field. Less than one hundred yards away, the back of a tall, yellow house. It was Dhaulagiri. I hadn't noticed that this apartment was so close, because it was not connected by any direct route to this building; getting there required a roundabout route via high-walled paths. But there it was, so close that I could see two of the children—Samir and Dirgha, it looked like—playing on the rooftop terrace.

I turned back to the owner.

"You're right," I told him. "I do need this apartment."

I spent my first night in the apartment five days later. It was freezing. Despite the cozy feel of several acres of marble, I could see my breath. Since I was used to living in cramped quarters and, in fact, felt more comfortable that way, I set up camp in one room, with a small desk, an Internet cable connecting my computer directly to a telephone wire outside of my window, and a mattress on the floor with the thickest blanket they would make for me. On the bright side—and this was a very bright side indeed—I had indoor plumbing.

Best of all, my balcony overlooked one of the largest and most important Buddhist stupas in all of Nepal: Swayambhu, draped in colorful Buddhist prayer flags. The stupa, or Buddhist shrine, looked a bit like a white upside-down funnel. It was known in most guidebooks as the Monkey Temple, named by the hippies who had come in the 1960s for the hundreds of monkeys running around the neighborhood. I would watch them as they leaped across rooftops and I would chase them away when I saw them hanging off my Internet cable line. They often brought it down with them, cutting off my connection to the outside world.

Like any good tourist, I had visited the Monkey Temple during my first trip to Nepal. I had never seen so many of the little beasts in my life. They were small and light tan in color. The smaller ones were like large, nimble cats; the larger ones, though, were the size of toddlers—toddlers who could run up the side of a house and chew through wire. They were enthralling.

Sharing a neighborhood with them, however, was a different story. I quickly developed a love-hate-hate-really-hate relationship with the monkeys. I loved watching them. They were so human, yet moved with impossible grace and agility. Other days, though, I would go out on my balcony to have a peaceful lunch away from my computer; I would step away for an instant to get a drink and come back to find that same agile, graceful monkey tightrope walking across a telephone wire with an egg salad sandwich in one hand and a fistful of potato chips in the other. I told Viva, who had fifteen years of monkey stories, about the sandwich-stealing monkey, and how I had felt like challenging it to a fistfight. "Listen, no joke, Conor—you fight a monkey, you better *mean* it," and related a cautionary tale that would make anyone think twice before fighting a monkey.

The neighborhood was, however, usually very peaceful, at least when the monkeys were not engaged in lunch piracy or hand-to-hand combat. Tibetan Buddhists, a common Diaspora in Nepal, were inclined to live as close to the stupa as possible, which meant I lived next door to a monastery. The deep bells rang just after dawn every day. In America, it would have driven me to the brink of insanity; here, it was my alarm clock.

When I was feeling particularly motivated, I would join a river of maroon robes, the low-chanting Buddhist monks, as they circled the massive stupa clockwise every morning at sunrise, spinning the hundreds of prayer wheels, the shape of large soda cans, mounted on the exterior walls of the temple. They may have originally been red, but the paint had been worn away with the touch of thousands of hands, hands that touched the Sanskrit topography on the metal wheels. It took a good twenty-five minutes to complete the circle. Branching out from the stupa there were few roads, only narrow paths weaving between the houses, patrolled by the monkeys and stray dogs and men carrying rusty scales attached to old bicycles, offering to trade an equal weight of potatoes for scrap metal. It was not far from the backpacker district of Thamel, but it felt a world away.

I described all of this in great detail for Liz. I wanted her to be able to picture exactly where I was.

"That's so great that you found a place so close to the kids!" she wrote.

"I know—that's why I took it."

"It does kind of sound like a mausoleum, though," she pointed out. "Like you should be sharing it with a dead dictator or something."

"I've got two extra bedrooms. I could throw him in one of those. Maybe hold daily viewings, charge a few rupees," I suggested.

"I'd pay that."

I found myself hoping that Liz noticed the similarities in our senses of humor, and that she was laughing at my jokes from nine thousand miles away.

A month earlier, I had asked her why she had chosen India. Secretly, I hoped she would respond with "No reason! Why, are there any other good countries near India? Because it makes no difference to me at all." But she didn't. Instead, she talked about how inspired she was by Mother Teresa, by the nun's compassion, her faith, her selflessness. She wanted to see where she had lived and worked. It made sense. Unfortunately.

Liz and I had been writing for seven weeks. She would be flying to India in a month. If I didn't say something now, I would lose any opportunity to meet her. But I could not bring myself to invite her to Nepal. It felt so forward, somehow. How easy it had been to meet women in bars, women that barely spoke my language. Yet with the one girl I wanted to meet, I was paralyzed with embarrassment to ask her to visit. So I began to drop hints that she should really visit Nepal.

"You know, I remember when I came from India to Nepal the first time," I wrote. "Such a short and inexpensive flight from Delhi!" Another time I described the neighborhood, concluding with: "But it's too difficult to explain over e-mail—you really have to see it for yourself, in person, to appreciate its beauty." She assured me that, by the way I described it, she felt as if she had already been there. Which, frankly, didn't help me at all.

My apartment, the mausoleum, gave me an idea. I found an excuse to e-mail her about it again, and lingered on the fact that there were three separate, distinct bedrooms, each one with a door and a lock, and how great it would be to have guests. I mentioned that two of my college friends, Kelly Caylor, and his wife, Beth, fellow University of Virginia grads just like us, were coming over Christmas break. I talked about how much fun it would be, in theory, of course, ha ha ha, if we all got together. She said that did sound like fun, and then changed the topic.

After a week or so of tough hiking, I reached the top of Kala Patthar, which offered a great view of Everest Base Camp (*pictured in the background*).

A view of the village of Godawari, where the Little Princes Children's Home is located, with the southern wall of the Kathmandu Valley in the background.

The boys of the Little Princes Children's Home called this the "pile-up"—it was a fairly common position. That's Nishal right below me and Santosh below him.
Photograph by Anish

The Little Princes Children's Home in Godawari, Nepal, as seen from the path.

(*Left to right:*) Raju, Nuraj, and Crazy Rohan, three of the youngest boys at the Little Princes Children's Home.

Raju (*lying down*) and his older sister, Priya (*right*), in their school uniforms.

Royal Nepalese soldiers were ubiquitous during the war, even in the playing fields in the village of Godawari. Boys from the Little Princes Children's Home play soccer in the background. *(Hriteek is in the blue shirt.)*

Women in Godawari working the fields.

The seven trafficked children that Farid and I found and began taking care of. *(Left to right:)* Madan *(with hand raised)*, Bishnu *(in Raiders shirt)*, Navin *(in baseball hat)*, Dirgha *(in hooded sweatshirt)*, Samir *(head barely visible)*, Kumar *(in bear shirt)*, and Amita *(in plaid)*. February 2006.

Jacky (*left*) with his wife, Viva (*right*), founders of the Umbrella Foundation.

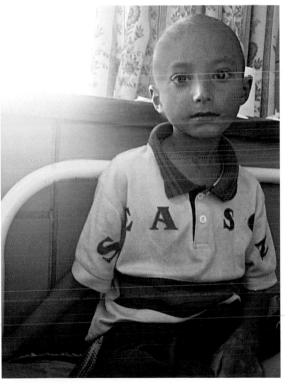

Amita, the only girl of the seven found children. This photograph was taken the moment I found her in a small village in western Kathmandu Valley. She was being held by the wife of a child trafficker. She was looking for water. October 2006.

Dirgha in the hospital on the morning he woke up.

The malnutrition ward of the Kathmandu hospital, where I stayed overnight with Dirgha and Navin. Parents stay there with their children because there are not enough nurses.

(*Left to right:*) Me, D.B. (who came to Humla with me), and my mentor, Anna Howe, celebrating the Tibetan New Year with D.B.'s family. Anna would eventually become a Buddhist nun.

The dirt runway in Simikot, Humla, where I began the search for families of trafficked children.

My team heads south into Humla on a month-long trek to find families.

Trains of sheep would come barreling along narrow mountain paths, a hundred feet above the Karnali River in Humla.

Residents of the small village of Ripa, Humla.

A view of the village of Ripa, Humla. Snow is visible on the upper mountains in the background.

Sitting with the parents of Anish, one of the boys at the Little Princes Children's Home, and my translator and guide, Rinjin (*left*).

Anish's mother, holding a photograph of the son she had lost years earlier.

Sitting with the mother of Amita, the only girl of the seven found children.

The mother of Rohan, one of the boys at the Little Princes Children's Home, holding a photograph of her son that I gave to her in her village in Humla.

Two local children whom I met in Rohan's village in Humla. They were brother and sister.

One of our porters preparing daal bhat, the twice-daily meal of rice with lentils eaten by the majority of Nepalese.

Upon returning from my trip to Humla, I went to see the boys at the Little Princes Children's Home and showed them the photographs I had taken of their parents, who now knew they were alive and well. Here I'm showing Rohan (*front, in hooded sweatshirt*) the photograph of his mother, who is holding a photograph of Rohan.

Farid with six of the seven found children. This was the day we opened our Next Generation Nepal (NGN) Children's Home, Dhaulagiri House, in Kathmandu. The seventh and last missing child, Bishnu, would not be found for another six weeks.

The younger children of Dhaulagiri House, the children's home opened by my organization, NGN, on their first day of school.

Carrying Amita outside her new home at Dhaulagiri House.

Adil, the youngest boy at Dhaulagiri House, wearing the new glasses we bought for him.

Leena (*front*) standing with her big sister Kamala (*back*). Leena didn't speak for the first five months she lived at Dhaulagiri House. She is wearing the oversized red hat that reminded me of a plunger.

Liz visited Nepal for the first time in December 2006, just days after we rescued thirty children. The children of Dhaulagiri House, especially the girls, clung to her immediately. Behind Liz is my visiting college friend, Kelly.

Gyan, of Nepal's Child Welfare Board, bringing two recently rescued children to the NGN Children's Home.

The first night in Dhaulagiri House for Bishnu, the last of the original seven children whom Farid and I were finally able to rescue.

Tilak (*left*) was a young boy who didn't have a home. He followed me out of the Child Welfare Office. The Umbrella Foundation, next door to our NGN Children's Home, had room to take him in.

Liz traveled to Nepal a total of five times to visit the children and me.

Leena, the girl who didn't speak for five months, sitting in Dhaulagiri House, happy at last. *Photograph by my photographer buddy Dave Hogan*

When we opened the children's home, I got the sense that her attitude was changing, that she was thinking more seriously about visiting. Every day I told her more stories of the six little kids in that big house. A week after we had opened the house, I gathered up my courage and wrote to her. I suggested, ever so gently, that, if she had time, only if she had a couple of days free and nothing to do, if she wanted to, she was very welcome to come visit Kathmandu and meet the children. Only if she was bored in India. Or whatever.

Her response blinked into my inbox. I went out on the balcony. I came back in. I got a glass of water. I walked back to my computer. I clicked on her reply.

"You know, I would really love that. I would love to meet the little ones, they sound amazing," she wrote. "And I bet I could get them to pile up on you so that you couldn't move. That would be fun to watch. . . ."

I made myself wait fifteen minutes before responding, then wrote something along the lines of, "Yes, they're amazing! And they love pileups! Come visit!" which I deleted before sending because it sounded too eager. I changed it to: "That would be wonderful—you'll love them. I'll look forward to it!" Those two sentences must have taken me another twenty minutes, trying to get the tone just right.

Liz was coming to visit. For the rest of the afternoon, I couldn't stop smiling. At least until I realized, in a panic, I had to see the carpenter, the one who made bed frames, immediately. And the sheet-maker. And the blanket-smith. And the pillow-constructor. The other two bedrooms in my apartment were completely bare. Aside from my bed and my computer, I had almost nothing. But I would fix that. I was expecting visitors.

Part IV

INTO THE MOUNTAINS

November 2006–December 2006

Five

FARID AND I BOTH lived in Kathmandu now. I had my apartment, and Farid had taken a small room—a former pantry, judging by the size—on the ground floor of Dhaulagiri House, where he would be the house manager, looking after the kids. He wanted to live in the house for at least a few months to keep a close eye on the kids, day and night. I offered him one of the bedrooms in my apartment. I was lonely there. Except for being icy cold at night, it didn't feel much like the Nepal I was used to back at Little Princes. Farid laughed at my suggestion.

"I could never live in this place that you live, Conor," he said. "It is far too big! It is like a cathedral! It is not homey!"

I agreed with him there. The apartment was wonderful in that it was located close to Dhaulagiri House, but I would never feel comfortable there. I had always loved living at Little Princes Children's Home, but Dhaulagiri would not have enough room for both Farid and me once the house was filled with children; there were only six there now, but there was room for perhaps twenty or so more. So Farid lived in Dhaulagiri, and I lived next door, spending much of my time at the children's home.

We made frequent trips to Godawari to visit the Little Princes. During those visits, Farid and I told them all about Next Generation Nepal. We told them our goals, about trying to rescue children like them in order to give them a home.

But there was one thing we kept from the children. We did not tell them that for the previous six weeks, I had been quietly preparing for a mission into the mountains of Humla. I was going to try to find their parents, as well as the parents of the six children.

Farid helped put the finishing touches on my strategy. For safety reasons, I told very few people I was going. Golkka was a powerful figure in Humla. We knew he had threatened physical harm against Anna Howe and others who put his operation in Kathmandu at risk. In the remote northwest part of the country, there was virtually no rule of law, and I would not have the protection of an international organization. He knew who I was. If he knew I was going to Humla, it would not be difficult for him to disrupt my mission, even to attack me openly. He had much to lose by my success.

Before leaving, I had to compile all the information I could from the Little Princes. I had lots of photos of them already, plus critical biographical information, such as the names of their villages (as far as they could remember) and the names of their parents. Unfortunately, many of the children were taken when they were too young to know their parents by any name except mom and dad. In conversations, I gently prodded them for any details they could remember about their villages or their families, anything that could help me track down their families in that vast remote region. I also collected this information from the six children we had rescued.

I kept my leaving a secret from everybody except Farid and Anna. But there was one boy I couldn't resist telling: Jagrit. I trusted him. More important, I knew that if I probed him for information on Humla and his family, he would probably uncover my plan.

Jagrit was giddy when I told him.

"You bring back apples from Humla for me, sir?"

After all this time, he still called me "sir." It drove me nuts, and he knew it. He tried to change it, to say "brother" like the other children. He had gotten to the point to remember to say "Sorry, brother" when I corrected him, then minutes later he would revert to "sir." I wondered if I should start calling him "sir," too.

I had learned a lot about Jagrit in the previous two months. He had been taken from his family when he was five years old. Unlike most of the others, Jagrit was a true orphan; his parents had died within a year of each other when he was a boy. His file was unique in that it contained death certificates for his parents. Viva had found him, along with two dozen others, in a destitute, illegal children's home near the trash-infested river that ran through Kathmandu. He now lived in the Umbrella home next door to our own Dhaulagiri House.

"No, Jagrit, I'm not bringing you back any apples."

"Why no?" He had a way of shouting everything he said.

"Too heavy—I'll bring you back one. Maybe. Maybe not."

He considered this. "You go to my village?"

I told Jagrit that I was going to Humla, but I did not exactly tell him why I was going, and he did not exactly ask. I would be looking for the parents of children under our care, but his would not be among them.

"Which village is your village?" I asked him.

"Jaira, sir. Jaira," he shouted.

I knew Jagrit was from Jaira, but he liked to tell me. He said it with pride, as if the fainter the memory became, the more fiercely he guarded it.

Later, studying the map of Humla and planning our route, Jaira was the first place I looked for. I desperately wanted to find somebody for him, a family member, somebody that knew him, or knew of him, or knew of his parents—anything to bring back and show him that he was not alone in this world.

"Yes, I'm going to your village as well, Jagrit."

"You bring me back apples from my village, sir. They are very, very tasty."

"No chance."

"You are lazy boy!"

"One apple," I told him. "If you're lucky."

◇

I KNEW THIS WAS a risky trip, I just didn't know how risky. Nobody knew. Not Anna, not even D.B., my Humli travel companion. We had planned on leaving earlier in the month, but the official peace agreement between the Maoists and the government had not yet been signed. Without that official truce, I would not be able to go, I couldn't take the risk. In the meantime, winter was fast approaching. Once the snows arrived, all travel into and out of Humla would come to an abrupt halt until springtime. All through November I watched the news and the weather with growing desperation.

But on November 22, 2006, I didn't even have to open the newspaper. The headlines were thick and large, aware of their place in history: "Peace Treaty Signed." I checked the weather: The snow had not yet arrived in Humla. A window of opportunity had been flung wide open. There was no telling how long the truce would hold. D.B. called me minutes after I had opened the paper.

"Are you ready, Conor?" he said. No explanation was necessary. I was ready. We set our departure for a few days later.

That night, Farid and I stared at the map of Humla. I had never seen a map like it. I was used to maps with roads crisscrossing, with names of cities and towns and villages, their populations indicated by the size of the font. This map had almost nothing on it. Not a single road. All travel would be done on foot. An occasional dot, a village, appeared next to the river, separated from its neighbor by wide, empty spaces where topographical lines squiggled around, almost on top of one another, indicating that there was virtually no flat ground in the entire region.

Together we tried to estimate how long it would take to travel the distances, over the passes that Anna had spoken of, but without seeing the terrain, it was almost impossible to guess how difficult it would be. The closest approximation I had were the treks we had done, up to Everest Base Camp and along the Annapurna circuit, both challenging, but both lined with tourist infrastructure to allow for frequent breaks. Humla would have none of that. Plus, there was the added worry that the snow would arrive when I was deep in the region, which would shut down the airport. The runway could only be cleared by hand, a near impossible task with constant snowfall.

There were no phones outside the district headquarters of Simikot, the village with the airstrip, so there was no way to communicate once I reached Humla. There would be no way to tell Farid if something went wrong. We didn't define "wrong"—we didn't need to. It could be injury, kidnapping, or worse. We decided to set, for lack of a better term, a panic date. Taking a conservative estimate of how long we thought it would take me to move through the region, we came up with December 18 as the date I was likely to return, give or take a day. I would make every effort to get back by then, as it was also the date that my friends Kelly and Beth were coming to visit me. The panic date was set for December 22. If I was not back by then, Farid would assume something had gone wrong, and he would send a team to look for me.

The night before I was going to leave, I wrote to Charlie Agulla, my old roommate from the University of Virginia. I told him I wasn't sure what this trip would be like. Most likely it would be safe, I said, if not terribly successful. Most important, I told him about the panic date. I told him that if I hadn't gotten in touch with him by then, he should call my family, whom he had known for years, and let them know the situation.

Charlie wrote back within minutes: "And what situation would that be, exactly?"

I was putting him in a difficult spot, I knew that. "Ask them to get in touch with Farid," I told him.

The last thing I did that night was write to Liz. We had made plans. She would arrive in Kathmandu on December 23 and stay for two full days. She would return to India on Christmas morning. She had my cell phone number to call when she landed in Kathmandu. I told her how much fun we were going to have, together with my married friends from college, our implied chaperones. But I had to also inform her that there was just the tiniest possibility that I would get held up. If I missed a flight or something, I told her, there was a chance I might not be there *exactly* when she arrived. Not to worry, though, Farid would have my cell phone and would introduce her to my friends, and I would surely be there the next day. At the latest. I made this out to sound like Plan D, the backup plan to the backup plan to the backup plan.

By that time, Liz and I had been writing several times per day, back and forth. It was as if we were just across town from each other. I told her not only things that I thought would impress her, but things that I knew wouldn't, like my original reason for coming to Nepal: to impress people. When we spoke about our past relationships, I told her that I had been terrible to my girlfriend in Prague in the final months of our relationship, hurting her enough to make her break up with me; it was the easy way out. It was something I had trouble getting over, even three years later.

Liz revealed to me that she had been married in her early twenties. When the marriage ended a few years later, she also stopped attending church. She told me that she couldn't imagine what kind of church would want someone like her. She was scared and embarrassed—who in their mid-twenties was *divorced*? she recalled thinking at the time. She felt it would be too hypocritical to sit in worship when she was so broken. "But God used that time of great sadness to reclaim me, to redeem me," she wrote. "Things that are broken *can* be made whole."

Now, as I wrote to her about my plan to go into Humla, I spoke vaguely, in circles. We often tried to crack each other up. In this e-mail, though, I couldn't bring myself to joke around. I was determined not to worry her. In the last e-mail I received from her before I flew to Humla, she wrote: "I know that what you're doing is not completely safe. I am going to try not to worry and I am going to try not to think about it too much. I very much hope that I see you on the twenty-third."

"You will," I wrote. "You think I'm going to miss my one chance to meet you?" and, with heart pounding, I signed it "Love, Conor" for the first time, quickly clicking the SEND button before I could delete it.

◇

THE NEXT MORNING, JUST after dawn, I took a beat-up taxi to the Kathmandu airport and met up with D.B. I had not spent much time with him. I knew only that he was committed to helping his country, especially his native Humla, and that he was Buddhist. D.B. had his own list of children whose families he would be seeking on behalf of the ISIS Foundation. Going into Humla together served a critical purpose; by joining our two teams, we created one eight-man group. The larger the group, the better our security against not only the Maoist threat but also the potential danger that Golkka might have trafficking cohorts operating in the region who would not want us to succeed in our mission.

D.B. and I had our plane tickets. Our bags were packed. There was no departure board at the airport, but a handmade sign told us that our flight was leaving on time. I put in a last call to Farid, an early riser, to check in on the six children. He assured me they were fine. I could hear the envy in his voice. He wanted to be on this trip. For two years, the children at Little Princes had been telling us stories about Humla. They repeated the same stories, simple stories reflecting memory weakened by time, until we could tell them ourselves.

The story that stayed with me was one told by Bikash. He was taken by the trafficker and was forced to walk many days with several other children. He walked through valleys he had never heard of and past villages whose names were unrecognizable. One day, he noticed the homes he passed were different—larger, and made of a harder, smoother substance than the dried mud he was used to.

The group came around a mountain pass, and Bikash found himself standing on a path, wider and smoother than any he'd known. He heard a noise, a buzzing sound. He looked into the distance, down the hard, flat trail. From far away he could see a man approaching them, running. But not just running—running faster than Bikash had ever seen a human being move, barreling toward them at preternatural speed. Bikash froze, mesmerized by this world where, he recalled thinking, men ran faster than wolves. With a roar, the man raced past, atop a machine that he didn't recognize. The man was riding a motorcycle.

I was brought back to the Kathmandu airport by Farid repeating his question on the phone.

"Your flight should leave on time?" Farid asked again.

"I think so—I have my ticket, I was told the flight is leaving on time, and I just saw the pilots."

"Okay. If the flight does not go today, we must have buffalo momos for lunch at that Tibetan place. I have a very big desire to eat momos today, Conor."

Farid knew Nepal well. He knew that nothing was ever certain, not even with a plane ticket in hand and a flight ready to depart. In fact, I had stopped using the word "sure" altogether unless it fell between "if you drink tap water" and "wake up on an operating table." The only time we could be certain that the plane would take off that morning was the moment the plane actually lifted off the ground, continued on an upward trajectory, and flew away from Kathmandu. Anything short of that was mere speculation.

Few places in the world can teach forbearance like Nepal. Let's say, for instance, that I asked somebody to buy me some bananas from the shop next door. In fact, let's say that I asked him to buy me bananas a week ago—then I reminded him hourly over the next few days. On that one billionth time that I reminded him that he promised to buy me bananas, the man would most likely respond with something to the effect of: "It will definitely happen today, my friend. I swear to you on the life of my son—your bananas will be bought today, in the next hour for sure. Erase all doubt from your mind. In fact, it is actually done already, even as we speak it is being concluded, as sure as the sun rose in the east this morning those bananas have been purchased. They belong to you now—the shopkeeper has no rightful claim to them any longer. You can open your mouth now in preparation for consuming this banana, which is here, right now. It is in my hand and on its way to your mouth, so I hope that you are ready to enjoy this fine banana. Your teeth may now begin to close as the banana is now in your mouth. How does it taste? Is it very fine?"

What that man really means is: "What bananas?"

The flight did leave that day, but there was a delay. Because D.B. and I were the only passengers, they converted the interior of the plane into a cargo area, putting down the seats and filling the plane with sacks of rice. Humla was three years into a drought; they needed all the food they could get.

Sitting in a cracked plastic seat in the passenger lounge, I was relieved that none of the children, save Jagrit, knew where I was going. This mission was beginning to feel very real, and there was enough pressure without twenty-four children back in Kathmandu waiting for me to return with news of their parents.

◇

EVEN FROM A LOW altitude, weaving between the mountains, one would never guess the world below us was inhabited. There was not a house in sight. The landscape in the dry season was a quilt of rusts and golds, split down the middle by the Karnali River running north to south. Not an inch of flat ground, at least not visible through the airplane's narrow window. As far as I could see it was just wave after wave of hills and snow-capped mountains extending to the horizon and into Tibet, just a few miles to the north.

D.B. pointed out his village, but I couldn't spot it. I listened to his description of an invisible cluster of mud huts and thatched roofs—his uncle's house, the one-room primary school—and followed his finger, pointing to a village that blended into its surroundings. He noticed my blank stare. No matter, he told me, I would see it up close soon enough. But first, we would set down in Simikot, the district headquarters situated ten thousand feet above sea level—and hopefully the one place in Humla with flat ground.

The first thing I identified below us, moments before hitting it, was the landing strip at Simikot. It was dirt. I thought that was only in movies, dirt landing strips—reserved for drug runners or dinosaur-infested islands.

Moreover, there was no airport to speak of. The door of the prop plane opened while we were parked on the runway and local men started unloading the rice. I craned my neck to scan the sky behind us; it seemed like an awfully dangerous place to park a plane. Nobody else seemed bothered, however, so D.B. and I climbed out with our bags. We had brought gear for the men who would be joining us, down jackets and boots so that they would not be walking in flip-flops. Sadly, flip-flops were the typical footwear for porters in Nepal, even at high altitudes.

One of the men saw us getting off and put down his sack of rice to give us a hand. He tentatively took my backpack, glaringly modern in the present surroundings, contemplated it for several seconds, then put it on upside down. He clipped random buckles together tightly and haphazardly until the pack was gripping him like a frightened octopus. He carried it past the runway and up to the only guesthouse in Simikot. The guesthouse was run by a local nonprofit organization. The man in charge of one of the projects, Rinjin, was not much older than me. He greeted D.B. with a hug. As it turned out, they were brothers-in-law.

D.B. and I began putting together our teams. We wanted eight men in total, including ourselves. He would lead one team of four and I the other. That way, if we needed to split up at any point to find specific children's families we would each be well-equipped. This meant, for me, that the first order of business was finding a guide. D.B. had suggested on the plane that Rinjin would be a good candidate. The moment I met him, I agreed; he was perfect. His English was excellent, and he had earned the trust of the villagers in southern Humla through his work on local hydroelectric projects, trying to bring electricity to the region for the first time. I needed him. The problem was, he was busy with a full-time job, and I would need him for three weeks.

I had tea with Rinjin, warming ourselves next to the fire after our evening daal bhat. We talked late into the night. Rinjin understood the importance of what we were doing. He asked me in many different ways why I was doing this for children in Nepal. Why not somewhere else? Why not helping in my own country? I had no good answer for him, except to simply say that in Nepal, nobody else was taking care of them. What other reason was there?

As we said good night, Rinjin took my hand and told me that if I, an American, was willing to take this risk for the children of Humla, then he was duty-bound and honored to take it with me. I thanked him. And I secretly loved how he had said it; I could not imagine an American outside of the marines talking about being duty-bound and honored in the service of his country.

I had my guide/translator. Moreover, Rinjin recommended an excellent porter and said he would arrange for him to join us. But I still needed one more to round out my four-man team. Rinjin told me the best person for the job was a young man named Min Bahadur, a member of the help staff at the local UNICEF outpost in Simikot. As I was already planning on meeting with UNICEF the next day, I would discuss it with him then.

Puspika, the head of the three-person UNICEF office, knew of Golkka. They had been trying to stop him for two years. She warned me to travel in a large group. She said she hoped I had not told too many people where I was going; even in Kathmandu, Golkka had a way of learning about these things. The roots of his network ran deep in southern Humla, she told me, and they would not be happy to learn that we were educating families about the dangers of sending their children away with Golkka's men in hopes of a better life for them.

During our conversation, a tall, lanky young man in his late twenties came in and served us tea with a happy grin. Puspika thanked him. When he left, I noticed she had a smile on her face; the man's grin was contagious. I realized that this was the man Rinjin had been speaking about. Puspika confirmed it a moment later.

"You know, that man who just served us, his name is Min Bahadur," she said. "He has been working with us for eight years. There is nobody I trust more, and nobody who knows the region better. If you can wait three days, our office will close for the holiday and he can join you."

I thanked her, but explained that we had to leave the next day. The snow was coming soon. She nodded, understanding.

"I will ask him for you, then. I will leave the decision up to him," she said, standing up. I thanked her for her time and thoughtfulness, and left to meet D.B. I found him at the local market, a wooden shack selling only rice and lentils, with no vegetables except for a few potatoes. Southern Humla was so poor that we would carry our own rice and lentils, knowing it would be difficult for villagers to spare anything. Our porters would bear the load.

In my own bag, which I kept close to me at all times, I was carrying something equally valuable: a blue waterproof folder containing photos and short bios of twenty-four children. It was the only information I had to go on, and I had read it through so many times I had practically memorized it.

The next morning we were ready to head south. As we sipped our tea outside, clutching the steel mugs to warm our hands against the chill of the morning, I watched as a smile spread across Rinjin's face. I turned around to see what he was looking at. Walking up the path was Min Bahadur, cloaked in a heavy jacket and flashing his contagious grin. He was coming with us.

When we finished our tea, D.B. spoke to Rinjin in Nepali for a few minutes, then turned to me.

"We have one more stop to make—you remember?" he said.

"I remember."

It would have been difficult to forget. Before we could travel into southern Humla, before we could even leave the borders of Simikot, we needed the permission of the Maoist leader.

The peace agreement in Nepal had been signed the week before I arrived in Humla, but the Maoists had already established their presence in Simikot, setting up in a small wooden house next to the marginally better-constructed army headquarters. It was a surreal sight, the red hammer and sickle flying just a few yards away from the Nepalese flag. The rebels now worked literally next door to the very buildings they had spent years bombing under the cover of night.

I walked into their building. It was discomfiting, to say the least. The United States government had sided with the king's government in the conflict. That meant my government had provided them with military aid to fight the rebels. The Maoists had no love for Americans.

But there was no avoiding it: the road to the children's families led through that door. Southern Humla was Maoist territory and had been for ten years. We were not sure if most of the rebels—former rebels, as of a few days earlier—would uphold the new peace treaty. Or, for that matter, if they were even aware the treaty had been signed.

Like everyone else in the high-altitude village, the Maoist leaders sat outside where they could be warmed by the sun. They sat in a row, four of them, on broken plastic chairs, waiting for us. Even the rickety chairs were a luxury—Humli people sat on woven mats on the ground. Chairs were usually reserved for wealthier individuals and government officials. The Maoists were behaving like the rightful heirs to the royal regime.

The Maoist district secretary sat looking like a man confident that he had earned the respect we were paying him by our visit. He wore a simple gray woolen hat that peaked about six inches above his head, stretching out his already thin features. The three officials at his side wore no jungle fatigues and carried no guns.

We greeted them respectfully and took the two empty chairs next to them.

I did not have a translator, but I understood pieces of the conversation, and I watched D.B.'s body language. He was humble and respectful and introduced me early on, conveniently failing to mention my nationality. They picked up on the omission and asked him directly where I was from. D.B. told them I was Irish. Technically that was true. I had brought my Irish passport and left my American one in Kathmandu.

D.B. told the story of Humla's children, what was happening to them, how they were being taken from their villages and abandoned in the streets of Kathmandu. The Maoists paid me little attention. That was a good thing. D.B. would almost certainly be allowed into the region; he was a local, after all. Whether I would be granted the same access was unclear.

One can only listen to a discussion in a foreign language for so long before it becomes achingly dull, even, apparently, if one's entire purpose for being there depended on the outcome of that discussion. This is especially true if you are sitting in the midday sun. Two hours later, my eyelids were sliding closed when the men leaped up and vigorously shook my hand. It scared the bejesus out of me to wake up to a throng of Maoists lunging at me, but I recovered in time to stop myself from instinctively hurling defensive, groggy punches at our hosts, an action that would likely have been something of a setback to D.B.'s diplomatic efforts. I shook hands with the men while D.B. picked his bag up off the ground. I caught his eye.

"That seemed to go okay," I said in a low voice.

"Better than okay," D.B. replied quietly, zipping up his bag. "You'll see."

He was right. That evening, an envelope was delivered to us by a local boy. D.B. took it from him, waited for him to leave, then carefully withdrew the single page inside. I saw from the light of his flashlight a document with red letterhead that was, surprisingly, written in English. It read "Communist Party of Nepal (Maoist)." The rest of the text was in Nepali. D.B. translated it for me. Amazingly, it detailed our exact mission: to find the families of the lost children of Humla. Most important, it instructed all Maoist cadres in the area to assist us in any way.

"Well—that certainly can't hurt," I marveled.

"No," D.B. said, smiling. "It certainly cannot hurt."

◇

WE SET OFF THE next day. The trail appeared to drop straight down. It reminded me of those short-breathed moments skiing, at the beginning of a run, peering over a sheer drop. I couldn't see how anybody got down this thing. Min Bahadur was first over, and I saw that he had jumped down onto a switchback that crisscrossed the mountain in broad, sweeping strokes. The Karnali River twisted two thousand feet below.

This was what the Humli would call a hill, but I called a mountain. To the Humli, mountains were the Himalaya, requiring ice axes and crampons—and oxygen tanks for the international climbers. Southern Humla was ringed by these snow-capped monoliths. These were the foothills of the Himalaya; the trail south would follow the Karnali River. Our path, the only path in the entire region, was narrow, wide enough for one person. It was slippery with mud and loose shale, and it rose so sharply in some places that you needed to grip the boulders and pull yourself up. I lost my footing several times on the first descent. Each time, Rinjin grabbed the straps of my pack and caught me. He took his job as guide seriously.

My knees and thighs took enough of a beating on the downhill that the flat ground felt almost relaxing, like I had landed on a moving walkway. I looked back up the mountain. Coming down was difficult; going back up would be worse. Luckily I had almost three weeks before I had to worry about that. Less, if we kept this pace.

A few minutes later, we were at the Karnali. We would have to cross it to continue south, since the only path was on the western side of the river. There was one problem: the Maoists had blown up the bridge.

The Maoists had destroyed almost every bridge in Humla in order to keep the army out. When villagers or bomb-toting Maoists bound for Simikot had needed to cross, they were ferried on makeshift cables. Men stood at each end of a cable strung over the river and pulled people across, collecting a few rupees for their service from each passenger. We were eight men with full packs; the men could expect a decent payday. One by one we climbed into the small metal containers suspended twenty feet up—the steel cage was an upgrade since the conflict, I was told—and traversed the river.

The porters led the way along the small single-track paths that had never seen a wheel, which had been carved out by the feet of villagers and long convoys of sheep and children chasing after stray buffalo. For hours we saw no villages at all. We moved at a terrific pace; even Min Bahadur, normally happily chatting to the other men despite bearing the heaviest load, had gone silent. I could barely keep up with them, and it wasn't just their superior strength and stamina. The two-hour descent and subsequent three-hour speed-walk had taken a toll on my knees.

Winter afternoons in Humla give way quickly to evening. By six we had reached our destination. It seemed to be the only destination unless we were prepared to sleep outside—the next shelter was many hours away. Rinjin told me the place was called Bokche Ganda, though the only thing I could see was a single lean-to, the kind I used to make as a child in the woods behind my house, except this one was large enough to sleep twenty men and didn't look like it would come crashing down on me the moment I climbed in with my comic books. I pulled off my boots, watching the men make a fire with maddening effortlessness. In my experience, making a fire required several hours of pained labor, virulent cursing, and about forty dollars' worth of lighter fluid. I would not survive one day here alone.

The porters served up enormous plates of daal bhat, boiling hot right out of the fire, which we ate while sitting on the cold ground. I crashed immediately after the heavy meal, listening to the men chatter into the night, drinking tea and stoking the fire to keep warm.

Even just a few hours into southern Humla, it was clear how parents here could be cut off from their children in Kathmandu. It took days to get anywhere. Poverty was everywhere; most villagers were fed by the World Food Programme. There was no electricity, and houses were one-room mud huts. There was virtually no medicine: the health posts had been abandoned. If villagers had to move around at night, they lit their way using flaming torches, like they were hunting Frankenstein. I didn't know these places still existed.

We broke camp at dawn. It was still very cold, even having descended three thousand feet from where the plane dropped us off in Simikot. The surrounding mountains were so high that the sun wouldn't reach us until after 9:00 A.M. We had tea and biscuits to warm up before we started moving; the morning daal bhat would be cooked in a few hours when we stopped for a break. We had a full day's walk ahead of us.

As I sat up in my bed of scattered hay under the lean-to, my back ached. It was stiff from the cold and from sleeping on the ground. Climbing out of my sleeping bag, though, I discovered a far worse problem: a sharp pain in my knee. I took a few excruciating steps and sat down on a rock.

I couldn't believe it. Half a day into a three-week journey on foot with men who speed over these trails as if on Rollerblades, and I was hobbling and wincing in pain. It wan't the pain that bothered me, though I was pretty unhappy about it; it was the knowledge that there was no medical attention for miles. If I continued to hike at that pace, I could seriously damage my knee and would have to be carried out. That really, really could not happen.

Fishing around in my medical kit, I pulled out two strong painkillers and swallowed them with tea. I wrapped a bandage tight around my knee to stabilize it, then tried walking again, boosting myself up with my walking poles. Thank God for my walking poles. I had bought them at the last minute on Anna's advice; now they were suddenly critical to my mobility. Even with the poles, though, I could do little more than hobble.

Embarrassed, I broke the news to D.B. and Rinjin. They were kind and concerned about my health, and made sure I was sitting down before they went to talk among themselves. D.B. came back and sat down next to me.

"We can go back to Simikot, Conor. I will take you myself—we can walk as slowly as you need. Walking uphill will be easier than downhill, we can reach Rinjin's guesthouse by tonight," he said.

"I'm fine, D.B. I'm slow, I know. I don't want to slow everybody down, and I know that I will. But I can keep going if the others don't mind." I hated to ask that; I felt like a whining little brother. But it was the only way I could continue.

He nodded and went back to tell the others. I saw them looking over at me as they packed up the camp. I couldn't meet their eyes.

Keeping my leg straight and leaning so heavily on my poles that I was petrified they would snap, I was the first of the group to set off. I was determined to prove that I would not slow us down to a crawl. I gripped my poles, stayed focused on the rocky path, and blinked away the tears of pain welling in my eyes, grateful that nobody was in front of me to see. I said a silent prayer, asking God only for the painkillers to kick in, and swore that if I ever made it back I would name my first child "Walking Poles."

◇

TWO DAYS IN, RINJIN stopped and pointed south, where the river curved.

"We reach there, we will be very close to Ripa," he said, patting my arm. I was leading the eight-man team—D.B. insisted on it. It was the only reliable way to keep the group moving at my slowed pace. As we approached a path leading up the side of a cliff, D.B. wanted to make sure I wasn't left behind.

I walked slowly along trails carved into the cliff walls. To my left was a sheer drop one hundred feet down into the river. In a way, I felt like I already knew Ripa. Bikash was from that village, as was his brother Ishan and several other kids from Little Princes. They spoke about it often. They told me of the steeply sloping terraces leading down to the white water of the Karnali, the cluster of mud huts built almost on top of one another, the nearby woods where the children collected herbs and spices for their families to sell. I wondered if the images they had painted would bear any resemblance to the real thing.

Min Bahadur barked out a single word. My daydream vanished. I had no idea what the word meant. I looked back. All seven men in our team had thrown themselves against the rock, as if they and the granite cliff wall had suddenly become magnetized. I heard Rinjin shouting a translation, but I didn't wait for it. I pressed myself against the rock as hard as I could. The ground shook. I felt them before I saw them: a herd of perhaps a hundred goats, laden with what looked to be rice-filled saddle bags, came streaming around the corner of the cliff trail. How they kept their footing I had no idea; I only knew that I couldn't keep mine. I gripped the rock tightly, terrified, and felt the surge of animals race past me in a cloud of dust, chased by a shepherd who ignored us completely.

I was still gripping the rock when Rinjin approached me, telling me it was safe to let go.

"If you see a herd like this, it is important to stay to the inside," he said, his hand tight on my shoulder, staring at me.

"I got that—stay inside when I see the goats. Thanks."

"Otherwise, you will end up in the river," he clarified, pointing down, in case there was any doubt. "The goats, they do not fall. Humli people, we do not fall. But you, you fall."

"Yep, I saw that. I saw it just now, with the goats."

"You did very well. It is very good you did not fall. You climbed very high on that wall, like a monkey," he said, looking up at the cliff wall.

"Yeah, well, I almost peed my pants, so—"

"You have to pee?"

"No, I don't have to—no. No, I'm good. Let's keep going. Thanks."

◇

WHETHER ANY OF THE children's families still lived in Ripa, I had no idea. But I was about to find out. The sky was graying as we entered the village up a sharp rise in the path. A cluster of mud huts was perched on a terraced slope, just as Bikash had described. Most of the huts shared walls; they were built practically on top of one another.

It had been an agonizing day, pounding on my inflamed knee for eight straight hours. Ripa, to me, was Shangri-La. It was the Four Seasons. I felt the pain more acutely knowing I was going to stop soon, and I hobbled openly for the first time, relieved we would be staying the night.

I was now last in the line of eight men, though Rinjin stayed just a few feet ahead of me. Walking through the narrow spaces between the huts, I was suddenly enclosed by villagers. They had seen us coming—or me coming, anyway. My pasty arms were pale enough to be seen for miles—they must have looked like light sabers next to the complexion of my colleagues. The villagers gave me a wide berth. Most gawked at me from their roofs. They shouted the occasional question at D.B., the leader of our pack, and the questions were clearly about me. I felt like a caged baboon being wheeled through some nineteenth-century town on its way to the circus tent.

Absorbing the stares of the villagers, I had no inhibition about staring right back at them. The women wore large, gold-plated nose rings and earrings and dozens of beaded necklaces. Some of them were gripping oar-length poles, poised to pound them against smooth, round stones, the middle of which were carved into a bowl, though I couldn't see what was inside—wheat, I imagined, to make flour. Other women were lugging wicker baskets on their backs stacked high with firewood. As is customary in Nepalese villages, the men seemed to be doing little but squatting on the ground, drinking tea, and watching the women work. Certainly they were not looking out for the babies; that job was left to the daughters, who were carrying the little ones on their backs, wrapped in handmade blankets of rough cloth.

D.B. stopped. He squatted down next to a man sitting in front of his door and spoke to him. The villager said nothing but listened to D.B.'s monologue for several minutes. He put down his tea, and without a word he got up and motioned for us to follow him. The village was small, and soon we were in front of an almost identical mud hut, the only difference being that it was whitewashed. It had a low door, next to which was a log with steps hewn into it, leading up to the roof, where there was a stack of hay and a woman weaving baskets. A man squatted in front of the door wearing a dirty white turban, smoking a pipe that he cupped in his hand.

The turban was the giveaway: this was a medicine man, a village elder. D.B., Rinjin, and I sat with him while D.B. explained our mission. We told him we had little information about the children, only a few names of parents. We believed there were families in Ripa, but we couldn't be certain. The information I took from the children was sketchy at best. I had little in the way of accompanying documentation. Sometimes the child remembered the name of their village, sometimes not. They were often too young to know their parents' names.

The elder asked to see the photos of the children. He studied them, listening to the names associated with the clean faces, well-groomed hair, and secondhand western clothing. They bore little resemblance to the children hovering nearby, donned in little more than rags, craning their necks to see what we were looking at. The man invited us to stay with his family. He would make a fire and his wife would cook our food for us. That was typical in Humla: as poor as they were, as much devastation as they had seen, they didn't think twice about opening their home to strangers.

We ate daal bhat inside the man's two-room hut, lit only by the small fire in the middle of the floor, which blackened the walls and ceiling. I was breathing smoke and air. The light reminded me of campfires and ghost stories from when I was young. In the corner, on a low bed, was an elderly man, naked except for a blanket, lying on his side and staring at the fire. I was the last to finish, despite concentrating on getting food down my throat as quickly as possible. I don't know how they did it, eating it when the daal was still literally boiling on the tin plate. We stepped outside and washed our own dishes in a bucket. Rinjin, D.B., and the porters all gathered around the fire, joined by several villagers who had remained outside, waiting for an opportunity to finally figure out what we were doing there.

I was led to the shed by the son of the family. The shed was just another room attached to the house, but smaller. He entered first, motioning for me to shine my head torch inside. He cleared the shed of the crude wooden tools— farming instruments of some kind—and opened his hand toward the door, inviting me in. I went in. My backpack was already near the door, my sleeping bag unrolled by one of the men. It would be a tight squeeze with all of us in here, but I would worry about that later. I lay down, making a pillow of my smoky fleece, and fell asleep almost instantly.

◇

I WOKE TO THE sound of heavy rain and the scrambling of two of our porters, who had been sleeping outside. Moments later they piled into the shed. It was uncomfortably crowded before—now it felt like an ill-conceived attempt at a world record. We huddled closer to squeeze them in. Feeling guilty that the foot of my sleeping bag now seemed to be inside somebody's mouth, I extricated myself from my bag, pulled on some rain gear, and stepped outside. It was still dark. But by the moonlight I could make out the tops of the hills nearby, just five hundred feet up from the village.

Something was wrong. The crests of the hills should have blended into the night sky, even in the moonlight, but they stood out like a cheap oil painting. I continued to stare at them and let my eyes adjust. Houses came into focus; the river appeared. Still, I stared at the hills. A moment later, I realized what was wrong, and my heart sank. The tops of the hills were covered in snow.

That was very bad news. It meant that Simikot—and more important, the airport runway—was snowed in. I had been warned, but I had held out hope that we would get lucky, that the weather would hold off. Now it looked like I would be trapped there for the rest of the winter, unless I walked out. It would take ten days just to reach a road.

These thoughts passed through my mind as I stared at the snow-covered hilltops hovering like a pale blue cloud against the night sky. Hope drained out of me and scattered away like dandelion seeds. I squeezed back into the shed, climbed into my sleeping bag, and prayed I would find just one parent to make this all worthwhile.

◇

SOMEBODY WAS SHAKING MY sleeping bag. I cracked open my eyes. Rinjin was standing over me, his unmistakable figure backlit against the dull light visible through the open door.

"Come outside. Somebody is here to see you," he said, and walked back out the door.

I stood up slowly, clenching my teeth against the pain in my knee. Piling on several layers, I stepped out into the dawn. Ten feet away, surrounded by half the village, sat a man and woman. The man was tall and thin, his eyes sunk slightly into his cheeks; or maybe it was just the appearance from holding his head down. But the mother, a plaid scarf tied around her hair, was looking directly at me. She had teardrop-shaped eyes, and her cheekbones came out like smooth shelves. Rinjin walked over to me to introduce them.

But there was no need. I knew exactly who they were. These were Anish's parents.

"The elders called them here. They heard we have news of their son," Rinjin said. He looked at me expectantly. "Do we?"

I didn't answer. I walked back into the shed and took my small daypack, the pack I kept near me at all times. I set it down outside and pulled out the blue folder I had prepared the week before, when I was at Little Princes, listening to the children, including Anish, yelling right outside the office door.

Flipping through the photos, I could see that all eyes were on me, trying to see through the folder, to see what this stranger had with him. I found the right page. I slipped it out of the folder. Stapled to the page was a photo of this woman's son. I removed it and handed it to her.

It was instant recognition. She cried out, and the group crowded in to see. She touched it to her head, as one does with a sacred object, and broke down sobbing, two hands on the photo, thumbs pressing into it as if she was trying to enter the picture herself, to touch the boy with the oil-slicked hair parted down the middle, flashing his wide grin. The father gently took the photo from her and held it inches from his face. Then he too began to cry.

The assembled crowd erupted with chatter. I dug into my pack for my notebook and sat down beside the parents. Rinjin sat next to me, and we began our first interview. I needed to understand what happened those years ago when they lost their son. Who came to take him? How much did the family pay? What were they promised in return? Did they have any idea where their son was now?

Each question instigated a short dialogue between Rinjin and the father. At first I thought Rinjin was clarifying the question, but that wasn't it. The questions were straightforward.

"What is he asking, Rinjin?"

Rinjin gave a frustrated sigh. "It is nothing. We can speak about it afterward. Please, continue," he said.

I continued. The interview took almost an hour and a half, just to elicit responses to what I considered simple questions. The answers were vague, reluctant. I asked Rinjin for follow-up on almost every answer the father gave. When I felt like I had all the information I would get, I asked Rinjin to translate a message for the father. It was a single message, but I instructed my guide not to sugarcoat it. Rinjin smiled grimly at the expression, getting its meaning. I spoke to both the father and mother, though the mother never looked me in the eye. I said this: They had put their son's life in danger. What they did, sending Anish away with Golkka, was reckless. It was a miracle Anish was alive at all, let alone safe in a children's home. If they did this again with another child, that child would almost certainly be lost forever.

Rinjin didn't sugarcoat it. The mother wept; the father stared into space.

I didn't like telling them that. I wanted to be a hero, to rejoice with them, to make this the scene in the movie where the music swelled and the parents gave me a tearful hug. But I worried. In a way, my coming here validated everything Golkka had done. He promised them their child would be safe, get a great education, stay healthy. And Anish was safe, educated, and healthy. I had to make them understand that he was all these things in spite of what they had done, not because of it. Above all else, we had to prevent this from happening again, and that required hearing a hard truth.

They stood up to leave, thanking me profusely, thanking Rinjin, thanking our porters. I returned the gesture, hands clasped together. And I asked Rinjin to take a short walk with me, to get away from the small crowd, just for a few minutes.

"What happened back there? Was he not understanding the questions, or did he not want to answer?" I asked him.

Rinjin shook his head. "Neither. I would translate your question exactly. He would ask me to repeat it. I would. Then he would think for one second and then he would ask me the same thing, every time."

"Which was what?"

He stopped and turned to me. "He wanted to know what the right answer was. He wanted to know what answer he should give so that you would keep his child alive, keep feeding him, keep sending him to school."

We didn't speak for a while. We stared together down toward the white water at the turn in the river, past the children running in the distance, leaping off the dormant farmed terraces where wheat would be planted in the spring. I felt terrible. Worse than terrible, I felt caught. I would maybe never have my own children, but I suddenly understood exactly what this father had seen when I walked into the village. He saw his son's benefactor, the person who would decide Anish's fate. He must have thought I was interviewing him on behalf of his son, determining his child's worth based on his answers. Four years after Anish's disappearance, his heart must have pounded with every question, terrified of getting one wrong and wondering what the consequences might be.

I would have to be more careful. My interviews would begin with reassurance, not interrogation. I would still be honest at the end—that was for the safety of the children. But I had lacked humility in front of parents who had sacrificed so much to save their son. I vowed not to make that mistake again.

D.B. and I spoke with families throughout the day. I took breaks to play with the children. They stood at a distance, respectful but dying to interact. When I came over they all shouted a sentence that they had clearly been working on together, a group project.

"Please one photo draw!" they cried, pointing at my camera. So I wasn't the first westerner in the village. I set them in little groups—first the girls, then the boys, then the young ones, and so on. Each time their smiles and roughhousing ceased immediately and they stood bolt upright, the Official Royal Portraits. As soon as I took a photo they collapsed again, and lobbied for photos with this boy, or these three children. They never asked to see the screen, which meant the last westerners through here had not had a digital camera. I wondered when that was. I was happy to continue to take photos, without the flash to conserve my battery. Now that I saw them more clearly, they were so similar to the children I knew in Kathmandu. They *were* the same children, really. Chance, age, gender, and probably other factors I would never understand kept them here while their brothers and sisters were taken.

By evening, we were finished. The elder's wife made us tea, and I sipped it alone, away from D.B., Rinjin, and the others warming themselves by the fire. I wanted to process everything I had seen and heard that day. I had spoken with the families of Hriteek, Bikash, and Anish from Little Princes, and Navin and Madan, the two elder boys of the seven children. Only in Humla did I learn they were brothers. But for now, I was trying to reconcile this village, this life, with the children I knew at Little Princes.

Anish's father was coming back. I saw him approaching down the trail. I was ashamed to catch his eye after our interview that morning. I had been honest, but I had also been unfairly harsh, practically lecturing him and his wife, as if I had every right in the world. I didn't walk to the fire—he could speak to Rinjin and Rinjin could pass the message on to me. I pretended not to see him, staring down into my steaming tea.

But he didn't go to Rinjin. He walked directly to me. He stopped a few feet away from me, waiting for me to look up. When I did, he greeted me with a bow of his head, and handed me a small plastic bag. He bowed his head again, then smiled for many seconds, as if he wanted to say something but knew I would not understand him. Without a word, he turned and walked back the way he had come.

I watched him go up the path. I caught Rinjin looking at me, then turn back to the fire. Then I opened the bag. It was walnuts, covered with honey, bits of the hive still on it. It was a gift, the only thing he had to give. A lump formed in my throat and stayed there until I fell asleep that night.

◇

ROHAN'S MOTHER SAT WITH us in the village of Tumcha. Rinjin was telling her the story of how Sandra found her son, how the boy ended up at Little Princes. He knew it well enough by then that I could afford to be distracted and look around. Tumcha was different—sunnier. Ripa, where we stayed for two full days before setting off early this same morning, sat below a mountain. By three in the afternoon, the village was in shadow. Tumcha, though, was built into a more gently sloping hill. It was 4:00 P.M. now, and the sun still reflected so brightly off the haystacks that I couldn't look at them.

Rinjin handed her the photo of her six-year-old son. Most parents broke down when they saw their child. Not Rohan's mom. Her reaction was the exact opposite, and somehow I was not surprised. Her eyes lit up and she laughed out loud. Her laugh carried chords of Rohan's laugh, the hilarious, borderline-maniacal laugh that earned him the nickname Crazy Rohan. Whenever I got bored at Little Princes, I would look for Rohan and ask him to tell me a story. He would spin an impressive tale on the spot, inspired by whatever object or person was closest. If Nuraj was playing cards nearby, the story would be about how Rohan and Nuraj one day had to fight fourteen evil men who were trying to hurt Hriteek, who was currently playing catch with himself on the other side of the room, and they would ride their motorcycle and fight them, simultaneously. The stories always featured Rohan on a motorcycle. The best part was that he laughed all the way through the telling. Also, every story—without exception—involved some kind of dance interlude. I would have given anything to see Rohan and his mother together.

I loved meeting the parents of the Little Princes. The similarities between parent and child were remarkable, like stepping into a time machine and seeing the child twenty years in the future. But I also loved the interviews because it meant I didn't have to walk. Hikes between villages could take as long as ten hours, stopping to rest and have a midday meal, and I was in constant pain. The ligaments in my knee were on fire. I recognized the pain from a bike injury in Sri Lanka the year before. When it happened, I took nine days and did nothing but sit in a chair, looking at tea plantations and reading books—and even then it was barely tolerable to put weight on it. This injury was worse, but there could be no stopping. I rationed my painkillers, saving them for after steep climbs and sharp descents. I stayed close to the others. There were times when the path split, with one rising up the mountain and one running parallel below it, and I did not want to have to backtrack if I went the wrong way. The mere thought of taking an unnecessary step was demoralizing.

At one such fork in the path, I followed Rinjin down. With everything on a slope, there was no "left" and "right" in Humla—directions were given as "up" or "down." Suddenly pebbles were raining down on me. I looked up to see, twenty feet above me, a tiny girl on the path above us. She was calling down to me while absentmindedly smacking a branch at the hindquarters of an enormous water buffalo, trying to get him to move. The buffalo looked nervous, as though the next step it took on the shale was going to carry it right off the path and create a one-buffalo avalanche. I had a vested interest in this not happening because the behemoth was positioned directly over my head. Panicked, I turned to Rinjin.

"Rinjin, you gotta tell her to stop hitting that buffalo! That thing's gonna come down on us!" I was practically shrieking.

Rinjin smiled. "She is calling to you—she wants to know your name," he tells me. "She is very sweet. . . ."

But I was gone, hobbling frantically up the trail, walking poles flailing. Behind me, I heard Rinjin tell the little girl that my name was Conor and that I was a very nice man.

◇

NEAR THE VILLAGE OF Mundi, several hours after my embarrassing buffalo-induced panic attack—the porters giggled about it for hours; I could hear them mock-screaming in low voices behind me—we set up camp in a former Maoist headquarters. It was a solid wooden structure by Humla standards: two floors, three rooms, built on a plateau just above the river. The owner of the building told us that one day the rebels came and declared that the house was now theirs. He was not about to argue with armed Maoists. The walls of his building were now covered in Communist propaganda both inside and out. Some of it, curiously, was written in English.

Every night up to that point, all eight of us had slept on floors next to families from the villages we visited. It was always an imposition on the family; but we had little choice, and they were eager to pay us back in some way for caring for their children. This night would be the first we were not staying with a family. The building was empty; the owner told us that the Maoists had left a week earlier and hadn't returned. The location was ideal: it was next to one of the few remaining bridges, and being near the river, we could wash in the icy water. We gambled that the Maoists would not return. At night, though, we were more cautious than usual. One man stayed awake and was relieved by another. Whatever sleep I had was uneasy, broken by fears—some rational, some not.

The next morning, Min Bahadur was gone. I walked outside looking for him. He was nowhere to be found. I saw Rinjin walking back from the river, and I limped down the hill to intercept him.

"Min Bahadur—he's gone. I can't find him."

Rinjin was drying his face with a worn towel. He slung it over his shoulder before answering.

"He saw from files that one child is from village of Puma," Rinjin said. "Min Bahadur says he can get there quicker by going over high pass, alone, and bringing back mother of the girl. I'm sorry, I cannot remember this girl's name right now, I gave the document to Min Bahadur. But he will bring the mother back. She will meet you here."

Five hours later, I was sitting with a woman and her sister. There was no mistaking this woman for anybody other than the mother of little Amita, the only girl of the seven children. Most of the seven children didn't speak about their parents. Amita was different. She spoke of her mother often, about what she and her mother had done together, that her mother had taught her how to sew and prepare rice, that they had never left each other's side, until Amita was sent away, to flee the Maoists, to get an education. It was rare for girls to be given this opportunity, and her mother had sold her animals to give her daughter a chance at a better life. Instead, Golkka had left her with Krish and Nuraj's mother, where Farid and I had found her almost a year earlier. Since then, Amita had been asking to go back home.

Now, I was face-to-face with her mother. I wanted to hug this woman. She looked so much like Amita. She also reminded me, somehow, of my own mother. Not in her appearance, but in the look she gave me, that expectant and fearful look my mother wore every time I saw her at the airport: excited and terrified at the same time, worried that maybe something had happened to me at the last minute—maybe I hadn't gotten on the plane; maybe I was in some room somewhere in the world, hurt, unable to get home.

Amita's mother had that look now: thrilled at the possibility of news of her daughter but terrified that the news might be bad, that her daughter might be sick or hurt or lost. I wanted to comfort her like I comforted my own mother. I wanted to tell her that her daughter was a shining star in our lives, that we adored her. I wanted to tell her that Amita missed her deeply, that she only wanted to come home, that nothing and nobody could ever take her place in her daughter's mind. All that would come soon enough. Now, I only greeted her, as I did every parent, with a namaste, and kept a respectful distance.

D.B. acted as translator for our conversation. I had told him. much about the seven children over our long days together, and he knew these children were the reason I had returned to Nepal. I had confided that, before I came up with the name Next Generation Nepal, I had considered the name Seven Babu, the Nepali term of endearment for young children.

The mother took the photo of Amita in one hand while clutching a tiny baby, Amita's newborn sister, in the other. Joy spread across her face, through her entire body. With D.B. conducting the interview, I captured the moment in a photo. It became one of my favorites from the hundreds I took during that trip. D.B. asked me if he could tell her the whole story of her daughter, beginning to end. I told him he could, and I watched as he explained how we had come to find Amita, wearing old clothes and no shoes, living in the single-room shack in Kathmandu with Krish and Nuraj's mother and six other children from Humla, doing little but waiting for the next chance to eat. Like the others, she had been reluctant to come out of the dark when I had first come to see them. But she was bolder than the other children, a natural leader in a place where leaders are rarely women. Amita not only came out of her shell, she brought the others out of theirs. We worked to find a safe home for her, and thought we had. Then she and the other children disappeared. It would be months before we found her again, alone on the road, carrying those two empty bottles, uncared for, looking for water. It was a miracle we found her at all.

I watched as the mother's bright smile faded and tears spilled down onto her baby. D.B. spoke calmly, with love in his expression, but he spoke plainly. She needed to understand the danger her child had been in. We had to at least try to prevent her from sending her next daughter away with the same irrational, impossible hope shared by so many mothers in Humla. Amita was safe now. She was going to school. She was eating daal bhat every day. And she missed her mother.

After two hours with Amita's mother, it was time for her to start the trek back to her village. She needed to get back before nightfall—walking at night was dangerous. She clasped her hands together in thank-you to me, and was about to turn when she seemed to remember something. She reached into the sling that held her baby and pulled out a bag of three hard-boiled eggs. She spoke quickly to D.B.

"She say that she meant to give you these earlier," he explained. "But she was too excited to hear news of Amita and she forgets. She asks your forgiveness. They are for you to eat."

She smiled and pointed to the eggs, putting her hand to her mouth. It was always difficult to accept these gifts, knowing how little the parents had and what it must cost them. But I also knew that this was for them. They needed me to know how much their children meant to them. And I did, long before she remembered the eggs.

I thanked her, and she turned around. I wanted to follow her home, to sit with her and have dinner with her. She was a mother, in every sense. She exuded it. In those minutes, in the exchange between us, I saw just a little bit of what Amita must have missed so terribly, and it made me homesick.

◇

ON OUR SECOND NIGHT at the former Maoist encampment, we were woken by the sound of loud, drunken voices. We rose together, quickly. The voices got louder. They were approaching from across the bridge. Now there were only four of us: D.B. had taken his team to a village five hours south to look for the families he had been charged with finding by Anna Howe and the ISIS Foundation. My team of four stayed behind because of my knee. They would return in two days. It was four of us against however many men were now stomping across the rickety bridge toward us.

Rinjin, who was on watch when we heard the men, quickly grabbed our bags and dug through them. He pulled out every flashlight we had and thrust them into our hands, two per man. He whispered an order to the two porters, then turned to me.

"Hold one in each hand. Spread your arms as far apart as they go. Point them at the bridge," he whispered. "Do not turn them on yet." He moved several paces away from me and did the same thing with his flashlights.

I realized what Rinjin had done—we would look like eight men, not four. Still the voices came closer, and for the first time I heard aggression in their tone. Something had set these men off, and there was nothing else on this side of the bridge but our house. They were coming for us, but why? How had they known we were even here?

Suddenly my stomach knotted up. The man in the camouflage jacket.

He had shown up when Amita's mother had left; he had come all the way up to us to listen in on what we were doing. It never occurred to anyone in our group to tell him to leave—men came up to us all the time to listen to interviews, to find out what we were doing there. But this man was different. He seemed irritated that a foreigner had been speaking to Amita's mother, and told off one of our porters. The porter, not one to back down, yelled at him to get lost. He was outnumbered by our team, and he sulked away. But I saw him the next day as well, walking past our camp. He must have noticed that our group was smaller. He watched us for a few minutes and left.

It had to be him. And he had brought friends. I tried to remember if I had said anything to him, given him a nasty look, anything. It didn't matter. It was *who* I was, what I represented, not what I had done to him personally. I was a foreigner, and foreigners had helped the Nepalese government fight the Maoist threat by offering aid. What was I doing in their territory, interfering? Even now that the Maoists controlled this region? Now, even when the royal government had lost, been overthrown? It wouldn't take much to convince some drunken former rebels that they had a unique opportunity, here in the dark, to teach me a lesson.

We turned on our flashlights and held them out; I looked into the darkness where the bridge should be, then up and down at our guys. Rinjin spoke loudly to our porters, who barked angrily back at him, interrupting each other. This was part of it, to make sure they knew we were several men. I kept my mouth shut, but my head was exploding.

The clamoring over the wooden bridge came to a stop. The drunken shouting died into whispers. They must have seen that the situation was not as the man in the camouflage jacket had described. There were not four of us, there were eight. And even drunken Maoists were not eager to start something they could not win. Who knew if the foreigner was even among them?

Rinjin and the porters also quieted. Together we stared into the still dark. My heart pounded. I hoped Rinjin knew what he was doing.

Several tense minutes passed, and the footsteps receded, back across the bridge. One of the porters kept watch for the remainder of the night. We did not hear from them again. But I didn't fall asleep again for a long time. I hoped that would be the last of the danger in this mission.

◇

D.B. AND THE OTHERS returned the next afternoon. Knowing we would break camp soon and might not have access to the river for several days, I walked down to the water for a much needed scrubbing. Halfway down, I found Rinjin speaking with a man I had never seen before, squatting on the ground in typical Nepalese style. I stood above them, bar of soap and towel in hand, for few minutes, then sat on a rock next to them. Neither one acknowledged me —they seemed lost in intense conversation. Finally I interrupted, frustrated at being ignored.

"I'm not clear who this man is, Rinjin," I said. I was cold. I recognized that this was making me irrationally irritable. It was only 3:00 P.M. and the sun had already dipped behind the adjacent mountain. I pulled out my hat from my daypack.

"He is the postman," Rinjin said slowly, sensing my irritation. He'd had a longer day than me, having gotten up early to prepare the rice and daal over the open fire, yet he seemed incapable of losing his patience. "He is a postman from the village of Jaira, but his post office is here."

I knew that we were nearing Jaira, Jagrit's village. But I had thought we were still quite a distance away.

"So Jaira is what, his postal route?" I wondered if the term was the same in Nepali.

"Yes, exactly," he said.

"How far are we from Jaira?"

"Maybe nine, ten hours walking. For you. Shorter for him. "

The postman was looking through the photos of the children that Rinjin had taken from my bag. He did not recognize any of them, and he could not read the profiles, since they were written in English. I was accustomed to villagers being curious about the files, but I was reluctant to let strangers study them. Rinjin was sensitive to this as well; he took the photos from the postman after only a few minutes and handed them back to me. In the past few days I noticed Rinjin becoming more protective of the children. I flipped through the profiles and found Jagrit's. I scanned it for the names of his father and mother. I did not bother with Jagrit's name itself; everything was traced by the name of the father. I was hoping the postman might have known him.

Rinjin read the name of the father off the photocopy I had of the father's death certificate. The postman's eyebrows jumped. He had known him— quite well, it seemed from his reaction. This was good news, as it would make our trip to Jaira more efficient if the postman could tell us which part of the village to go to and to whom we should speak. I took out my notebook and opened to a fresh page. I told him through Rinjin that we were heading to Jaira in two days, explaining that we were looking for families of children living under our care in Kathmandu, and we were trying to get as much information as possible about this boy. I started to ask if he knew of any living relatives of the father when the postman interrupted me to ask why we weren't going to visit them ourselves?

I looked up from my notes and paused for a long moment.

"Visit who?" I asked him.

The postman named the father and mother.

Rinjin and I said nothing. There must have been some kind of mistake. I pulled out their death certificates and handed them to Rinjin. Rinjin took them from me and held them out to the man. He pointed at the names on the certificates and asked the postman to be absolutely certain we were talking about the same people. Of course, he told us, puzzled. He had known them since he was a boy.

The death certificates had been forged. Jagrit's parents were not only alive, they were just a day's walk from where we sat. If it wasn't so tragic, I would have laughed at the absurdity of it. Here was a boy who had grown up believing his entire family was dead, who had been shown evidence of it on government-stamped documents. And yet all it took to disprove it, to alter the course of this boy's life, was to go to his village and check if his family might actually still be alive. I was struck by how viciously the civil war had torn this country apart. Children had been taken by traffickers and the door to their village had been slammed shut by the Maoists. Nobody could get in or out, even to check if their family members were still alive. I felt suddenly overwhelmed by the amount of work that needed to be done in Nepal. But in that moment I also felt focused. I had a single task in front of me. My young friend in Kathmandu needed me right now, even if he had no idea how badly. If Jagrit's parents were alive, I was going to find them.

◇

I WOKE UP BEFORE the others. Lying in the dark, unable to fall back to sleep, I thought about Jagrit, about what I would find at the end of the day, about the postman's reaction. I tried to imagine what the trail would be like that day, whether it would rain, what the condition of my knee would be. These thoughts, unhampered by any stimuli save the sound of men breathing, had free rein and kept me awake. I got up and went for a walk in the predawn light down to the bridge and stood in the center, watching the wide river race beneath me like God's treadmill.

After an hour, a fire sprang to life back at our camp. I climbed back up the slope to help prepare the tea.

Later, on the path, I could feel a difference in my knee. I measured it by the length of time I could go in the morning before it caught fire, before the long thick nail was hammered in, just below the kneecap. That morning it was fifty-five minutes, a new record. But the going was tough that day. I had been drinking steadily, and I was out of water. The path had taken us up, away from the river. Rinjin handed me his own bottle.

"You can use your pills in this," he said. He was referring to the chlorine tablets I carried with me. I had never drunk unpurified water in Nepal, and I was not about to start when I was a week's walk from a hospital, no matter how pure the Karnali looked. Yet I was in no position to refuse his offer. Humli men were strong, they could go without water. But the more dehydrated I got, the more I slowed us down. I took the water and dropped in the tablets. They would work in twenty minutes. I cheers'ed Rinjin with the canteen.

"Thanks."

"It is nothing."

It was far from nothing. We had been walking for six hours, including an hour's rest during lunch, rice cooked over an open fire on the side of the trail. I was exhausted. And things were about to get worse: D.B. was waiting for me up the trail. I caught up with him and sat down on a rock.

"How is your knee, Conor?"

"Much better than before. Still moving slowly, but better," I said.

He nodded, looking down at my knee. Then he met my eyes. "Rinjin told me about the postman, and about Jagrit. This is the same boy you told me about? The bright one from Umbrella?"

"Yes, same boy."

He paused. "I would very much like to find the family of this boy. But there is a chance that the postman is not completely . . . accurate. In Humla, we often confuse relations. We call cousins brothers, for example. This postman is not lying, but he may be confused between the father and brother," said D.B.

"I don't think so," I said. "We even asked him about the mother, he said it was definitely the right person."

D.B. smiled, and nodded again. "Yes, you are probably right," he said. "Anyway, we are not far now."

But the way he said it, sympathetically, told a different story. D.B. doubted the parents were alive, and he knew this region and the culture. He was uncomfortable telling me; he would not have said anything unless his doubts were well-founded. In a matter of minutes my spirits plummeted. I had allowed myself to get excited about finding Jagrit's parents alive, about returning to Kathmandu with this extraordinary news. What if his family really was dead? What if I couldn't even find his uncle? I continued to sit on the rock. The team didn't move, but waited respectfully up the path, where D.B. had rejoined them.

As I sat there, I allowed my mind to wander to Liz. In that moment, I remembered a short e-mail she had written to me a couple of weeks before I'd left for Humla. Apropos of nothing, she had written this:

> This morning, on the crowded train to New York, a man in the
> row in front of me sneezed. The woman in the row behind me said
> "God bless you." He could not have heard her, since I barely heard
> her, and the train was packed. But the fact that she said it gave me a
> sense of the innate goodness of man.

I remembered reading that e-mail and thinking I wanted to be near somebody like that. I wanted to be near somebody who could hear somebody sneeze and somebody else say "Bless you" and be able to conclude that human nature is, at its core, good. I wanted that kind of optimism in my life all the time. I wanted it to rub off on me. I wanted to see the world like that. I needed it right here, right now, sitting on this rock.

I got up and walked up to the men.

"Ready?" I said. They got up and loaded their packs, and we continued up the trail toward the village of Jaira.

Three hours later, D.B. pointed out Jaira. It was an hour, maybe less, along a traverse, downhill slightly from where we stood. We stepped off the path for a herd of goats barreling toward us from behind. I would hardly have even noticed them if the shepherd hadn't slowed down just as he passed me, coming to a full stop for perhaps one full second to stare at me before jogging after his goats. They raced on toward the village.

Forty-five minutes later, we arrived. I sat down. Rinjin and Min Bahadur would find the parents. They could do it more efficiently than I could as they spoke the language and maybe even knew some people in the village. Besides, it gave me a chance to rest. By now I was used to people gathering to stare at the white man propping his leg up, unwrapping a bandage from his knee, touching it gingerly. There was no alone time in Humla, not for me. Going by past experience, I would have at least an hour before Rinjin appeared with the first parent. I rested my head against my backpack and closed my eyes.

The shepherd stood above me. I recognized him from the trail—he wore a thick, dark red scarf around his neck. Rinjin and D.B. were speaking several feet away. They saw me stir and walked toward me, still talking.

"Hi there," I said to the shepherd, dusting myself off as I stood up. I had taken to greeting people in English—out of laziness, partly, but also because it discouraged them from trying to start a conversation. Sometimes it even thinned out the group. The shepherd didn't move.

Rinjin came up to me. "Sit, Conor. We will stay here," he said.

"I'm okay," I assured him. "I can walk, I just needed a rest. Did you find anything on the father?"

Rinjin looked confused for a moment. Then, leaning into my ear, whispered. "The shepherd *is* Jagrit's father, Conor."

◇

SINCE MEETING THE POSTMAN, I had imagined this moment. Now, face-to-face with him, I was positive this was the father. Rinjin had confirmed it, and the resemblance was uncanny. This was the moment I had been waiting for. Yet I suddenly found myself having no idea what to ask Jagrit's father. For his part, he just looked back and forth between Rinjin and me, genuinely confused as to who we were and why I needed to speak to him. I talked to him about where he was from, his wife's name, and so on to establish that we were talking to the right person. It was him, there was no doubt. I asked him if he had a son.

"Yes—his name is Khagendra, he lives with me," he told me.

I waited. He did not say anything else. Rinjin, who often conducted much of the interview himself by now, knowing my questions by heart, purposefully waited for my next question.

"Ask him if he has any other sons, besides Khagendra," I said. Rinjin translated the question.

The father said nothing. He stared at me, as if trying to work out why I was asking that particular question. Rinjin repeated the question.

The man nodded.

"Ask him if this other son's name is Jagrit—or something that sounds like Jagrit. Hold on—that might not even be his real name. How can we possibly know—"

Rinjin cut me off, putting his hand on my forearm. "Just let me ask him." He translated the question.

Again the man said nothing. I watched him press his lips together so tightly it looked like they would never open again. Then he nodded again.

I took out the photo of Jagrit and handed it to Rinjin, who handed it to the father.

The man stared hard at the photo, holding it up to his eyes for what felt like several minutes. Then his hands, still clutching the photo, dropped slowly to his lap. Tears fell, absorbed by dusty trousers. Rinjin leaned in, as if to comfort him, but never touched him. I felt like an intruder in an incredibly personal moment. I wanted to give him time, let him go see his wife, take a few days to take this news in, to come to believe it in his heart and understand how his life might change, how his son's life might change.

But our time was limited. It was always limited. I was meeting parents and doing the equivalent of throwing a bucket of cold water in their faces with the news of their long-lost children, then asking them tough questions and recording their answers, all within the course of an hour or two. I watched them come alive when I told them their children were safe. I watched them die a little as they relived the loss of their child to a child trafficker. It was intimate and overwhelming and I felt, over and over, unqualified to be doing this job. But there was nobody else to do it.

Jagrit last saw his parents when he was five years old. The boy in the photo was fourteen.

I never had any intention of showing this man the document I was now pulling out of my pack. I hesitated for a moment, then handed it to him. The father took it from me and stared at it blankly. He was illiterate. Rinjin gently took it back and read it aloud to him. I waited for him to finish. The shepherd's head hung down as if a weight had been slung around his neck. A man he had met just an hour earlier had just read him his own death certificate.

"Your son believes . . ." I started to say, looking to Rinjin for guidance. "Your son, Jagrit, he believes that you, and his mother, and the rest of his family, are dead. He has always believed that. That document you are holding—your death certificate—we have the same document for your wife. It is an official government document. It was forged by the man who took your son."

The man said nothing, but looked back up at me. His eyes closed slightly, as if he has received too much information to process.

Rinjin was watching me. "I will ask him what happened," he said, motioning for me to open my notebook.

The father recounted the whole story. His eyes never met ours, but stared into space. I couldn't understand the words, but he seemed to travel back in time and watch the entire event unfolding in front of him. He spoke of the government official who told him he had seen potential in Jagrit as a young boy, who promised to put him in a top school in Kathmandu. The official had asked the family to provide a large sum in advance. The father waited to hear news of his son. Weeks became months, and months became years, until one day there was no hope left. It was as if his wife had never given birth to the boy, as if he had never held that bright young child, his firstborn son.

Rinjin and I were riveted. I felt like I had lived the story with him, watching from afar, seeing the father—the shepherd—and his small son, Jagrit, together first, then saying good-bye, not understanding it would be for the last time. When the father finished, I closed my notebook. We sat together for a while, silent. The father stared at the ground. Then he said something to Rinjin without looking up.

Rinjin translated. "He is asking if you will tell Jagrit that they are not dead."

"He can tell him himself," I told Rinjin. "He's going to write him a letter."

We stood fifty feet away and watched while the father, sitting with the village schoolteacher, the only literate man in the village, dictated a letter to his son. When he was finished he walked over and handed it to me, folded several times into a tight square with Jagrit's name written on the front in Sanskrit. I didn't ask what he wrote. Rinjin wanted to know if I had any more questions for him.

"No, it's okay, he can go," I told him. It was a two-hour walk back to his house, outside the village, and it was already getting dark. "Wait . . . tell him his son—tell him he is an amazing kid. Everybody loves him. Make sure he understands that."

Rinjin told him. The shepherd, Jagrit's father, smiled for the first time. He clasped his hands together in a silent thank-you, and set off up the trail.

◇

THE EXTRAORDINARY CIRCUMSTANCE UNDER which Jagrit's father, the dead man, came to life gave me a glimmer of hope for two of our other children: Raju and his sister, Priya. We had always thought them to be true orphans. Back at Little Princes we did anything we could to help the children keep a connection to their families. One of those things was helping them write letters to their parents, even if they might never see them again. All of the children did it, even Raju. It was Priya, his sister wise beyond her seven years, who explained to her brother that they could not write letters, that they had nobody to send them to because their parents were not living. That was a difficult day.

But now there was a ray of hope—a dim ray, perhaps, but a ray. Their parents might still be alive. I almost did not want to think about it, the idea was so overwhelming.

I charged Min Bahadur with getting to Lali, the village of Raju and Priya, across the river and to the northeast. He was the strongest in our team and knew the region better than anyone. He could make it there and back in less than two days. I gave him all the information I could about the two little ones and sent him off, unburdened by packs so he could move quickly.

We watched him leave, then continued our journey south. I tried to put Min Bahadur and his search out of my head, but it was difficult. The walks were long and lonely, and I had hours of time with my thoughts. I imagined a father picking up Raju the way I picked him up, of Priya helping her mother cook for the family, of the two playing together in the fields and lying between their parents at night, warmed by their body heat.

At the end of the second day, Min Bahadur caught up with us in a village called Tulo. He immediately sat next to Rinjin and spoke to him softly. Rinjin listened intently. Then he called me over.

"Their children's names are Raju and Priya Atal? You are sure?" he asked.

"I'm sure." I held my breath.

"Min Bahadur found those in the village that knew them," he said. "Four years ago they got very sick. . . ." Rinjin paused, then shook his head. "I'm sorry. They are dead."

◇

THE FIRST TIME I ever had food poisoning, I was in a hotel room in Jacksonville, Florida. I woke up with it after an evening at a seafood buffet, and stumbled to the bathroom. My flight to New York was departing in less than three hours; I didn't leave the bathroom for the next fourteen. I lay curled up on a nest of towels, my face resting against the cool tub, sucking water from the tap, wondering how I was going to survive. The cleaning lady stopped in, thinking I had vacated the room, and I just had the strength to croak out most of "Come back later!" before my stomach seized up again so it came out as "Come back—*blaeeegh*!" Vomiting, for me, is a loud affair. Decibelwise, I might compare it to the inside of a sports bar in Boston the moment the Patriots score a Super Bowl–winning touchdown with three seconds on the clock after coming from six hundred points down. The cleaning lady couldn't get out fast enough.

That was a spotless Marriott in the United States. Now I was in Humla, and it was only a matter of time before I got sick. Sure enough, I was struck down two weeks into the journey. I was usually able to sleep through the night, exhausted from the day. But one night my eyes popped open from a dead sleep. I needed to get outside. Like, ten seconds ago. It was pitch black in the hut and there was a family sleeping beside me, so I controlled my overwhelming urge to bust out through the wall like the Kool-Aid Man, and instead shuffled gingerly toward the door. Not gingerly enough, as I found out when I accidentally kicked a sleeping chicken across the room, causing a holy panic in the claustrophobic space. I felt my way out the door, then it was just a matter of how far away from the house I could get. Not terribly far, as it turned out.

Already weakened from days of walking and dehydration, the food poisoning felt like it had the power to kill me. It was difficult to hold down any food at all, which was dangerous because I was expending an enormous number of calories each day. My team learned to watch for signs that I was about to stumble or even collapse. We couldn't afford to stop; we were already behind schedule because of my knee. And with the snow, we would have to start thinking about other ways out of Humla. I tried to keep my mind off the fact that if further complications developed there was no help, no hospital, and no easy way out.

With my new illness, I was experiencing a level of discomfort I didn't know existed outside of passing kidney stones. Food poisoning causes the body to evacuate everything it can, as rapidly and inconveniently as possible. To make matters much, much worse, in Humla, there were no toilets. And when I say no toilets, I do not merely mean a lack of comfortable indoor plumbing—I mean no toilets. I asked "Where is the toilet?" on my first day in southern Humla, and was told: "No." I don't think I had ever gotten that response before. It shouldn't really be a yes-or-no question, after all.

◇

THREE DAYS LATER I was on the mend, able to eat daal bhat for the first time. I even encouraged the others to walk ahead, though Rinjin insisted on staying behind me. We had been walking for two hours when I came over a crest to find D.B. and the rest of the men sitting on rocks, looking down the valley. He smiled when he saw me, and came back up the path to meet me.

"You see the mountain there? The last one, very tall?" he pointed down the Karnali River, to a mountain about the size of the one we had descended the first day when we had landed in Simikot. I nodded.

"At the top is Shreenagar," he said.

Shreenagar. It was the last village; the last two families were up there. But two days earlier, Shreenagar had become something else as well. It had become a way out of Humla. The World Food Programme (WFP), the UN-sponsored agency active in the region, was making rice drops at the top of that mountain by helicopter. With a helicopter, I could catch a ride out. I could get to Balaju or Nepalganj or wherever they were going. It didn't matter. Wherever they were going would have a road or an airport. I had been in Humla for almost three weeks. I had done what I had set out to do. It was time to go home. One more day to the mountain, a three-hour hike straight up, and I would be at the helipad.

We took our time, stopping for lunch with some men fishing in the Karnali. My stomach turned at the idea of eating fish, but for the other men, fish was a rare treat. We decided not to start the climb until the next morning, when the sun would hit our side of the mountain and warm us as we hiked. By the time we began the ascent up the switchback trail, I was feeling stronger than I had felt in days.

Dhananjaya was the man responsible for this region for the World Food Programme. He saw us coming up the trail and came down to meet me. I told him about our mission, and about my knee. He confirmed that Simikot was still snowed in—WFP was able to land there by helicopter, but no planes were coming in our out.

"You are very lucky, Conor," he told me. "Tomorrow our last helicopter of the season arrives. I am going home as well, also back to Kathmandu, to my family. We can easily fit you on board. I know the pilot, he will be interested in your story."

Kathmandu sounded so sleek, so modern sitting in this village. I looked at my watch. It was December 15. Remarkably, after everything that had happened in the past three weeks, I would be home early, in time to meet my college friends coming to visit, and a few days before Liz arrived in Nepal. I couldn't wait. I had spent so many hours thinking about her. On several occasions in the past three weeks Rinjin had caught me smiling.

"You are thinking about a woman, I think," he said the first time, laughing and jabbing his index finger in my chest.

"No," I said instinctively, somehow embarrassed that I had been caught. "I was just thinking about an e-mail from a friend of mine." Technically, this was true. At that moment, I was thinking about an e-mail. I didn't mention that it was from Liz. She had written to me in the middle of the night, her time. It was the middle of the afternoon where I was, and I had written back immediately, asking her what she was doing up at that hour.

"Oh, it's kind of embarrassing actually," she wrote. "There was this crazy thunderstorm tonight, so Emma, my big lug of a yellow Labrador, jumped into bed with me because she was scared. It took me, like, forty-five minutes to fall asleep again, and just when I did, Emma rolled over in her sleep and fell out of the bed with this really loud thump and I jumped about ten feet in the air. So I'm letting her sleep in the bed now and I'm on the couch so I decided to e-mail you to say hi."

I loved so much about that e-mail. I loved that she lived alone with a huge Labrador, a dog that leaped into bed with her during thunderstorms. I loved how she told the story of Emma falling out of bed. But most of all, I loved that when she was awake in the middle of the night, she wrote to say hi to me, as if we were best friends, as if we had known each other for years.

I would be meeting Liz in a matter of days. I had trouble focusing on anything else, including preparing for my last interview, an evening interview with the parents of a boy from Little Princes named Ram; my mind was on the helicopter, on getting back to Kathmandu. But Rinjin showed up with not only Ram's parents but three generations of his family, from a one-year-old baby to a grandmother of indeterminate age. It was a perfect final interview, a lasting image of an entire family surrounding a mother who held one single photograph of an eight-year-old boy from Little Princes, a boy who was anything but an orphan.

Just after dawn the next morning, I said good-bye to my team. Most of them would accompany D.B. to a few other villages to help him complete his work, interviewing the parents of children Anna had asked him to find. All of them, including D.B., would remain in Humla for the winter. This was their home. Rinjin offered to stay with me, but I insisted he begin the long trek back to Simikot.

We took one last group photo, overlooking the mountains in the gray dawn. I said good-bye, filling an envelope with twice the salary I had promised the men and asking D.B. to divide it among them. I watched them set off on their quick descent down the mountain, unburdened by the hobbled, food-poisoned Irish-American. Min Bahadur turned and gave an awkward wave—a western gesture he must have learned from me—before disappearing out of sight.

For the first time, I was alone in the mountains. It was a strange and suddenly very lonely feeling. I became friends with Dhananjaya, the WFP guy. We'd had dinner with him the night before. He told me the drought had gone on for the last three years; the Humli people needed much more assistance in order to survive. But WFP had dropped all the rice they had. It would last through the winter, and the program would continue in three months. Dhananjaya would be back then.

I hiked up to the makeshift helicopter landing area at the crest of the mountain, an area flattened by the hands of the villagers by chipping away the rock. The helipad was a twenty-minute walk up from the village. At the top, I dropped my backpack and leaned against it. I pulled out my well-worn book, *Carter Beats the Devil*. I was on my third time through it since first arriving in Humla; I practically had it memorized. The helicopter would arrive within the hour. I put down my book. There would be endless time to read when I was on the flight home, in the airport, back in Kathmandu.

For almost three weeks I had been so focused on finding families, on wondering what the weather would be like that day, wondering how I would get out of Humla, that I had spent little time just sitting and enjoying the landscape in this remote corner of the world. The view, now, was spectacular, with the river far below and the dramatic snow-covered Himalaya in the distance. I hoped that I would make it back to Humla one day, not for such an intense journey, but instead to visit the children who might one day be able to go back to their own families. Staring out at that panorama, I realized this was a fitting place to say good-bye to Humla, a place that had brought such difficulty and pain, but also such joy in meeting the children's parents. I leaned back against my bag and watched the sky for the helicopter.

◇

AN HOUR PASSED, THEN TWO.

Ten hours later, I was still at the helipad. The helicopter had not come. For the last four hours I had stared at the horizon, too distracted to read. It was a mind-numbingly boring day, blistering hot in the sun and freezing in the shade. I hiked the short distance back down to the village. Dhananjaya, who was waiting in the village, knowing the helicopter would not leave, without him, was frustrated and apologetic. He offered to let me stay the night in the house where he was staying. In the storage area beneath the house sat two hundred and fifty tons of rice from the World Food Programme, ready to be delivered to impoverished local villagers. I accepted his offer and crashed early.

Just after dawn the next morning, I returned to the landing area. I was frustrated to be delayed. Now I would arrive on the same day as my friends, unable to meet them at the airport after they had traveled halfway around the world to visit me. I apologized silently to them. It was frustrating, knowing I could not tell them why I was late. I was grateful that I had at least been able to warn them that I might be a day late if I was somehow delayed getting a flight home. But it was still extremely irritating, being so close, and having to wait another few hours to leave. I recognized how trivial it all was in the grand scheme of things; I had spent almost three weeks wandering through this desperate country, meeting villagers who had virtually nothing to their name, who had lived through ten years of war, and here I was moaning about having been held up a single day. I tried to put it in perspective, but I failed. This helicopter better be on its way here, at this moment, I recall thinking. I'm going to close my eyes, count to ten, and I better hear the helicopter coming. I began counting as slowly as I could, waiting whole minutes between each number. I opened my eyes. Nothing. I sighed, and closed my eyes again. Okay, this time I'll count to twenty, I decided.

The helicopter did not come that day. Nor did it come the next day, or the day after that.

For five days, I waited on the mountain, on the rocky surface, in the sun and in the shade. The helicopter did not come. By the end of the fifth day, I was near despair. It was torturous to sit for hours on end watching the sky, willing a helicopter to appear. There was nothing but mountains, waves of them as far as the horizon. The landing pad started to feel like a raft in the open sea. I was as far away from civilization as I had ever been in my life, and I had no idea how I would get back.

In my days there, I got to know the children of Shreenagar. They would come up to the landing spot and watch the sky with me. The same six children always visited me. By the third day, they were up at the coarse-graveled helipad by 7:00 A.M., waiting for me to arrive. We couldn't communicate, but it was nice to have company. I would pace back and forth, and they would pace twenty feet behind me. I would sit on a rock, and they would find a couple of rocks fifteen feet away and squeeze onto them, the older boys claiming the best perches. A few hours later I would be throwing small stones off the side of the mountain; just a few feet away, they would be throwing stones, aiming at the small, isolated trees and shrubs clinging to the slope among the low, winter-browned grass. When I went for another lap of the flattened area and saw them huddling, I knew they were planning how to approach me. They waited until I drew closer, then the eldest stepped out from the tight circle and into my path.

"You . . . daal bhat—" he began, pointing at me, then his mouth. "Helly-

cota." He pointed to the sky—helicopter, he was saying—then back at himself, then at me again. "Running . . . me . . . you," he said. From the eager
pantomiming of the boys behind him, I understood that he meant that I
should go down to the village to have daal bhat for lunch, and if the helicopter
came, he would come running down to get me.

I looked around at the boys, and they stared at me, waiting for my
response. I couldn't resist; I said "Ke?" which is kind of like "Huh?" because
I knew that they would erupt back into this grand charade to help me understand, and frankly, it was the only entertainment I'd had in a couple of very
boring days. I made them do it two more times until they caught on that I was
messing with them. Then I took them up on their offer. Anything to break
the terrible monotony of the day and that empty sky.

On the third day, Dhananjaya asked if I would like to help with some of
the distribution of the rice. I was happy to assist, having lived freely off the
Humli people for the past three weeks. More important, I wanted something
to do, a task to keep my mind occupied. We helped villagers load up their
allotted twenty kilos of rice into panniers strapped to their goats—the same
kind of crazed goats that almost took me off the cliff wall early in my journey.
We watched the men drive their trains of goats out of the village and east-
ward, over the mountain pass, sometimes walking up to two days straight,
back to their own villages.

Late in the day we had an unexpected visitor to the food distribution
site. He walked slowly toward the villagers loading their sacks. They stopped
what they were doing and moved away. I was in the house at the time, taking a break in the shade, but I could see it happening through the open door.
The man wore fatigues, a local leader of what should have been the defunct
Maoist army. I stayed inside, out of the way. I no longer had my document of
protection from Humla's Maoist district secretary— D.B. had taken it with
him when he left—and I was far from Simikot.

I heard them talking outside. The Maoist's voice was agitated, incensed.
Dhananjaya's was calm and reasonable. Their conversation couldn't have
lasted more than half an hour, but when Dhananjaya came in he looked worn

out. He collapsed onto the bed, took a few deep breaths, and told me what had happened.

"He demanded five hundred kilos of rice," Dhananjaya said. "I looked to see if he saw you—I am very glad you were inside. It would have made things much more difficult if he had seen you. He just wanted the rice. For his men, he said. I did not ask him what men. I knew what men. I told him no, it was not possible, the rice was for the villagers. I was very nice with him. He did not accept this answer. His men needed to eat as well, he told me. He could not deny them. This Maoist, he was armed. What could I do?" He paused, expecting an answer.

"What *did* you do?"

"The only thing I could do. I gave him the key to the storage room. And I said 'Take as much as you want. Please just do me the favor of telling me how much you will take, since every grain must be accounted for and I must inform the United Nations of how much is missing.'"

"Whoa—that's good," I told him. It *was* good. The Maoist would know that stealing food would be a violation of the ceasefire. And that he would undoubtedly bring the wrath of his leadership down upon him if he defied the UN, jeopardizing the peace process over a few bags of rice for some men who were no longer part of an official army. "So what did he say?"

"I do not know the words in English. I would not translate them even if I did," he said, smiling. "But he left. With no rice."

◇

ON DAY FIVE, THERE was a change in the sky. For the first time in weeks, I saw planes far overhead. They were heading north. That could only mean one thing: The airfield at Simikot had reopened. It had not snowed since that night in Ripa. In three weeks, the men of Simikot must have managed to clear the runway by hand.

We had a difficult choice to make, Dhananjaya and I. We could wait for a helicopter that might or might not come, or we could try to walk out, back to Simikot. We estimated in our condition it would likely be a four- or five-day journey if we went directly north. I counted the days on the calendar. It was December 20. Liz would arrive on the 23rd and leave the morning of the 25th. Even in the best-case scenario, I was all but certain to miss her visit.

Moreover, getting back to Kathmandu in five days was the *good* scenario. There was an additional risk to consider. If it snowed during our trek, the airfield would be snowed in again. That meant we would not only be trapped in Humla, we would have spent days walking north when the only way out of the region was due south. It would add at least a week to our journey.

Over tea, Dhananjaya and I made our decision. We would risk the trek to Simikot, gambling that it would not snow in the next five days. In truth, we felt we had little choice—it seemed the helicopter would never come. Dhananjaya was also injured, suffering from a bad back, so it would be a slow trek for both of us. As Dhananjaya asked our host to find us a porter in the village, I packed my bag. If I had left with Rinjin, I would be in Simikot right now, maybe even on a plane back to Kathmandu that day. I tested the weight of my bag, bouncing it a couple of times before dropping it on the ground. Then I went to find Dhananjaya.

Five hours after setting off down the mountain, walking north for the first time, Dhananjaya, our porter, and I arrived at the village where we would spend the night. We had not planned on walking so far, but three hours into our journey, when we were about to stop, we met a man on the path who changed our minds. It was a man Dhananjaya knew through the WFP. He was coming from the north, and he had news of the helicopter. He told us that the pilot had received orders to change his drop schedule. The pilot was distraught: he knew Dhananjaya was waiting for him, but Dhananjaya had no radio. There would be no more drops to Shreenagar for three months. I breathed a sigh of relief. At least we hadn't waited.

"But the helicopter has one more drop, Conor," Dhananjaya told me, translating what he had just heard. "It will be tomorrow, this man says. In Sarkegad."

"Sarkegad? That's still a day from here—what time will it land?" I asked.

"He does not know. It could be any time. But I think we must try for it. We can continue past this village, I know of another two hours away. We should get there before nightfall. Then tomorrow morning, we leave early." He smiled. "We may get our helicopter after all, Conor."

After an abbreviated night of sleep, we left at first light. Despite our hurry, it was too dangerous to walk the difficult trail at night. We hiked as fast as we could toward Sarkegad. We did not stop because we could not; Dhananjaya told me we had only a twenty-minute window from the time the helicopter set down to unload the rice before it would take off again. We had no idea when it would come. We were racing a clock, but with no idea of our deadline.

We trekked back along the narrow paths dug into cliffs high above the Karnali River. Trains of goats and buffalo cannoned toward us in the other direction, but by then I was instinctively hugging the rock and more sure-footed on the shale, having learned to compensate for my pained knee. The biggest problem was our porter. He was utterly unreliable—the single worst trait a porter could have short of homicidal tendencies. He lagged far behind us, and he had my water bottle. It was stupid to have left it with him, but it was an extra kilo, and I had thought he would be right behind me the whole time. Now we couldn't wait for him, but neither could I drink, and I was painfully dehydrated.

For seven hours we walked without stopping even to sit down. I was obsessed with the helicopter. I strained to listen to the air around us, trying to detect any sign of the aircraft. I was tired. To keep my pace I repeated a mantra: No helicopter before the village. For hours I repeated this to myself, timing my steps to the quick rhythm of the prayer, parched and hungry and not stopping, keeping a steady distance behind Dhananjaya who walked thirty feet ahead of me.

Coming over a ridge too carelessly, I quickly found myself sliding down the steep path, forced to use my beaten-up walking poles as brakes. I slowed my slide, but the noise of the tumbling shale seemed only to get louder.

I froze and looked up. Dhananjaya had stopped. He was staring up the valley.

Seconds later, the helicopter screamed overhead.

We were an hour from Sarkegad.

I walked ahead to where Dhananjaya had sat down for the first time in several hours. I sat down next to him. In my mind, I replayed the minutes of the last twenty-four hours. I replayed the moments I had lingered when I could have been moving, and the extra minutes we had taken getting packed up that morning, the minutes wasted looking for my misplaced water bottle before we set off from Shreenagar. Those minutes easily added up to an hour. An hour that could have put us in Sarkegad at that very moment, climbing into a helicopter.

Twenty minutes later, the silence was shattered again, and the helicopter raced over our heads, down the valley and out of sight. After weeks of silence, the mechanical roar was otherworldly.

Dhananjaya continued to stare at the horizon. He looked exhausted, beaten.

"We are very unlucky, Conor," he said flatly, and rose to his feet. We continued on.

We arrived in Sarkegad and collapsed. Dhananjaya could not continue. His back was hurting too much; he needed to stay at least a couple of days to rest. The difficulty of the day's trek took a lot out of us. I knew exactly how he felt. All I wanted was to lie down in the middle of a field and fall asleep. I had grown up in a culture of automobiles, never giving a thought to the fact that in much of the world distances are still covered on foot. We were still miles away from Simikot, and we were shattered.

"I know you wanted to make it farther, Conor, but we need to rest here. We have come very far today. Your knee is bad, I can see it when you walk. My back is very bad as well," he said to me. "I know many people here, we can stay with them. We will continue tomorrow, perhaps."

"I'm not staying," I said.

I wasn't sure what I meant by that, really. It just came out. I could not go on without him—I didn't know the way, it was getting dark, I did not speak the language of my porter, who anyway was completely exhausted and sat with his head slumped down. Yet I said it, and I meant it. I had to keep going. Alone, if necessary.

Dhananjaya tried to talk me out of it. The village elders joined us as well, and they tried hard to dissuade me. I did not understand, they pleaded. You do not walk in Humla at night. Even locals do not walk at night. You will get lost or attacked or slip off the cliffs; it is dangerous terrain even in daylight. You do not know what you are saying.

But I did know. I knew that if I waited, I was going to get snowed in again—it was only a matter of time. If I kept going, if I didn't stop, if I walked at a fast pace, there was a chance I could make it out. I had been cautious on my knee because even though it was feeling much better, I did not want to reinjure it and risk becoming incapacitated. Now, I didn't care, I would run if I had to. I just wanted to get out. The panic date was approaching, the date when Farid would alert the authorities and call my family to tell them I was missing. I couldn't imagine how difficult that would be on them; they were already worried. The only thing I could think about, though, was that I had to meet Liz. If she came to Kathmandu and left without my being there, that was it. We lived nine thousand miles apart. I knew, with absolute certainty, that I was looking at my one and only chance.

I told the elders of Sarkegad that I was continuing, alone and in the dark. I was getting back. There was no other plan, because no other plan included Liz.

Resigned to my decision, Dhananjaya set about helping me prepare to leave within the hour. Because my porter was as exhausted as I was, I hired another porter, a teenager, to join us so that they could share the load. Between the three of us, nobody had to carry more than twenty-five pounds. It was a paltry weight by porter standards, but I wanted to move fast. I said good-bye to Dhananjaya, promising to speak to him when we were both safely back in Kathmandu. And with that, my porters and I set off into the dusk.

Not long after leaving the village, we were walking in pitch black. Not long after that, the old flashlights used by the porters began to flicker. They were following a good distance behind me; when I turned, it was difficult to make out the faint glow of their lights.

My original porter was unsettlingly strange. I didn't trust him. Earlier that day he had lagged far behind; when I retrieved my pack I saw that he had gone through it. I could not find anything missing, and I definitely could not afford to accuse him in the current situation. I needed him. I heard him whispering to the younger man, about what I had no idea, but it gave me a bad feeling.

I took comfort in the fact that I knew at least where I was leading us to that night: the village of Unapani. I had stayed there before, and I knew we could stay with the family of one of our kids back in Kathmandu. I was concerned about food—we had none. I had left it with Dhananjaya for his return trip. But I was confident that somebody in the village would be able to spare something for us.

Seven more hours of walking, and we were cold and tired. My porters, walking close behind me now, stopped suddenly for no apparent reason. I turned and stared at them. They didn't move.

"Why are we stopping? We are going to Unapani," I said in my limited Nepali.

It took me a few tries to understand what they were telling me: This *was* Unapani.

I looked around. We were standing next to a small, locked hut. There was nothing else but darkness and the sound of the river next to us. This was definitely not Unapani. Unapani had many houses. I knew because I spent two days there. I fumbled for words to try to make myself understood, and I heard them repeating the same sentence over and over, struggling to make me understand.

Then it hit me, what they were repeating. As the translation took shape in my head, my stomach dropped through the earth. This was *Lower* Unapani. We had gone the wrong way. The village I was thinking of was directly up the mountain, invisible to us, with no trail that I could find in the dark. That was where the houses were, where food and shelter were. In our shattered condition, almost unable to take another step, it would take hours to find the trail and hike up the mountain.

It was 10:00 P.M. We couldn't continue. We hadn't eaten in nine hours, and two of us had been walking since 6:00 A.M. Even the new porter slumped down beside the older man and leaned his head on the bag. I sat down beside them. I reached into my bag and pulled out our last two tangerines and passed them to the men.

There was nothing we could do. I had no clear idea where we were. I rested my head in my hands, closing my eyes and wishing it would all go away. We were already freezing; it was an especially cold night, even for December, even for Humla. Sleeping outside would be foolish. But without food we would not have the energy to trek up the steep trail to Unapani, and the next village was many hours away.

I switched off my flashlight to preserve the battery. Everything disappeared. For just over three weeks, I had been looking up at the same night sky in Humla. Living under the bright lights of the city, you forget about stars; it seems strange to think they are always there, above the fray. In my first days in Humla, I loved the fact that I was in that wilderness and could finally appreciate how heavenly it all was.

But now, I wanted very badly to be able to see that blank, smoggy sky over the city. I wanted the pollution and the noise and the electric lights blocking out the stars. I wasn't meant for this, I thought. I pretended I was, but I wasn't. I was meant for heated apartments and new car smells and high-caloric appetizers and friends with beers in their hands, inviting me over to watch college football. I wanted to be anywhere in the world except here.

Then, from up the trail, I heard voices in the distance. I must have imagined it. I turned my head, then stopped moving so as to not rustle my down jacket. I heard them again. We had been sitting there for maybe forty minutes. As terrible as our situation had been, it suddenly turned worse. The only men I knew to walk at night in Humla were drunk Maoists, perhaps armed. We scrambled off the path, into the field and crouched down to keep from sight.

I counted nine of them by their flashlights. They were speaking loudly and carelessly. I glanced back at my men, crouching behind me. They were straining so hard to understand the voices that they were practically holding their breath. The din got louder.

Suddenly I didn't care who it was. Our situation couldn't get worse. Nobody was going to shoot us. If they threatened us, so be it. I had nothing for them to steal. They were going somewhere, to shelter nearby, and they would eat. That was all that mattered right now. I wasn't staying in that field any longer. The convoy came closer and I heard the man in front laughing. I dropped my bag and rushed at them, crashing onto the path, landing five feet in front of the leader.

"What the *shite*!" he screamed, arms suddenly pin-wheeling backward as if trying to reverse time.

He was Scottish. I would have been less surprised had he been a porpoise. I had not seen a foreigner in weeks, let alone walking at night, let alone right there, right then. I stretched out my arms instinctively to catch him, but he crashed into the man behind him, who caught him. My porters burst out behind me. The other men yelled and tensed, ready to counter our ambush.

"Wait! Wait, no—wait, wait . . ." It seemed the only word I could come up with—I just wanted to say it enough times so they recognized that under this dirty beard and black fleece hat, I was American.

The Scotsman was back on his feet, still tensed. "Where th' hell did *ye* come from?" he shouted.

"I was here, in there—back there," I pointed to the field, my voice cracking. "We're a nonprofit, we're working with children." I fought to get out helpful words as quickly as possible so they would understand, so they would relax.

"A *wot*?"

"Nonprofit! I'm American!"

The man straightened up slowly, dusting himself off. He stared hard at me for a few long seconds, taking me in. Then he took one large step forward and held out his hand jovially.

"Right, then. I'm David."

They were part of a humanitarian mission, working for a Dutch anti-hunger organization. They had been delayed that day, and thought they could stay all together in Upper Unapani. Their contact there told them about this hut. It was a shelter for travelers, and he had convinced them to make the hike down to it in the dark, as it could sleep a dozen people. The owner of the hut was with them; he removed the padlock and swung open the door.

"Listen, would ye care te join us, then? We've got enough rice and daal to feed the lot of us and more. The lads back there from Unapani, they're makin' a fire and all. Ye and yer guys can stay here if ye like," David said. "Unless ye prefer to stay outside . . . though it's brutal cold, ain't it? Yer not one of them extreme types, are ye?"

"No—no, I'm not—we'd love to stay here, that would be great. You sure?" I asked in my American instinctive politeness that did not match the situation.

"Course! We'd be happy for the company!" he bellowed, waving us inside. He took my arm as I passed him. "It's a bloody riot though, ain't it? Meetin' here like this?"

A riot. That's what he called it. The whole thing was impossible. The hut was open, food was being cooked, a fire was made, and we hadn't moved a muscle. It was a miracle, wrapped in a Christmas bow and laid in my lap.

◇

I SAT OUTSIDE WITH David, my new best friend, feeling full and rested and warm by the fire. I leaned back against a log. My two porters had befriended the porters from the other group, and together they sat on the other side of the bonfire, staring into it and speaking energetically. One of them was lighting some kind of pipe that he held cupped in both his hands. The other men from David's group, foreigners like us, gathered on the porch of the hut, hands buried deep in the pockets of their down jackets, laughing over some story that I couldn't hear, their pale, foggy breath bursting from their lips like small steam engines.

I was telling David about my weeks in Humla, about the parents I had found and how stunned they were. That they seemed to have given up all hope. I told him I wanted to do something about it, though it would be difficult to reunite the children quickly, with such poverty in the region.

Poverty was something David's group knew about, having studied the region for some time before arriving for this fact-finding mission. They had only arrived three days earlier, and were also trying to leave in the next few days. But they had a radio with them in case things went bad, if they couldn't get back to Simikot or they needed a helicopter. David told me just in his few days there, he loved Humla—the people and the landscape. He loved the honey, which was a specialty of the region, he told me. And the apples. Everybody had told him about the apples. The apples were a highlight, he said.

"You tried the apples?" I asked him. "I know a boy—he's from a village a few days from here called Jaira—he never stopped talking about the apples."

"He's right, they're fantastic. I actually have a bag full of them—here, hang on," he said, and he walked over to his bag, grabbed one, and tossed it to me. I caught it, rubbed it on my dirty sleeve, and took a large bite. It was delicious.

"Was I right?" David asked, watching my expression. "I got a ton of 'em—ye want to bring one home for yer friend?"

I considered that. It was an incredible coincidence, having the opportunity to bring the boy an apple; it was the first apple I'd come across in Humla. But it occurred to me that it wasn't the apples Jagrit was always talking about. It was the memory of the apple, a five-year-old's memory of savoring that sweet taste, the only real memory he had left of this place. I wanted to help him keep that memory. No apple could ever live up to that. Besides, the letter from his father in my bag would be a far greater gift than an apple could ever be.

That night, we slept on the hard floor, softened a bit by scattered straw. I set the alarm on my watch for 3:30 A.M. We could only sleep three hours before having to set off again. We were not out of the woods yet. Simikot was still a good fifteen hours' hike from our hut. Fifteen hours in Humla meant two or two and a half days of hiking, due to the difficulty of the terrain. We didn't have that long if I want wanted to get back in time to meet Liz. We would need to cover that two and a half days' hike in a single day. We had to reach Simikot that evening.

I woke five minutes before my alarm went off. Climbing out of my sleeping bag, I woke my men, piled on several layers of clothing, and we quietly left the little hut. David had insisted I not pay them for the food. I scrawled a note of thanks and left it in his boots. Then we continued through the dark, still a long way from safety.

While the likelihood of snow had increased with each passing day, we had another deadline as well: we had to make it to the final river crossing, a day's walk from here, by 5:00 P.M. Because there was no bridge, we had to make sure we got there when men were still working who could ferry us across in that steel crate attached to a cable. I remembered from our first days in Humla Rinjin telling me that they worked from seven in the morning until five in the afternoon. If we got there and nobody was there to pull us across, we would be trapped for yet another day, and be forced to retrace our steps back to the lean-to at Bokche Ganda to sleep that night. Every day we delayed was a day the long overdue snow could finally arrive, sealing us into Humla.

The porters fell farther behind in the dark. I fought to control the panic rising in my throat during the long moments when I could no longer hear them, when I feared they had abandoned me, taken my backpack, which alone was worth more than these men could earn in a year. If that happened, I would be lost. In the end, my paranoia won; I waited for them. Looking for a place to rest, I could make out a kind of overhang in a cliff wall to my left, off the path. I started toward it.

As I approached it, I slipped on some loose stones, sending them tumbling off the path. Instantly, two pairs of narrow yellow eyes appeared beneath the overhang. Then low growls. Adrenaline pounded through me—I swung up a walking pole like a baseball bat, dizzy with fear, and stumbled backward, away from the growls, knocking more rocks down the path. The clamor broke the silence and a man shouted. Under the overhang, a hundred pairs of eyes snapped open. I heard my porters, behind me, shout to the man, and he shouted back, all drowned out by vicious barking.

It was a shepherd and his dogs, protecting his flock. The dogs were soon calmed by the man, and the rumbling of a hundred nervous sheep soon quieted. Their eyes, pair by pair, blinked out, and silence fell again like a thick blanket.

We arrived at the cliffs. There were several sets of cliffs, but these were different. The terrain was unmistakable, even in the dark. We had crossed a wide stream earlier where the path ended, and we clamored over stepping stones, large boulders strewn haphazardly. I could feel the terrain change then, too, emerging out of the forest and hearing the stream, feeling a cooler breeze from my left. It was the same kind of change now. The river had reemerged, but far down below us. To my right the world dropped away, and I felt myself instinctively leaning left, into the uneven granite wall.

I remembered this part of the path from my journey south. I had been nervous to walk it then, even during the day with Rinjin standing behind me, my own personal tether to the path. There were times when the trail simply fell away, destroyed by rains. You clung to the wall and leaped across small chasms. Rinjin would take one end of one of my poles as I jumped, lest I lose my footing on the gravel and end up a hundred feet down.

I was scared. I could handle heights, but I didn't like them. Rock climbing on sheer walls, even tied onto the rock, puts me into a glaze of sweat, but I can do it. But the height plus a slippery surface? Well, that is the stuff of nightmares for me. I wanted to wait until it was light to attempt this pass. It was one thing to be up against Maoists and dogs and the chill of the night; it was quite another to slip wordlessly off a wall and into the freezing white water far below, thousands of miles from home and family, and disappear without a trace.

But I couldn't stop, or I wouldn't be walking at night in the first place. It would be stupid to give up now, after everything I'd been through. With my left hand, I made sure to stay as close to the wall as possible. With my right,

I used my pole like a blind man, testing each step before I took it. And when I reached those small chasms, I controlled my breathing and imagined I was on a sidewalk in New York City, stepping casually over an indentation in the concrete. An hour later, we were past it. My jaw was sore from clenching my teeth the entire time.

The sky brightened, too slowly to notice at first, the dark blue giving way to a cold, dim gray. We still had many hours to walk, we were still exhausted, but the daylight rinsed the fear away, especially along the later cliff walls. Then, just after 4:00 P.M., I saw it: the bridge. The cable, the steel box. And the men sitting beside it, waiting to ferry people across. For the first time in days, I began to relax. It was still a steep ascent up to Simikot, ten thousand feet above sea level, but I knew at last, with certainty, that I would make it. Even if I had to crawl.

We strolled, unnoticed, through the village. I was covered in enough filth and scruff to be almost camouflaged. We headed straight to the guesthouse. Rinjin was not there, but his sister was. She said Rinjin had returned for a day, but had to leave again. I was disappointed—I had very much wanted to see my friend, to tell him everything that had happened since we parted ways. But I accepted the mug of tea from her, paid my porters, and sat in an old plastic garden chair, looking back down the valley, until she called me inside for daal bhat.

As exhausted as I was that night in Simikot, I couldn't sleep. I would catch a plane in the early morning, but only if it didn't snow that night. The clouds had arrived the day before, bearing more snow. Rinjin's sister stated this as a fact, in the same breath telling me I was very welcome to stay with them through the winter. I wanted her to take those words back, to suck them out of the air and incinerate them. The snow was here? *Now?* After all this? I looked at the sky. I hadn't noticed the dark clouds—I hadn't looked up in two days. But there they were, resting on the high mountains that separate Nepal from Tibet, black thoroughbreds quivering in the starting gate.

That night I sat in my sleeping bag with my head near the door, staring up and out at the sky. Where there should have been stars, there were none. I prayed, my head bowed and fingers tightly interlocked, that it would not snow, just for one more day.

The early light woke me. I scrambled up, hopping in my sleeping bag, and flung open the door. Clear, crystal, perfect blue sky. I couldn't recall seeing anything more beautiful in my whole life. I was going home. It was December 22. I had found the families of all twenty-four children.

◇

I SAT IN A small airport in Nepalganj, a town in the lowlands of southern Nepal, waiting for my flight to Kathmandu. I had three hours. I sat on the floor, legs outstretched, leaning against my backpack, keeping one hand on the cold marble floor to remind myself that I was on my way back to civilization. I still had only the one book, and I would be damned if I was going to open that up again. So I stared. I watched the people hurrying in to catch flights, I watched the bicycle rickshaw guys outside talking and laughing together until a passenger came out, when they turned into enemy combatants fighting for the fare, then went back to being friends. I watched luggage roll across the smooth surface, never having to be lifted by the man in the suit clutching the handle.

Across from me, on a bench thirty feet away, sat two boys with their father. The older one reminded me of Navin, the eldest of the seven children, the boy who I had sat with in the malnutrition ward of the Kathmandu hospital. It got me thinking about those kids and what I would tell them when I saw them. I looked forward to that, sharing photos and letters with the children from their parents. I couldn't even imagine what that would be like.

The boy's father caught me looking at his son and smiled. And kept smiling. The guy was absolutely beaming at me. I smiled back, and kept looking at the boys.

The father got up and walked toward me. There was something familiar about him.

Then suddenly, like a brick between the eyes, it hit me—the boy, the one who looked like Navin, *was* Navin. *The* Navin. The boy I had lost and then found. And his brother, next to him, who looked like Madan, was the real Madan. I leaped to my feet. The man walking toward me was their father; I had met him in my first days in Humla. We had sat on a pile of hay and I had shown him a photo of his sons. I had told him they were in our children's home, in Dhaulagiri House in Kathmandu, behind Swayambhu. And he had told me that he was going to go to Kathmandu. And he was going to find them and bring them home. I didn't think much of it—I had heard the same thing from several parents.

Well, he had gone, and he had found them, and now he was bringing them home. I got a rush of excitement thinking about him coming to the door and introducing himself to Farid, showing him the address on the piece of paper. And Farid greeting him and calling the boys downstairs. The boys running downstairs and seeing their father, after everything they had gone through, after being taken and abandoned and taken again and rescued and brought to the hospital and into their new home and, finally, wondering where they go from there. I couldn't stop smiling, imagining Farid's reaction to all of that.

I walked quickly to greet him, and together we went back to the boys. They hadn't recognized me immediately either, they hadn't expected to see me here, and I must have looked like a vagrant after weeks without a shower. They jumped up and wrapped their arms around my waist. I loved that feeling. I hadn't realized how much I missed the kids back at Dhaulagiri House and at Little Princes. Once you gained their trust they had no inhibition around you. The children used me as furniture, as a jungle gym, as a horse. And also as a surrogate parent, until the real one showed up. That hug by those two boys, with their smiling father standing a few feet away, lifted every last scrap of weariness I felt.

I brought the children and their father into the canteen to buy them a meal, and we sat together for the next two hours, saying little except with our hands, but smiling all the way through. I took a final photo of us together in the airport, then left them. We were all going home, just in opposite directions.

◈

EVERYTHING MOVED SO FAST in Kathmandu. It was strange to see cars, bicycles, and electric lights. For the first time since I moved to Nepal, I was the filthiest person walking down the street. I hailed a taxi and went straight from the airport to meet Kelly and Beth, who had arrived on December 18 and waited for me on faith that I would return to hang out with them. I found them at the guesthouse where they were staying until they could move into my apartment with me. They were sitting outside at a table, in the sun, drinking beers, and I managed to surprise the hell out of them. Before we went back to my apartment, we had a beer chilled in a refrigerator and served to us in a glass. It was perhaps the single best beer I'd ever had. Then I excused myself to find a pay phone to call Farid.

Farid was ecstatic to hear from me. He had big news: Dhaulagiri House had gone from six children to twenty-six. Just twenty-four hours earlier, Farid and the Umbrella Foundation had rescued twenty-nine children held for years by a child trafficker. Farid told the children about me; he said they were excited to meet me. Dhaulagiri House was a reality. We had actually started something.

I was about to say good-bye and return to my beer when Farid remembered one other thing. "Ah yes, one more good news, Conor—I cannot believe I forgot to say it already!"

"What's that?"

"I am walking to a taxi right now, to meet your friend, the American girl. She called me just before you— she has arrived a day early, and now she is on her way to Thamel from the airport. I arranged to meet her at Swayambhu, near your house, in an hour. I should bring her to your apartment, no?"

My heart vaulted out of my throat and splashed onto the floor. I said a quick yes and a quicker good-bye and rushed back to the table to my friends.

"Guys—we gotta go," I said, not even sitting down. I grabbed my beer and chugged it. The wonderful thing about friends you've known for fifteen years is that these things rarely require an explanation. Kelly and Beth chugged their beers and ran after me into the streets of Thamel and straight into the open back door of a taxi.

I only had a little time before Liz arrived. I spent three quarters of it taking the longest shower of my life—I was caked in dirt and grime—and I shaved. I looked in a mirror for the first time in almost a month. I had dropped about ten pounds. I had no nice clothes in Nepal, so I found the only fleece that wasn't filthy from my trip and put that on, smoothing it out in the mirror.

Just before 7:00 P.M., Liz Flanagan arrived at my door. She was beautiful, just as I had imagined. She smelled so lovely, her hair and her skin so fresh, so unlike the dust and grime of my last few weeks. She was here, in Kathmandu, at my door. All I could think in that moment was how very close I had come to not getting here, to missing this moment. This was the woman to whom I had told so much, who had lived through so much with me from nine thousand miles away. Even though we were meeting for the first time, we knew each other intimately. Liz waited a beat for me to say something, then smiled and took a step toward me and held out her hand. Without thinking I took her and hugged her tightly before she could even introduce herself.

Part V

LIZ

December 2006–September 2007

Six

T HE POLITE THING WOULD have been to ask my guests what they would like for dinner. I could not, however, take the chance that Kelly, Beth, and Liz would opt for traditional Nepalese food. I needed red meat. I needed beer. I needed French fries stretching to the horizon. We could have traditional food at the next meal. My friends took one look at me and agreed. On the way to the steakhouse in the center of Thamel, I chatted to my buddy Kelly while his wife, Beth, hung back and got to know Liz. I was thrilled that we were all there together; it took the expectations off what would have otherwise been a pressure-cooker of a first date: man walks twenty-seven hours in two days to get out of the mountains to meet girl who has just flown nine thousand miles for a visit.

Liz had booked a guesthouse room in Thamel, the backpacker district. She was only going to be in town for two days, and I wanted to spend as much time with her as possible. I wanted to invite her to stay with us, in my apartment, but I was afraid of coming off as lecherous. When I finally summoned the courage, I asked her in what was intended to be a breezy manner, but which sounded more like a strained songbird. I added, in a mile-long run-on sentence, that there were three bedrooms, one for her, her very own bedroom with a door and everything, and it would be easier to meet up than if she was in Thamel. She hesitated for a moment, just enough time for Kelly and Beth, heroes that they are, to leap in and insist that she stay with us.

Everyone waited patiently for me to coax the last shreds of food onto my fork, then we shared a taxi back to my apartment. They all had questions about my trip, and I had questions for Liz. I wanted her to keep talking, to hear her voice. But after only an hour, exhaustion caught up with me, and I actually started to nod off in midsentence.

I said good night to everyone and walked to my bedroom. I had been looking forward to sleeping between sheets for the first time in a month, but I didn't even make it that far. Devoid of energy, I fell on top of my bed, fully clothed, and slipped into a dead sleep.

I had underestimated the trauma of the trek to get out of Humla. Only fourteen hours had passed since I'd woken up to that clear blue sky. Since returning safely to Kathmandu, I had felt only joy—that I had made it out, that I had met my friends, that I had finally met Liz, that I was eating real food and taking real showers. Now, alone and shutting down, my mind began to turn, processing the last four weeks and especially the last few days. Nightmares ambushed me from dark corners. I was consumed by them, waking every few minutes in a sweat. Those moments of being awake brought with them floods of relief as I found myself in my bedroom, safe.

I don't know how much of the night passed like that. I do remember, though, being woken up by my own shouting. Fear dissipated again into relief, which quickly turned into paralyzing embarrassment when I saw that the light in the living room outside my door was still on. Liz was awake, probably reading. I wished with all my heart that I could have caught my panicked shout in a butterfly net, gently eased it back and let it out my bedroom window.

The door opened carefully, and Liz slipped in. I closed my eyes, mortified. She came toward me, completely unselfconsciously, and put a hand on my hand.

"You okay?" she whispered.

Her voice was absent of any judgment, free of the tinge of embarrassment you hear in somebody's voice when they are clearly embarrassed for you. She was concerned for me, and that was all. I was relieved. I took her hand in mind, intertwining our fingers. Neither of us moved.

"Yeah, I'm okay, thanks," I whispered back. She slowly slipped her hand out of mine, walked back out, and gently closed the door behind her. That night I had one more dream, far different from those nightmares. I dreamed that Liz and I were in Humla on a warm, breezy day. I poured a handful of hard, dry rice into her hand, and she poured it back into mine, and together we carried that rice slowly up the mountain.

◇

I WOKE UP THE next day, a Saturday, to find everybody already up and dressed. For the first time, I had slept through the bells of the Buddhist monastery next door. Farid was sitting at my computer in the corner of the living room, where my desk served as our office. He was talking to Liz, Kelly, and Beth.

He saw me come out, dazed, and he rubbed his hands together with excitement.

"Conor, you have a very big day today," he said, getting up. "I have told the children that you are coming to meet them, they are very impatient for it. Some are still very shy. And Dirgha and Amita have been asking me for many days when you were coming home. I told them we would be there one hour ago, but you did not wake up. So, they will be patient. It's okay, it's good for them to learn to wait for things, don't you think?"

Kelly made breakfast for everybody. After many months of hanging out with children, not to mention porters and guides and parents who didn't even speak much Nepali (Humli is a separate dialect) let alone my own language, it felt wonderfully odd to have a conversation in choppy, poorly enunciated English, accelerated by slang and splattered with inside jokes. I was still getting used to hearing Liz instead of reading her words, of hearing her responses to my questions seconds after they had left my mouth instead of hours later on a screen. Soon it was as if she had known us for years.

The five of us followed the small winding dirt path, enclosed on both sides by six-foot-high brick walls. Monkeys ran along the walls, leaping over our heads from one wall to the other. A few minutes later we emerged at the field in front of Dhaulagiri House. We left our shoes at the front door—a fundamental rule in any Nepalese house—and wandered inside.

Immediately I noticed there was something strange: the house was completely quiet.

"You sure there are thirty children in this house?" I asked Farid. The Little Princes home was usually quaking with shouts and general excitement.

Farid laughed. "Twenty-six. You'll see," he said.

The front hallway was empty. So were the dining area and the kitchen. In the living room, however, were about twenty children, ranging in age from maybe five to about eight, gathered together on the floor, leaning over beat-up notebooks and flimsy textbooks that resembled discarded coloring books. They were studying.

I put my hands together and said in a loud whisper: "Namaste, *babu*!"

Startled, they leaped up, the older ones helping the less coordinated little ones. They clasped the palms of their hands together and cried "Namaste, *dai*!" in an uncoordinated cascade. They saw Liz and cried "Namaste, *didi*!" and repeated the greetings two more times for Kelly and Beth.

Farid beamed. "It's very good, no? These are the younger children—the older ones are upstairs, also studying."

"It's amazing."

"It is our children's home, Conor," he said, both hands on my shoulders.

"It's amazing," I repeated. Dhaulagiri was filled with children, children who had spent years with a child trafficker until only two days earlier. Liz sat down next to one of the little girls, and I plopped down next to a young boy. He was writing the letter *b* in lowercase cursive over and over. He stopped and held his paper up for me to see.

"Very good, Brother," I said. Liz was complimenting the girl on her work; she had just written the word *house* for what looked like the hundredth time. The girl's face lit up, and she wrapped her free arm around Liz's leg, binding herself to Liz before continuing her homework.

◇

THE RESCUE OF THE children now living in Dhaulagiri, Farid told me, had not gone as planned. The plan had been for Gyan, together with Jacky and Farid and a policeman, to pick up the children from a notorious child trafficker. The trafficker had kept them for the last four years, showing them to foreigners and receiving donations on their behalf, which he then pocketed.

But the business had reached an end. Gyan had finally received legal authorization to take the children. The man promised the authorities that he would make sure the children were safely packed and ready to go when the police arrived. His concern, he assured Gyan, was the well-being of the children. He did not want them to be traumatized by the transition, he said. He had raised them as he would his own.

But when Gyan, Jacky, and Farid arrived, the children were not outside. They were not even aware they were going anywhere. The child trafficker made it seem as if our people had infiltrated his house and were trying to steal the children. He blockaded the children inside; outside he screamed to the neighbors that Gyan, Jacky, and Farid were abducting Nepali children to sell to foreigners. Neighbors came to his defense. Suddenly TV cameras were surrounding the scene. It was the beginning of a standoff that would last deep into the night. The trafficker periodically screamed at the cameras that the children were being sold, that Gyan, Jacky, and Farid were likely to kill them once they had taken them to America and Britain. He swore they would have to kill him first to get to them.

The police and Gyan decided the man would never give up the children willingly—he was going to make this as difficult as possible on the police and the children. The police pulled the trafficker aside and went in to rescue the children, who had heard the whole thing going on downstairs, and were terrified that men were coming to kill them. Gyan, Jacky, and Farid had no easy task getting them into the waiting cars to bring them back to Umbrella and Dhaulagiri House.

At Umbrella, the children were released into the arms of dozens of waiting children, led by Jagrit and some of the older boys. They took the hands of the still-frightened little ones and brought them inside. Farid and Jacky stayed away while the Umbrella children spoke to the children, told them that they'd had the same fears, the same experience. But that they were safe now, safer than they could even imagine, that they would be given their own bed and food and that the next day they would go to school. When they were given food and hot tea by the Nepali house mothers, they began to calm down.

Just two days later, Liz and I met these children for the first time. Several were still not talking. Some had shaved heads, the consequence of an overwhelming lice infestation. But many had adjusted quickly.

There were sixteen boys and ten girls in all.

"Bishnu's bed is still empty," Farid added, his voice thick with regret. "The last of the original seven children."

"And no word?"

"Word?"

"No news? About Bishnu?"

"No, no news. I ask Gyan every day. Every day, there is no news," he said. He shook his head. "It has been almost ten months—you know that, Conor? Ten months."

"I know."

We stood quietly outside Dhaulagiri, staring at the home, squinting at the yellow paint reflecting the bright sunshine, listening to the rustle of books and papers coming through the open window.

"Wait . . . it's Saturday—why are the children inside studying?" I asked.

"I told them to go outside!" Farid said happily. "I tell them, go play! But they are so happy about going to school, Conor! They want to do reading time now, on this beautiful day! It's crazy, no?"

"It's amazing," I said.

"I think you need a new word, Conor. That word is not so interesting.

You want me to find a new English word for you? I am a very good teacher, I give you good price for it. Friend price."

It was nice to be home.

An hour later, the children ran outside. There were now four girls attached to Liz. The other girls were tagging along behind, asking over and over to touch her long blond hair. Finally Liz sat down in the field and the girls went to work braiding her hair and gently playing with her earrings. The kids spoke little English, but as I had learned long ago, language isn't always necessary when interacting with kids. Liz sat on the hard dirt patch, children hanging off her, strands of her hair being accidentally pulled out from time to time in the braiding process. She looked up and saw me looking at her, and gave a broad smile, and mouthed the word "Yaaayy!" and laughed. We had spoken often of our shortcomings over e-mail with surprising openness. I knew I had much to learn about her. But at that moment, watching her with the children, she was perfect to me.

I noticed that Liz was paying particular attention to one little girl, the smallest one and the only one not trying to climb all over her. The little girl simply watched the others without emotion. Liz took her hand. The girl did not move, but let her hand be taken as she continued to stare at nothing in particular.

"Who is that girl?" I asked Farid, who had just come outside. He looked over to see who I was talking about.

"Ah yes—Leena. She is the youngest. It is very strange, Conor. She is like this all the time. I have not heard her say even one word yet," he said.

I watched Leena until I was pulled away by the little boys, almost none of whom I had met, to play a game like dodge ball, using a ball formed from rubber bands tied together. I agreed, and, almost simultaneously, was nailed in the back with the ball. Apparently I wasn't very good at this game.

We were now well into the afternoon. It was nice to be back with the kids. But there was still one child I had not spoken to, a child I really needed to see. It couldn't wait any longer. I asked Kelly, Beth, and Liz to watch the kids for a while, and I went back to my apartment. Inside, I grabbed my laptop, where I had stored hundreds of photos from my trip to Humla, and walked back to the cluster of Umbrella homes to find Jagrit.

◇

JAGRIT WAS SITTING ON a whitewashed wall, watching the other kids playing in the field next door at Dhaulagiri.

"Sir, I saw you are back from Humla—I saw you this morning. You were walking with that girl who is very very beautiful. This is your girlfriend, sir? You are very lucky!" he shouted in his normal conversational voice.

"No Jagrit—she's just a friend."

"How many apples did you bring me, sir? I do not see a bag—did you leave them at home? I'll come over and carry them myself—come, we go." He leaped down and playfully started dragging me toward my apartment.

"I brought you zero apples, Jagrit. I was going to bring you one, but I ate it myself."

He paused. "You ate one apple? You are lying?"

"No, I'm not lying—I had one a few days ago."

"Was it very very tasty, sir?"

"It was delicious."

His hands shot up in triumph. "I told you, yes? I told you!" He called over to his friends on the wall to translate the apple story. "You tell them, sir! You say them about the apple!"

"Jagrit, listen—I brought you back something better than an apple," I told him.

He turned back toward me. "What did you bring me?" He was genuinely curious.

"Come inside. I'll show you."

There was no easy way to tell a boy who had grown up believing his entire family was dead that I had, just ten days earlier, met his father. There was no easy way to tell him that I had a photo of his father holding his own death certificate, that I had a letter from him for Jagrit. There was no easy way to tell him he had a mother and a brother and sister, that they were all still alive and had never forgotten about him. That they had spent the last nine years wondering where he was, if he was even still alive. So I just opened up a long series of photos. I showed him photos of the postman who first told me of their existence, photos of the long trek to Jaira. And then I showed him a photo of his father, the shepherd. The man in the picture was holding a photo of Jagrit that I had given him. From beginning to end, I told him the entire story of how his family had come back to life.

Jagrit had never cried in front of me before. At fourteen years old, I imagine he considered himself too old for it. But now he could not stop. He stared at his father's face. Jagrit, choking with emotion, asked if his father had told me why he had given him up, why his mother had not fought to keep him. That began a long discussion of the children lost in Kathmandu, of how traffickers tricked parents into giving up their children. I told him the story as I knew it, and added everything that I had learned in Humla.

I pulled out my notebook, where I had taken detailed notes of my interaction not just with his father but with all the parents. The notebook was filled with the stories of shock, guilt, pain, and desperation. It was filled with mothers recounting the fear of living under rebel authority, of young teenagers with automatic weapons, of the moment they had learned their neighbor's child had been abducted and forced into the rebel army. The decision taken nine years ago to send Jagrit away was made under circumstances that he would never fully comprehend. I hesitated a moment, then handed the notebook to Jagrit.

"Everything is in there. Anything you want to know."

He took the notebook and opened it slowly, flipping through the pages but not reading them. Even for a boy as bright as Jagrit, it would take concentration to read in English. He didn't seem to have the strength. He held it up.

"My father in here, sir?" he asked. "You can show me the page?"

I took it back from him and turned the worn, smudged pages until I found the heading that read Jaira, Jagrit's village. I read him a paragraph that I jotted down quickly during the interview, while Rinjin was asking the father the first questions about his son.

Jagrit's father is a shepherd. I ask him about his son he doesn't seem
to know who I'm talking about. Seems confused. But there's something
in his reaction. Not sure what it is, almost like he's waking up and not
sure how to react. Rinjin mentions Jagrit's name to him again. He seems
to be nervous, expecting really bad news—think he's scared. Rinjin sees
it—he takes the photo of Jagrit and gives it to him and tells him his son
is safe. We are waiting on the questions, they can come later—right now
this is a father who is watching his son come back to life.

I stopped reading. "It goes on," I said. "We asked him how you were
taken, who did it. He said it was a man from the village, an important man
who said he could educate you." I paused, watching the boy. "You remember
him? That man, from when you were young?"

"I remember." Jagrit's voice was stiff. I didn't push him. Again, we sat in
silence for a few moments.

"I showed your father your photo, you know. He liked it. He thought you
were a handsome boy," I said.

"He say I am handsome boy?"

"He didn't say it. He didn't have to. I could see it," I said. "Of course, I
didn't want to tell him how wrong he was. . . ."

This got a small smile from Jagrit. "You really show him my photo, sir?"

"I really did, yeah."

"And you have photos, too? From him?"

"Not just of him—your village, too. From Jaira, and all over Humla," I
said. "You want to see them?"

For an hour, Jagrit and I talked and went through the photos, starting
with his father, then going through the whole trip so he could see more of his
village and Humla. He never let go of the letter from his father.

"You can make me a copy of the photo from my father, sir? For me to
keep?" His voice was tight. He was choked up.

"Of course. I'll bring it over tomorrow."

"Thank you." He looked down at the letter, not reading it, but just staring at it, as if it was some artifact that he didn't quite believe he owned. Then he said, "Maybe I sit alone for a while, sir."

For as long as I had known him, Jagrit had never wanted to be alone. But I would have wanted the exact same thing in that situation. I stood up.

"You're not the only one, Brother," I told him before I left. "There are many children like you in Nepal. The only difference between you and them is that they still think they are alone in the world."

I touched his head and walked out, gently closing the door behind me, leaving behind the sobs that grew fainter as I walked downstairs and out of the house.

◇

IN OUR LETTERS OVER the previous three months, Liz and I had come to know so much about each other, but in person, we initially found it hard to share our thoughts in the same way we had been able to over e-mail. But it took only that one morning with the children for us to open up. Now I could see her facial expressions, see the sympathy in her eyes and hear what made her laugh. Spending time with Liz felt like being at home—a childhood home that was so familiar you could walk blindfolded from room to room without even touching a wall. I had dreamed about sharing this experience with somebody. Not just in words and photos, but having them smell and feel and hear and taste it all. Liz was the perfect companion; she soaked it all in and she never flinched. She only wanted to experience more of Nepal, more of what I had been talking about in long letters to her over the past three months.

Just before sunset on Christmas Eve, Liz and I walked to the top of Swayambhu, or Swayambhunath, as it is more formally known. The sprawl of Kathmandu stretched like water to the hills, while monkeys ran around us in the foreground. The Kathmandu Valley had been, in fact, a lake until a mere ten thousand years ago. This hill on which the temple was built was once an island in that lake. The legend went that on the base of the hill where the temple was ultimately built, the Bodhisattva Manjushri, an enlightened being who predated the historic Buddha, had a vision of a lotus flower in the lake, at the site of Swayambhunath. Recognizing this place as worthy of pilgrimage, he cut a gash in the hills to drain the lake, making the Kathmandu Valley into habitable land and allowing access to the holy place on the hill.

Archaeologists, while perhaps reserving judgment on just how the site was created, agree that it has existed in some form for more than fifteen hundred years. On the top of the hill, in addition to the sixty-five-foot-diameter, hundred-foot-tall white stupa, are myriad statues, small temples, a monastery, monks, and monkeys, all wrapped up in a tangle of colorful Tibetan Buddhist prayer flags, which, with each gust of wind, spread prayers and compassion. The site is holy to both Buddhists and Hindus, and the architecture and statues reflect the shared importance.

In short, we stood at a focal point for Nepalese faith, religion, legend, and culture. It seemed a fitting way for Liz to end her trip to Nepal; she would be leaving the next morning, on Christmas Day.

"You have traditions? On Christmas morning?" I asked her, wondering if I could find some way of making her feel more at home here.

"The usual," she said. "Stockings, presents, long breakfasts . . . we go to church, if we haven't gone the night before, on Christmas Eve."

Of course—she was a Christian, so this holiday probably held a lot more significance to her than I was used to. "Shoot—sorry, I didn't even think about that, I'm a moron. Listen, I haven't heard of a church here but I'm sure there is one, I'll look it up when we get back to the apart—"

She cut me off. "It's not a hard and fast rule, Conor," she said. "The reason I was coming to India in the first place was to do acts of service on Christmas Day. It's a time of year to celebrate the life of Christ and follow His example. Spending time with the children would be perfect."

"Well, that fits in with our plan anyway. You know we'll be having daal bhat for breakfast, in that case, right?"

"It sounds perfect. Really."

I nodded. "Right. Christmas-morning daal bhat it is," I said.

Christmas goes virtually unmarked in Nepal. December 25, therefore, felt like any other day at the children's home. The children were not aware of the Christian holiday, so they did not understand the significance to Liz, Kelly, Beth, and me; the celebration of the birth of Christ, and our individual family rituals that went along with the day, including stockings and presents tattooed with happy snowmen. Instead of a church service followed by Christmas pastries, we were wrist-deep in slushy rice and boiling daal and dangerously curried vegetables, stuffing fists of it into our mouths. The children found all of this gut-rippingly hilarious, of course. It was, oddly enough, a perfect Christmas morning.

I said good-bye to Liz that afternoon. She waited in the security line at the airport, well in time for her flight back to Delhi and the group of friends with whom she was traveling.

"So . . . how much longer do you have in India?" I asked her.

"Two more weeks," she said, picking up her bag and moving slowly with the queue.

I nodded thoughtfully. She was four people away from going through the metal detector. My heart suddenly picked up its pace. I cleared my throat.

"You know, the kids would love to see you again," I said. "In case you're bored in India or anything. The girls loved you—it was so great to have you helping care for them and making them feel loved and welcomed. I know they would love to see you again." This was coming out less casually than I had intended.

"Well, I'd love to see them again too, Conor—they're wonderful."

"Yeah, they are, and they'd love to see you, I know it. . . ." I wasn't sure what else to say. "Listen, would you mind giving me a call when you get back to India? Maybe tomorrow, after Christmas? Just so I know you got there okay?"

"Of course," she said. "I gotta catch this plane—but Merry Christmas! It was so nice to finally meet you!" She opened her arms to give me a hug, and I hugged her, accidentally knocking over her suitcase in the process and knowing I should pick it up like a gentleman but not wanting to let go of that hug. I kind of kicked at it with my feet, but it didn't spring back up as I hoped.

Finally I broke the hug to bend down to get it. That was the end of our time together. It had passed neither particularly quickly nor slowly, just inevitably. And that made it painful. Two days together was an absurdly short amount of time. I knew it before she came, but I felt it now, in my chest. I hated to see her go.

She walked through the metal detector and waved back at me before disappearing down the corridor. I went outside, into the white water of hawkers and drivers and hotel representatives, and caught a taxi back to Dhaulagiri, where Kelly and Beth were. They would be in Nepal for another week, which I loved. But my mind was still with Liz. I had to see her again. I didn't know how or when. But I had to. I wondered what would happen if I just caught a flight to India in the next few days. What would she say? Would she want to see me?

I felt lost, rudderless. My last month had been focused on getting to see Liz. I had done everything to get back from Humla in time to meet her, wondering what it would be like when we finally met. Well, now I knew. It was perfect. We had spent all of sixty-five hours together. And I was crazy about her.

◇

I HAD SEEN THE kids at Little Princes excited before. I had never, though, seen a reaction like the one I got when I arrived in Godawari two days after Liz left. The children had obviously learned that I had gone to Humla, that I had found their families, and that I had photos to show them. A dozen of them were standing on the road, waiting for me to arrive. It was noon; they had been there since 9:00 A.M. There was an audible panic on the minibus when the other passengers saw the children charging our vehicle, as if we were about to get rolled down a hill by a gang of insane little people. The bus screeched to a halt and I was practically torn from the minibus, which then sped away, door still open. I could only imagine the relief of the other passengers that the children seemed only to be interested in the foreigner.

"I can't show them to you now, you crazy kids!" I shouted over the din.

The children seemed unable to comprehend how it could be that I had been off the bus for all of six seconds and they had not yet seen photos.

"I'll show them to you in the living room! In the *living* room! They're on my laptop! I can show you when you're all sitting down—" I stopped. There was nobody there. A trail of dust led to the Little Princes home.

I took my time walking down the path. Farid was right—it was good that they learned patience. I walked into the house, listening to the excited murmuring from the living room. I came in to find the children lined up in flawless rows, stock still, like little terra-cotta warriors.

"What are you doing?" I asked Santosh.

"You say you show photos when we are standing in living room, Brother!"

"I said *sitting* in the living room, you ninnies! Why would I tell you to stand?"

"We don't know, Brother!"

"For Pete's sake, sit!" I said. The children collapsed in a heap, laughing hysterically.

I set up my laptop on a little straw stool, turned it on, and clicked on the slideshow I had prepared. It was just under two hundred photos. From the moment the first shot of Humla appeared, taken of the landing strip at Simikot, the children pointed and chatted excitedly. As the montage took me into southern Humla and their villages, they were bouncing up and down, recognizing places from their early childhood, wondering if the people in the photos were people they knew, debating the names of villages.

I paused just before we arrived at the first photo of a parent. I knew that it was of Anish's mother. I made sure I kept an eye on him as I opened the photo of the woman, reddened eyes and tear-streaked cheeks, her wrinkled, field-toughened hands clutching a photo of Anish. She needed no introduction.

The boys went crazy. They jumped on Anish, shaking his shoulders and patting his head as if he'd just scored the goal to put Nepal into the World Cup finals. Anish, though, was completely still. Slowly, he leaned into the photo on the screen to get a better look, and a smile grew on his face. He noticed me looking at him, and he looked back at the photo. I saw it in his face. He was staring at something that, at last, was his very own, something that he would never have to share with anyone else in the house.

I related the story to Anish and the rest of the children of how I'd met his family, what they had said, and how his father had given me a gift of honey and walnuts, which I had savored after many meals of plain rice and lentils. The kids chirped in with additional commentary in Nepali, none of which I understood. But Anish's smile had changed from joy to something more like embarrassment. I bent down next to him.

"What is it, Anish? This is very good news for you," I said, hand on his arm.

"She crying, Brother," he said in a soft voice. He cupped his hand to my ear. "Other boys will make fun."

"She missed you," I whispered back. "And look around—does it look like anybody is making fun of you for your mother crying?"

He looked behind him at the boys, who were chattering away, unaware that we were even speaking. He shook his head. "No, Brother."

"I've got a secret for you, Anish," I whispered again.

He couldn't help but be intrigued by that. "What, Conor Brother?"

I paused, looking around dramatically to make sure nobody, except maybe nineteen other children, were within earshot. I whispered, "*Everybody's* mother cried."

He broke into a wide grin. "Okay, Brother—show more photos," he said.

We looked at the photos and I told stories for almost two hours. The children couldn't get enough. When we were finished I handed out the letters I had from their parents. They took them solemnly, as if receiving a knighthood. Then I took out an extra treat: I had printed out photos of their parents for each of them. When they saw the stack they yelped in delight and crushed around me. As I called out each name, a little arm would reach out of the crowd, accept the photo, and run off to a corner to stare at it.

I had passed out the last photo, the one to Crazy Rohan, when I saw that Raju and his seven-year-old sister, Priya, were still standing there. Priya was holding his hand, pulling him away.

"I am sorry, Conor Brother," Priya said, still tugging. "I tell him no photo for us, but he no listen."

It was as if somebody had pulled a plug, draining all the joy from my body. I thought back to the day I had sent Min Bahadur to go look for their parents, and the moment two days later when he revealed that they were, in fact, deceased. I recalled how deeply that had affected me then. Priya, the sweet little girl, had known her parents were dead. But it had opened a wound for her, and especially for Raju. I sat down so that I was looking up at them.

"It's okay, Priya—you take very, very good care of your brother, you know that? I am very proud of you," I said.

"Thank you, Brother."

"Raju—I don't have a photo for you, but I hope that next time we will have a photo, maybe of one of your uncles or aunts, okay?" I took his hand from Priya, and he wiped the tears out of his eyes with his free hand. He nodded.

Priya said something to Raju, he paused and then nodded again. "Brother, maybe can you show Raju pictures again?" she asked.

"Oh, yeah—of course, I'd love to. You want to see them, too?"

"Yes, please, Brother."

The three of us went upstairs to the rooftop, taking three small stools with us. I asked Bagwati to make milk tea for us. And I went through the photos again, all two hundred, telling them everything I could remember.

◇

THE TWO DAYS I spent at Little Princes were pure peace. It was like digging up a time capsule you had buried long ago and spending a few days living among your childhood toys and drawings and favorite hat and pretending, just for that time, that this was how it had always been and would always be, this simple life that floated safely along. We spoke about Humla constantly. The children helped me fill in some lingering questions. What were the women pounding as they slammed the oarlike stick against the rock, when there was no wheat? They were pounding dried, cooked rice into *churaa*. What were the men boiling in large pots that seemed filled with straw? It was tobacco, or something like it.

On the third morning, as I was helping the children get ready for school and preparing to head back to Kathmandu, I got a call from Farid.

"I have good news, Conor—but you will have to be patient. You will see it when you come home," he said, and refused to tell me anything else, despite my pleas. "Like the children, Conor! You are too impatient!" he said happily.

I arrived back at Dhaulagiri House. The children, as usual, were playing outside. They knew me now, and they greeted me with cries of "Namaste, *dai*!" from across the field. Farid was swinging the youngest boy in the house, Adil. He had a particular fondness for the boy because of his poor eyesight. We resolved to get him glasses; until that happened, Farid spoke louder to him so that Adil could follow Farid's French-accented Nepali to be picked up or swung around.

I waited for them to stop spinning. Farid and I were able to talk business in front of the younger Dhaulagiri children. Their English was not as advanced as the children at Little Princes, so we could say anything we wanted to in complete privacy. Farid was still gripping Adil's wrists but catching his breath before another spin when he told me the news.

"Your trip worked," he said. "You remember the father of Navin and Madan coming? You remember it was only a few days after you met him in Humla?"

"Yeah, I remember."

"More parents have come. Not parents of our children in Dhaulagiri, but the parents of children in the other Umbrella homes. Many, within just two days of one another, while you were in Godawari. They have come to see their children. Viva asked them how they found us and they showed us piece of paper with your handwriting, the address of our home. They could not take the children home yet, they are too poor, they are not prepared, but the children were so happy, you should have been here to see it. You would have liked it very much, Conor."

"That's fantastic!" I practically yelled. I was shocked that the trip had yielded results so quickly. I couldn't even imagine how excited the kids must have been.

"And you remember finding Kumar's father, yes?" he asked.

"Yeah—I brought back a letter for Kumar."

"He called this morning. He called Dhaulagiri, on the house phone with the number you gave him! Kumar was so excited that he fell down the stairs— the front stairs, there—and I was afraid he had maybe killed himself with his excitement, but he jumped up and ran ran ran for the phone. He told me it was three years ago he spoke to his father. Imagine, Conor! Three years in the life of a nine-year-old boy! I took a photo of it to show you—he had a very big smile."

I couldn't believe it. Even when I found the parents, I doubted, somehow, that connections could be made. It seemed impossible that we could actually affect any change in this country. Kumar's father must have walked three days to get to the phone in Simikot. And what an act of faith it must have taken to do that, trusting another person who gave him a phone number and a promise that his child was safe, three years after he had disappeared. Having no children myself, I had completely underestimated the lengths to which a father would go for his son. What a long three days that walk must have been for him, wondering if anybody would be on the other end of the phone. Then hearing this strange man calling his son by name, Kumar, and hearing a mad tumble down the stairs and a voice, older but uncanny, on the other end of the line. . . . I could not imagine how that felt for him.

I stood daydreaming about that moment as Farid spun Adil around outside the house, the boy's tiny body whirling parallel to the ground before Farid ran out of steam and he bent down to give the boy a comfortable landing. I didn't want to ask the next question—I was afraid of the answer. But I had to know.

"And Bishnu? Any news yet from Gyan?" I asked.

Farid straightened up slowly, leaving Adil laughing hysterically on the ground, begging for another ride.

"Nothing," he said, shaking his head. "I called Gyan this morning. I am worried, Conor. I am worried that the boy may be gone."

◇

THAT EVENING MY PHONE rang, displaying a number I didn't recognize. I was reluctant to pick it up; it had been a very long day. But I had learned that you never knew when an important call might come through. I answered it and heard, on the other end, through a sea of static, Liz's voice. It was January 2, almost a week since we had last spoken.

"Oh, hi!" I said, realizing that I had already set off in a nervous lap around the room.

"Hey, I'm in Mumbai—I miss you guys!" she said. "How's everything going?"

You guys? What did that mean, "you guys"? Did it mean the kids, or me, or me and the kids? This was fifth grade all over again, trying to guess if the pretty girl with whom I was infatuated liked me, too. Not that I was going to say anything to her, of course. My courage didn't extend that far. After a minute or two I calmed down. I had so much to tell her, and she was eager to hear it all. I had her on the phone for twenty minutes before remembering to ask her about her own trip.

"It's great—we've been having a blast . . . but I really miss being with you and the kids, and I was thinking, the rest of my friends are going to southern India tomorrow, and I don't really need to go with them—"

"Come here!" I practically shouted over the phone. "The kids would love to see you, they ask about you all the time!" It was true. The girls asked every single day, without fail, if Liz was coming back.

"Would that be okay? I wouldn't want to be a burden, but I would totally be willing to help with anything—"

"Don't be ridiculous—I would love it! We would love it, everybody."

"Okay . . . well, great! So, tomorrow, then? It's supereasy to get these flights right now—"

"Tomorrow would be great!"

She went and grabbed a piece of paper with flight information, and rattled off a couple of flight options, finally choosing the most convenient one for the following afternoon. Before she signed off, she said, "You know, I have to tell you—my friends that I'm traveling with here, they think I'm crazy to be going back to Nepal."

I knew what she meant. If I had told my buddies, with whom I had traveled halfway across the globe for a three-week vacation, that I was detouring off to meet up with a girl (orphans, I mean—meet up with orphans!), they would have given me endless hell about it. I didn't know if it was the same for Liz, but I had to assume it was not an easy decision for her.

"Well, listen, I don't think you're crazy. I'm really, really happy you're coming," I told her.

"Good. Me, too."

◈

LIZ AND I SPENT seven more days together. It felt perfect. Life was beautifully simple: get up, go hang out with the children, see some touristy stuff in Kathmandu, have a typical Nepalese lunch at some small café, pick up the children from school just around the corner, help them with their homework, spend the evening hanging out with them. On the second night we were there, Farid and I traded accommodations. From time to time, he needed a break. Neither of us took any time off, not even weekends, and Farid had the added responsibility of living at the house. He loved it, and he wouldn't have had it any other way. But about once a week, he would stay at my apartment, maybe watch a bootleg DVD on my laptop, and get a peaceful night of sleep. I would take his place at Dhaulagiri, putting the kids to bed and sleeping in his tiny room downstairs. I loved those days, mostly because I would wake up to the sound of kids running around early each morning. It reminded me of living at Little Princes.

We made the switch during Liz's visit, and she joined me in the house. She stayed on the top floor in the girls' room, which drove them almost mad with joy, while I stayed downstairs in Farid's room. I liked Farid's room. I had once offered him a room in my massive apartment, free of charge, but he preferred to live with the children. In his room, I detected something else as well.

Farid had spent almost two years in Nepal caring for children, and I had watched with fascination as he turned more and more to Buddhism. His small room had prayer flags and incense and a guitar, but was otherwise almost completely free of material possessions. He was focused on following a principle tenant of Buddhism to control one's desire for things. Staying in his room was like stepping into his life for a night.

That evening in Dhaulagiri, Liz and I were treated to a blackout. It was a common occurrence during the dry season in Nepal; electricity was mostly water-powered, and electricity cuts lasted anywhere from four to ten hours a day. Liz and I went through the pitch black house with a flashlight to find children holding tight to various beds or chairs like survivors of the *Titanic* clinging to debris, waiting to be rescued. With little to do but gather around a single candle in the living room, the children sang songs, calls and responses, with the boys singing one verse and the girls responding with the next. The candle barely lit the faces of the children; anyone in the slightest shadow almost disappeared.

But I could see Liz's face. Her blond hair picked up the glow of the candlelight, which fell on her cheeks and her eyes, and her neck disappeared into the shadows. The rest of her was almost invisible, as the children were piled up on both of us as if we were couch cushions. We lay there, crushed by the children's body mass in a way that felt so normal in Nepal; and I had the good sense to take note that, in that exact moment, with no money, no clean clothes, no electricity, no good food—just Liz and twenty-six children—I was as happy as I had ever been in my life.

Liz was able to relate to the girls in a way that I was never able to. They adored her. She was able to get them talking and interacting in ways that Farid and I were not. Besides being a rather lovely quality in a person, it was critical in helping see the children through the trauma they had so recently experienced.

No child in the house needed this attention more than little Leena. While the other children slowly cracked through their shells, Leena kept to herself. In the week that I had been watching her, she had never smiled, never spoken, never laughed, and never cried. Not once. She moved around only to follow her older sister, Kamala. Leena always did as she was asked, whether it was going to bed or doing her homework or helping with small chores around the house, but she never played with the other children.

I had never seen anything like it, but then I had never been around such severely traumatized young children. Farid and I spent many days discussing how to best care for her. Neither of us were psychologists; we had no idea what the "proper" treatment was. So we did what we always did—we came to the best decision we could agree upon and hoped for the best. In this case, all we could really do was continue to show her as much love and attention as possible, and hope that she found a way to surface out of her paralysis. Liz was wonderful with her. She spoke to her and held her, even as the little girl sat stone-faced. I loved watching Liz with Leena, watching her pour out love without expectation.

◇

OVER THE COURSE OF the week, Liz and I had long conversations and, unsurprisingly, found that we really liked each other. I'd had long-distance relationships before, living a couple hours away from a girlfriend. These relationships endured the distance because we had built up a strong enough bond that we thought it could stand up to the test of not seeing each other except on weekends, of speaking on the phone. I had spent a little over a week with Liz. We had only just admitted our feelings for each other. Now she would go back to DC and say . . . what, exactly? That her boyfriend— this guy with no money to his name whose voice she had just heard for the first time a week ago—lived next to a children's home in Nepal, nine thousand miles and eleven time zones away, with no immediate plans to return to the United States?

The day after she left, I wrote an e-mail to Charlie, my college buddy back in the States. I told him this: "I'm not saying I proposed to this girl I just met. But I am saying that I understand now why people get married: it's because they meet Liz Flanagan." Charlie's response was simply one complete line of question marks and exclamation points.

Liz and I wrote back and forth probably a dozen e-mails per day. When the fatter monkeys weren't bringing down my Internet cable, we also spoke on the phone. (Good old Skype!) Because of the radical time difference, I would call her at exactly 7:30 A.M. her time each day; that call would serve as her alarm clock. We would talk again at her lunch break, when I was going to sleep. We often talked for up to three hours a day. That was our relationship.

Two weeks after Liz left, I went to an English-language bookstore in Thamel and bought a Bible. As I took the rupees from my wallet to pay for it, I told myself it was so I would get to know Liz better, maybe even impress her with some knowledge of her religion.

But as I took it home, I knew it was more than that for me. Just as living in this extreme environment had drawn Farid to Buddhism, I was being drawn to Christianity. I decided not to tell Liz that I'd bought it; contrary to my initial instincts, it was suddenly very important that she *not* think I had done this for her. Instead, I spoke to Farid about it the next day, after staying up late reading the night before.

"I think it is a very good thing that you bought a Bible, Conor," Farid said, after we had put the Dhaulagiri children to bed and gone downstairs to make tea. "I cannot say why. But I think I know you quite well, and I can only say this makes sense to me, that you did this."

I was happy to hear Farid say that. He was unlike any person I'd ever met. Everything he said mirrored his beliefs perfectly, and he never seemed to worry how this would sound to others. He was interested in the truth. Finding that truth was the thing that had first brought him to Buddhism, as he explained to me later that evening.

"I never understood why there was so much suffering, Conor," he said. "Even in France, I never understood. Buddhists recognize it. They see life as purposeful. Everyone is trying to escape this . . . I think the word is cycle, yes? . . . this cycle of suffering and rebirth, to achieve this Nirvana, they call it. I never had any religion, I never thought about it. Then when I came to Nepal, I spent more time with the children and I saw so much suffering. The question reawakened in my mind. Why do we suffer? I began to learn about Buddhism, and I knew—for me—it was right. This answer to my question had always existed, but somebody had just lit a candle and showed me that answer." He paused. "Does that make sense? I am not sure how to explain it so well in English, maybe."

"You explained it perfectly."

"It was the same for you? With Christianity?"

"Yes, partially," I said. "Except for me, I already knew about Christianity. I went to church when I was little, the age of Raju and Rohan and the others. I knew there was something about it, that God was real, that this was the truth, but nobody else around me seemed to think it was the truth. Nobody I knew was a Christian, and I let that influence me for my entire life, until I came to Nepal. In Godawari, with the Little Princes, I found myself praying sometimes—did I tell you that?"

"You told me, yes."

"And, to me, it felt right, it felt comforting. Then I met Liz, and she's a Christian, and I thought, you know, this is a very good opportunity to redis-cover God. Because I can learn more about Liz at the same time," I said. I couldn't help smiling at that. "That must sound strange, no? That the cata-lyst—the thing that turned me back toward Christianity—was a woman?"

Farid laughed. "Conor, I know you, and I believe that God must have sent Liz to you. He knew you would pay attention if she came to visit, no? I don't think He is offended."

"Exactly! You're joking, but that is what I thought, too!" I said.

"I'm not joking, truly," Farid said, still smiling. "As I said, Conor—when you bought that Bible, I knew you were doing the right thing for you. We both saw that light, I think. We just saw different things in the light."

I liked that idea. I also liked that both of us were completely convinced that what we had seen was the Truth, and we could speak about it so openly with each other. Under this one roof, we had a Buddhist, a Christian, and two dozen little Hindus. And we couldn't be happier.

◆

ON JANUARY 30 I was sitting with Leena, watching the little boys play soccer. The days were warm enough, as long as you stayed in the sun. If you ran around in a crazed pack chasing a ball, all the warmer. There is nothing quite like watching young kids play soccer. It must be the same around the world—a scrum forms around the ball, it pops out, hammered off some-body's toe with a grunt, and the scrum swivels their collective heads around like a family of periscopes, spot the ball, and fly toward it, en masse, as if by gravitational pull.

I could not tell if Leena was finding the same enjoyment. As usual, she had not even acknowledged me when I walked into the house, nor had she responded when I picked her up and carried her outside to watch the match with me on my lap. I felt like a child with a fancy doll. She was at least watch-ing the game, though. Any stimulation had to be a good thing, I thought. I was about to lift her onto my shoulders when my cell phone rang. It was Jacky.

"Hey, Jacky—I'm just next door at Dhaulagiri, watching the kids play socc—"

"Conor, I need you. Right now," he said, cutting me off. He told me to meet him at Kimdol chock, an intersection of quiet streets next to us that circled Swayambhu.

It was unlike Jacky to be so abrupt and insistent. I left Leena with her big sister and ran the five minutes to the intersection. Jacky was impossible to miss, with his straggly, mildly dreadlocked graying hair among the shorter Nepalis and Tibetan monks. He saw me coming and got into the backseat of a waiting taxi. I jumped in on the other side, and the driver, already given directions, took off toward the center of Kathmandu.

"Where are we going?" I panted.

"Gyan just called—he has Bishnu," Jacky said. "He says we must hurry."

I could hardly believe it.

Gyan's office at the Child Welfare Board was characteristically mobbed. He sat at his desk with an assistant leaning over his shoulder, pointing out the relevant place on a document that would help Gyan make a decision that would likely change the future of the family standing in front of him. I did not envy his job. I envied it even less because he was paid almost nothing; this was a civil service he was giving his country, a duty performed by his father before him, something expected of a man of his talents. He bore a heavy responsibility.

We waited inside the office for a few moments before Gyan noticed us. He made eye contact with me and motioned to the far corner. There, through the forest of distraught mothers and crying children, was a barrel-chested man standing in front of a chair, as if refusing to sit on principle. He had a tidy haircut and wore casual western clothes, a sign of wealth. I ducked my head to get a better look. In front of him, sitting at his feet, Indian style, was a boy of six, with sharp Tibetan features and smooth bronzed skin, gazing at the floor.

It was Bishnu.

Less than five minutes later Gyan managed to make his way over to us and pulled us into the hallway. Speaking quickly, he related the situation: Bishnu had been working for the last ten months as a domestic slave. He was sold by Golkka to a local hotel, where he worked twelve hours a day washing dishes. There, he was discovered by a bank manager who was a client of the hotel, a relatively wealthy and powerful man by Nepalese standards, who bought the boy from the hotel for the equivalent of perhaps eighty dollars. He took him to work in his own home. The story was similar in many ways to what had happened to Kumar. Gyan was vague when I asked him how he had persuaded the man to come in, and I had learned not to press him on such issues. I had to force myself to remain calm at those moments, not demand that the man be arrested for enslaving this young boy. The important thing now was getting the boy into Dhaulagiri House, where we knew he would be safe.

"Okay, we can bring Bishnu back in a taxi," I said. "Jacky, can you wait here while I get one?"

"Wait—there may be a small problem, Conor sir," said Gyan, putting a hand on my elbow. "The bank manager—the man in the corner, standing up—he does not want to give the boy up."

I stared at Gyan, incredulous. "He doesn't want to give him up? Surely that's a nonissue, Gyan? You can compel him, can't you? He's already here, for God's sake."

"Yes, I can try to compel him. But I cannot arrest him right now; I do not have the correct papers. If I try and make force with him, he may leave this office with Bishnu now and disappear. He has already said Bishnu is better with him. It is best if we can persuade him to give the boy up by his free will," he said.

Gyan watched my reaction. We had been through this before. Either I had faith in him or I didn't. Gyan had done very well to get the man here in the first place. I imagined he had used some thinly veiled threats about police visiting the bank manager at his home, a public embarrassment that the man was probably eager to avoid. Maybe Gyan didn't have the right papers to arrest the man or even compel him to release Bishnu, but he sure knew how to bluff. Whether he could convince the man to actually give Bishnu up to us was another story. We were about to find out just how far Gyan could push his bluff.

"Okay, Gyan—whatever you think is best," I sighed.

He stepped back into his office, indicating that we should stay where we were. "I will call the man here—we will leave Bishnu inside."

He returned a minute later with the bank manager. The man stood two inches shorter than me but a solid foot wider at the shoulders, as if he wore an ox yoke under his jacket. He did not smile when he was introduced to us, and ignored our greeting. Instead he spoke quickly to Gyan in what was clearly some kind of diatribe about western intervention in the case. Gyan declined to translate for us, opting to speak softly to the man. I started to interrupt, but Gyan, not even looking at me, lifted his hand just slightly toward me—the sign to keep my mouth shut. I realized that anything I said at this moment was only going to enrage this man. He already looked ready to pop. All we wanted was the boy, and Gyan was working on getting him for us.

This dialogue went on for ten minutes. The families inside, forced to wait, grew restless. The bank manager swayed between relative calm and severe agitation. Jacky and I leaned in, trying to glean a clue as to where the conversation was going. Gyan alone remained utterly calm, speaking in a low voice, his hand on the man's shoulder.

Finally, after an unusually long monologue by Gyan, the man hesitated, then gave a single reluctant nod and grunt. He looked Jacky and me up and down. He had softened from his original position, that was clear. He nodded once more as Gyan continued to speak, then cut Gyan off with a single word. The manager walked back inside, helped Bishnu to his feet, and walked back out to the hall where we were waiting.

Gyan turned back to us. "He will let the boy go into your care. But he wants to see the conditions where Bishnu will live. You do not have to show him inside, just the outside of the house, so he knows you have other children and are committed to Nepal, that you are not simply taking Bishnu back to your country. Would this be acceptable?"

I wondered why this man was so intent on keeping the boy. Surely Bishnu was just a servant? It gave me pause as to whether we were doing the right thing. A year ago, if I was in this position I may have decided the man could be trusted. He seemed to genuinely care what happened to the boy. I had to allow for the fact that I might have been making a mistake. Maybe Bishnu really was safe with this man. Maybe this was the boy's one chance to have a foster home.

I couldn't risk it. By then, I had seen too much. I had seen instances of Nepali men and women talking with pride of the poor boy or girl they had taken into their home, only to discover that yes, the child was being cared for and going to school, but was also being treated as an outsider to the family, as little more than a servant, working all hours of the day without pay, cooking and cleaning for the family. Was that wrong? Were they better off living as a servant, with the blessing of their mother or father who had given them away? Was it better to get an education than to live with one's own family? These were the questions I had asked myself in my time in Nepal. It was, as Gyan always said, a difficult country. There were no easy answers.

But I knew one thing for sure. I knew Bishnu would be safe with us. This man might be a loving father to the boy, providing him with a home. Or he may have just been upset that we were taking his piece of property. I was not going to take the chance. We would take him with us. If that meant fulfilling Gyan's conditions, then that was what we'd do.

I looked at Jacky. "Does that sound okay to you? He can come and see the house?"

"Yes, if that is the condition, I think it is okay, no?"

"I think so too," I said, and turned back to Gyan. "Fine, we will go together. And then he'll leave the boy with us?"

"Yes, he will leave Bishnu with you. He knows he may get in trouble if he does not."

I noticed that the man was listening. He understood English, at least a little of it.

I clasped Gyan's hand. "Thank you, Gyan. You've done a great thing. Really."

"You have also, Conor sir. And you, Jacky sir. Always you do great things for children."

I looked down at Bishnu, who was looking up at me with surprised recognition. The man, looking from Bishnu to me, spoke to me in broken English. "He say he know you," he said. "How you know?"

"We met one year ago." I smiled at the boy, who was now smiling openly right back. "It is very nice to see him again."

Then the four of us—the bank manager, Bishnu, Jacky, and I—walked out of the government offices together. As I was leaving, Gyan took my arm and pulled me back and spoke in a low voice.

"Conor sir—be careful. I have seen this very often. I think he will give up the boy. But whatever happens, do not trust this man. Bishnu is not his family. You understand?" he said.

"I understand. We'll be okay," I said, with more confidence than I felt.

Outside the offices, there was a line of the usual beat-up taxis waiting on the street. The bank manager indicated that he would follow us, with Bishnu, on his motorcycle. I nodded and opened the door of the taxi. I was getting into the backseat when I noticed another boy, about Bishnu's age, standing behind me. There was nobody around him, no parent or any other children.

It took me a moment to realize that he was waiting to climb into the taxi with us. He clutched a tiny battered suitcase the size of a large lunchbox.

I called back to the bank manager, waiting on his motorcycle for us to lead the way.

"*Dai,* you know this boy? He is your son?"

The bank manager craned his neck to see the small figure standing next to the taxi. The boy had gone around to the other side and was now reaching up, tugging at the door handle.

"I never have seen him," he said with a shrug.

I realized what had happened; it was hardly surprising, really. With so many children coming and going in Gyan's office, the boy had followed the wrong people out. Many children were there with distant aunts and uncles and cousins who had suddenly discovered they had guardianship of an orphaned child they had never seen before. In the confusion, the boy had likely thought the bank manager was his relative. Meanwhile, somebody upstairs was panicking. I asked Jacky to wait for a minute while I took the boy back to make sure he found his family.

Gyan was back at his desk, and now there were two new families surrounding his desk, one mother making a scene while others grew impatient waiting their turn. Bored children wandered through the legs of the adults. Gyan saw me walk back in with the boy and hurried over to me.

"Gyan, I'm really sorry, this boy followed us out—his parents must be panicked, if they even noticed he was gone for the last few minutes," I told him, looking around the office for some sign of recognition from a mother or father.

Gyan smiled sadly. "No, Conor sir—Tilak is also from Humla. We found him living alone. He has no parents. He must have followed you when he saw you taking the other boy. . . . You can take him, perhaps?"

It was not really a question. The boy had no home. In Nepal there were no safety nets, no system where all children were cared for in an orderly manner. If we had the means to care for a child without parents, then that is what we would do. The woman who had been yelling at Gyan a moment earlier was now tugging at his arm, seconds away from turning hysterical.

I reached down my hand. Tilak took it without hesitation, completely trusting. I led him through the decrepit government hallways and back outside to where the others were waiting. We walked up to Jacky, waiting in the front seat.

"Jacky, this is Tilak. Can he come with us?" I asked.

Jacky didn't even blink. Umbrella had rescued almost two hundred children just like this.

"*Mais bien sûr!*" he cried enthusiastically to Tilak, who clearly spoke not a word of English, let alone Jacky's heavily accented mix of French and English. "Come, Tilak! You are sitting with me." He lifted the boy and his suitcase into the front seat of the taxi and onto his lap. The five of us drove back to Dhaulagiri and the other Umbrella houses.

Tilak had a new home.

Things did not go as smoothly with Bishnu. After showing the bank manager the homes, we went into the small Umbrella office, next door to Dhaulagiri. Just before we went inside, I asked Farid to bring over the remaining four children who had lived with Bishnu when we first met him. In two minutes flat, Kumar, Samir, Dirgha, and Amita were running across the field toward us. They stopped short in front of Bishnu. They said nothing but only stared at him, and he stared right back. The bank manager asked the children if they knew Bishnu. They all nodded. This seemed to make the bank manager more agitated, as if he were losing his grip on the boy.

Farid took Bishnu's hand and led him out into the field where he could play with the other children. Jacky, the bank manager, and I went inside the office to speak.

Immediately I sensed a serious problem. The man would not sit down. He paced back and forth, shaking his head at every word that came out of our mouths, then pounding on the table and pointing at us and cursing in Nepali. Jacky shot me a look; he had seen this before. He confirmed in French what I was thinking, that there was going to be a big problem. The man stopped pacing and looked at me.

"I take boy my house. He is mine, not yours," he said. He strode toward the door. I moved so my back was against the door.

"*Dai,*" I said, respectfully, my palms facing him. "I am sorry, but this is not an option. Bishnu will stay with us. We appreciate you taking care of him for this long, but he belongs here." I slid one foot back until it was jammed against the door.

The bank manager's jaw tightened. He pushed my hands aside and grabbed the doorknob and yanked at it. The door moved an inch before hitting my heel. His hand came off the doorknob and he stumbled backward. Furious now, he regained his balance and flung himself against me. I was ready for this. Using the door as leverage I threw myself back against him and pinned him hard against the wall. But I was no match for his strength and weight. He grabbed my throat and slammed me back against the door. I wouldn't let go of him, and he was pushing me against his only exit. But I had no idea what I was going to do next. I couldn't hold him forever, he was much stronger than me. If he got out—and he would get out—he could physically grab Bishnu. Once he had the boy it would be impossible to stop him without harming the child.

Jacky, who was behind him trying to pull him off me, suddenly let go and lunged for his cell phone. With one hand gripping the man's arm, he scrolled frantically through numbers and pressed a number. He held his phone tight as the man wrenched around trying to get us off him. After several interminable seconds, I heard Jacky say, "Yes, hello? . . . Hello? . . . Yes, sir, this is Jacky Buk, with Umbrella Foundation, we met . . . yes, exactly . . . yes, I am well, sir, but we have a situation right now and I need your help very badly—a man is here who is trying to take one of our children," he said, panting with exertion.

The bank manager seemed oblivious to this phone call, intent only on getting out the door. But I was mesmerized by it, wondering who on earth Jacky could possibly need to call right now.

"Yes, sir, that's correct," Jacky panted into the phone. "Yes, sir, he is here, we are speaking with him now . . . yes, sir, I am putting him on the phone now," Jacky said. He released the bank manager's arm and took a step back. He touched the man on the back and held the phone out to him.

"Sir, the mayor would like to speak to you," he said.

The struggle stopped. The bank manager pushed off me and turned toward Jacky, panting and looking between him and the phone, trying to work out if this was some kind of trick. I was trying to figure out the same thing. Still Jacky held the phone out.

The bank manager snatched the phone out of his hand and said a gruff "Hahlo?" into it. He was silent for a few seconds. He then launched into Nepali. Almost as soon as he began he was cut off by a raised voice on the other end of the line, audible from where I stood. He stared at the floor. After a couple of minutes, he said a cursory good-bye, clicked the phone closed, and placed it on the table. Without a word, he took the doorknob again. I looked at Jacky. Jacky waved me out of the way. The bank manager walked out to his motorcycle, put on his helmet, and without so much as a glance back he drove off. We never saw him again.

I walked back inside to find Jacky lighting a cigarette. We stared at each other for a second, and both burst out laughing.

"You know the mayor of Kathmandu?" I asked, collapsing onto a chair. "Are you serious?"

"*Bien sûr*—we rescue many children, Conor. The mayor approves of what we do here," he said with a smile. "He gave me his card some months ago. But I admit, this was the first time I had called him. I am surprised he picked up. But very happy. It was a very good decision, I think, no?"

I just shook my head in wonder. Jacky had guts. Later that evening, we would learn from Gyan, who already knew what had happened, that the mayor had threatened to call the chief of police and send every single policeman in Kathmandu to descend upon that office if the bank manager did not leave immediately.

I had no more doubts. We had gambled by taking the boy, but the man's decision to quickly flee convinced me that he had been keeping Bishnu as a servant, nothing more. Bishnu was safe at last.

◈

I WALKED OUTSIDE TOWARD where Bishnu was sitting in the field, building a small house with Dirgha and Amita. Bishnu had watched the man leave, yet had not gotten up, had not even reacted. He turned back to his old friends from that shack on the Ring Road and continued building the house. Bishnu never spoke of him again—further evidence that he had been a servant and nothing more.

Farid was watching them from a short distance away. I walked over to him, and he heard me come up.

"I don't think that was very easy, no? I could hear you shouting from outside," he said.

"No, not so easy," I said.

We watched the kids try to balance a roof of heavy twigs over the tiny stone walls they had just built.

"We have all seven children," Farid said, trying the words out, slowly, as if trying to convince himself it was really true. "Who would have believed this? You?"

"I didn't know," I said, truthfully. "I guess I didn't really believe it, no."

"I didn't either," he admitted. "I hoped, but I thought it might be impossible."

I considered that. "You know who believed it?" I said to him. He shook his head. "The only person who believed this was going to happen was Liz. She kept telling me over and over."

Farid smiled and turned back in time to see the little house crumble under the weight of the twigs.

Seven

LIZ AND I CONTINUED writing, often up to twenty times a day. I wasn't the only one interested in Liz's life; the Dhaulagiri girls were thrilled that I was able to bring them daily news about her. They asked about her two or three times a day, always with a sly insinuation that we were more than just friends. It became their favorite topic. I assured them, in what I felt was a reasonably good lie, that of course we were just friends; otherwise we would be married. For a young Nepali girl from the village, this was airtight logic. You were unlikely to have even met your husband before your arranged marriage to him, let alone have dated him.

"Then you *want* to marry Liz Sister, yes Conor *dai*?" they crowed.

"*Friends,* girls. We're just friends. You can ask Liz!" I said. Then I would quickly e-mail Liz and remind her to tell the kids that we were just friends when she wrote to them. The children loved it when she e-mailed them; they would scour her letters for clues that would give away our budding romance.

"Yes, Conor, I remember it from when you reminded me two days ago. And when you reminded me the day before that, and the day before that."

The Little Princes, well, they were a different story. They knew me too well; I couldn't keep anything from them if I tried. I tested out the same line on them, and the boys laughed as if I had just told them the single greatest joke in Nepalese history.

"Brother, your lie very terrible! We have seen many American movies now. We know not much arranged marriage in your country," Santosh said, wiping the tears from his eyes. "We meet Liz on her visit. She very very beautiful. You very love her, Brother! You love her!"

I denied it vigorously. But the fact was, from the moment Liz left Kathmandu in January, I had been working to get her back. I went about it cautiously, being sensitive to the fact that she would have to take a week off work, buy a ticket, and fly halfway around the world. So I dropped small hints, telling her all the things that were happening with the girls, how much everybody missed her, how much warmer the weather was getting now that it was March. She responded cheerfully, but never came out and said she would come.

I had confided in Viva about the issue a couple of days earlier. Viva was like family, a cross between a mom and a big sister. She knew I was crazy about Liz, she had seen it when we all met for tea on several occasions in January. I asked Viva what she thought might be going on in Liz's head.

"Conor, it constantly amazes me how dumb men can be," she said in her Northern Irish brogue as she put down her tea. "For God's sake, *tell* her you want her to visit. Women want to be pursued, not have their feelings danced around. You want her to come? Be a man. Better yet, be a French man— right, Jacky?"

"*Ah oui,*" Jacky murmured, taking a drag off his cigarette.

"Ask her to come. Demand it, from your heart. My God, how do you not *know* this stuff?"

So I did. I told her in my next e-mail that I would love it if she came to visit me. That I knew it was a long way to come and expensive and everything else, but that I really wanted to see her. The next day, she told me she had gotten the e-mail and started to check flights. I didn't let her off the hook until she had committed to a time: mid-April. She wrote that she would love to come then. Good old Viva.

I went over to Dhaulagiri to tell Farid the good news. As I was leaving, I ran into Leena in the foyer, alone as usual, staring out the front door. She was wearing her woolen maroon hat. The house maintained its chill with remarkable efficiency, regardless of the temperature outside. The hat was clearly too big for her; it was difficult to get clothes donated that fit the children exactly right. This particular hat, though, stuck up well off the top of her head. The elastic in it, meant for clutching a much larger cranium, was pulled together at the top, in a kind of cone shape. It reminded me of a plunger, and that made it entirely too tempting to pass up. On my way out, I took it and plunged it up and down on her head, making a sucking noise.

She giggled.

I froze. It was the first sound I had ever heard her make. I whirled around to see if Farid or anybody else had heard it. But no, we were alone in the hallway. When I looked back down at her, she had moved. But not just moved—as it took me a moment to comprehend: she was running very slowly away from me, looking back and waiting for me to chase her. So I chased her. She burst out laughing and took off for real. We ran all around the house for a full ten minutes. Farid came out of his room and did a double take as she sprinted past. He too froze, not wanting to break the spell. I scooped up Leena and carried her, smiling and giggling, over to Farid, and delivered her into his arms.

Farid was wide-eyed. "That is amazing," he said, shaking his head.

"It is amazing," I said.

And just like that, from one day to the next, after months of not speaking, Leena had broken through her stone casing. She was a happy little girl.

◇

IT WAS MAY 2007, and I was going on another mission. I had planned it for just after Liz's visit, knowing that I would be out of contact for two weeks. Our seven days together in April had passed quickly; watching her leave again was crushing. The short times together were glorious, but the oceans of time between brought me down at some point every day. But we had made a decision during her visit in April: we would commit to each other. We would try to make our relationship work, painful as the distance promised to make it.

Now I was going off, back into the wilderness to find more families, this time to the Nuwakot District, just north of Kathmandu.

As in Humla, I had many hours alone with my thoughts. I thought about the last conversation I'd had with Liz before leaving. It was tense. All we had to keep our relationship together were e-mail and phone conversations over a static-filled Internet connection. We were not sure when the next time we would see each other would be. And now I was going away for two weeks, cutting us off completely. I think we were both surprised at how deeply we were affected by the thought of not being able to speak every day. On those long treks through Nuwakot, I allowed myself to daydream about her, to replay our conversations, to think about what we would do the next time she came to Nepal, whenever that would be. She was already almost out of vacation days.

I was in love with her. I thought about her constantly. I missed her. She was my best friend. Yet I never saw her. I mulled over different solutions, different ways I might be able to get her to visit or find ways of visiting her. But in the end, we lived nine thousand miles apart, and I just didn't know if we could ever overcome that. Worse, I was afraid she might be thinking the same thing. I knew that there were other men lobbying to date her. Rich guys, guys with impressive jobs in DC. I knew that she had turned them down, and she always told me how much she wanted to be with me, not with them. But they were there, and I wasn't. I began to realize that love wasn't always enough. I walked slower than usual that day, unable to shake that depressing realization.

Two weeks later, I was back in Kathmandu. In the final day of my mission, I had come to a decision that I was anxious to share with Farid. We met down at the local tea shop, where we spent most of our time when we were not with the Dhaulagiri kids. I started by filling him in on the details of the trip, about the seventeen families I'd found. Farid listened for a long time, and paused before responding, studying my expression.

"You did very well, Conor. Seventeen families. You should be happy," he said. We had spent almost two years together in close quarters—he could tell when something was bothering me.

"It's not that, I am happy, the trip went well—but I think that I need a break. I was thinking that I might go back to the States for a bit, maybe six weeks. There are two NGN fund-raisers going on, I could help with those," I told him. "But what would you think? I'm worried it would be a big burden, managing everything from here alone, no?"

He didn't hesitate. "Of course you should go, Conor! We so rarely take breaks, and you remember that I took one last month?"

He was referring to a two-week trip into the mountains he had taken to live among the Buddhists in the Khumbu region of the high Himalaya, the home to Everest, to learn more about the Buddhist culture in that beautiful mountain setting.

"I can see it, you need this break," Farid continued. "Go visit your family. And I think you want very much to see Liz, no?"

"I really do, yeah. I think we need to have a talk."

"So go! We are fine. We have a very good system. We have our staff. The children are fine. I am very happy to do this alone. You were here before me, you remember? It is time for your break," he said. "And I think Liz will be very happy to see you, too."

"She better be," I said, taking a deep breath. "I'm going to ask her to marry me."

Eight

I RETURNED TO NEPAL after six weeks in the States, bearing photos of Liz and me from the day I proposed to her. The kids went berserk at the news.

"She really say yes, Brother? You are very sure?" asked Anish.

"I am very, very sure, Anish."

"And her father? Her mother? They also say yes?"

"Yes, Anish—everybody said yes. Her mother said yes, her father said yes, she said yes. We are getting married."

Only Priya and Yangani, the two girls, asked for details on how it happened. I told them that I had taken her down to the dock at her father's farm, her favorite place in the world, after getting permission from her father.

"You sit on one knee, Brother? Like this?" Priya asked, getting down on one knee and holding up an invisible ring. She must have seen it in a movie.

"Yes, exactly like that. And I said 'Elizabeth Lyons Flanagan, will you marry me?'"

The girls squealed.

"Do not forget about the dog, Conor," Farid said. He had heard this story a few times now, and sat, amused, on the couch on the far side of the room, watching me regale the children.

Emma, Liz's dog, had followed us down to the dock on her father's farm, where I proposed. Somewhere between "Elizabeth" and "Flanagan," Emma decided it was a good time to belly flop off the floating dock. Eighty pounds of dog hit the water just two feet away, soaking both Liz and me. Liz was laughing so hard that it took me a moment to work out if she had actually said yes. This became, predictably, the best part of the story for the kids. They made me tell it twice.

Farid and I spent a couple of days down in Godawari at Little Princes. I had missed them. But then it was time to get back to work. Our mission to find families would continue.

◇

FARID AND I BECAME more efficient at finding families in remote areas. We knew how to put together search teams and assemble the supplies we would need, and we knew how to ask the right questions. Actually reuniting the children with their families, though, turned out to be a much more complicated beast. Every parent was overjoyed to find their son or daughter again. But when they learned that their child was being well taken care of, they were suddenly reluctant to take him or her home. Nepal is a terribly poor country; it is a challenge to support a family.

I understood the parents' perspective, but it put us in a difficult position. We were committed to doing what was best for the children, and the children were desperate to return home. We believed they had a *right* to be raised in their own homes, in their own communities—a belief shared by UNICEF and virtually all major child protection organizations. NGN existed to protect that right. Yet there were countless reasons why a child might not be able to return home. For example, one of their parents may have remarried; in Nepal, under those circumstances, the new stepmother or stepfather would rarely accept any children from the previous marriage. Sometimes we suspected abuse by an uncle or cousin. On several occasions we learned that the parent was actually aiding a child trafficker. All of these circumstances would put a returned child at risk.

One issue we thought we could overcome was the financial problem. By offering an impoverished parent a monthly stipend to help support their child in their own home, the family would be reunited, and it would cost us less than supporting the child at Dhaulagiri House. When a mother came to visit her son and indicated that she was eager to bring him home but would have difficulty paying for his food and education, we calculated how much she would need and offered her monthly support. The boy was reunited with his mother, and we monitored the situation closely.

It didn't take long to conclude that this solution would not work. As it turned out, by supporting a family under these circumstances, we were, in effect, rewarding precisely those people who had chosen to give their children to traffickers. We learned that this was likely to inspire neighbors to send *their* child off with a child trafficker, hoping that they might miraculously end up in the hands of a Western nonprofit organization. Never mind that the great majority of these children never returned; the neighbors focused on the one child who *did* return safely and whose family was now being mysteriously rewarded for it.

Reunification was going to be much harder than we thought.

◇

A BREAKTHROUGH CAME, AS it always seemed to, at the tea shop.

Farid and I were talking about Solo Khumbu, the region in northern Nepal that spanned the tallest part of the Himalayan range—the home of Everest. Farid had made several trips to the region to spend time alone in the Buddhist villages, where he could stare at the stars and meditate with the monks. I was describing the glacier I had seen near Everest Base Camp, a long mass of ice and rock that was, at the same time, both unmovable and unstoppable.

"It's like this work," Farid said, with something between a laugh and a sigh.

"What, unmovable?"

"Unmovable, exactly," he said. Then, after thinking about it for a moment, he added, "But you know, maybe also unstoppable. Everything just moves more slowly than we are used to, Conor. We cannot see the progress sometimes, I think. Maybe 'Nepali time' is a real thing," he said.

"Nepali time" was an expression I heard probably once a day. It was always said by a Nepali who was well behind deadline, always to a foreigner who couldn't understand why the deadline hadn't been respected. Nepali time meant that everything moved slower in Nepal. I imagine many countries around the world have a similar expression.

Farid's comment was profound. We spoke about Nepali time with disdain, as an excuse for laziness. Often it was, of course. But maybe, as Farid had suggested, it was more than that. Maybe it was the pace at which things *had* to move here. We had thought that reuniting children with their families should have been straightforward—either they could go back or they couldn't. But what if it was more complicated than that? What if we were giving up too soon? What if, Farid suggested, instead of pressing a parent to take back a child when they visited, we slowed the process down? What if we just let a parent visit their children, with no pressure to take their child home?

Remarkably, this worked. Success was still rare, and we had to cultivate the relationship with the parent over a number of weeks, but it was worth it. Two of the children from Dhaulagiri, a brother and sister named Puspika and Pradip, were visited by their mother no fewer than six times in eight weeks. On the ninth week, she came and asked if she could bring her children home. We were helping families become reacquainted after years of separation.

Gradually, a few more children found their way home. Two cousins from Dhaulagiri, Kunja and Agrim, after spending two weeks with their mother over the course of several months and visiting the local school in their village, were able to return home. We continued to search for families. Nepal is such a difficult country to get around that Farid would be gone an entire week and come back to report he had managed to locate only three families. It was painstaking work. But the results were worth it.

◇

"WHAT TIME IS YOUR FLIGHT?" Farid asked. It was a morning in late September, and there was not a cloud in the sky. The rainy season was officially over.

"Five o'clock," I said. It was nearly inconceivable that I was leaving Nepal.

Liz and I had tried to find a solution where she could live in Kathmandu with me. We had gone so far as to find a house next to Dhaulagiri; Liz had even gotten her dog, Emma, properly vaccinated for the big move and found somebody to rent her condo in DC. But it was just too difficult. Liz had been unable to find work in Kathmandu, and she had a good job back in the States. I also had to admit that returning to the United States was probably the best thing for NGN as an organization, since I would be able to fund-raise more effectively from there. We already had a great staff in place in Nepal to carry on the work. The difficulty for both Liz and me was knowing that we would be far away from the children.

My biggest concern was finding someone to replace me as country director. We needed somebody who could work well with Farid, somebody who shared our values, somebody who the children loved. We just couldn't imagine who that could be.

Then, out of the blue, Farid called me one day and told me to meet him at the tea shop. The tea shop was run by Tibetans and served one dish: momos. Momos are similar to Chinese dumplings: steamed dough filled with vegetables or, as we preferred them, water buffalo. I came to find him sitting at our usual table—the only table outside, a dangerously unstable, rickety thing—sipping tea, staring out at the quiet street that encircled Swayambhu, near our children's home, watching the Tibetan monks walking around a massive prayer wheel the size of a small car. They would turn it three times clockwise before moving on around the stupa or retreating back into the monastery just next to my own building. He had ordered me a lemon tea, which now sat next to him, steaming.

"Conor, I hope you are prepared for this discussion," he said.

I sat down and took a cautious sip of my tea before adding a spoonful of coarse brown sugar from an open bowl on the table. "What discussion?" I asked.

"I am going to prove what karma can do for you," he said, his voice deadpan.

I put down my tea. The woman brought out two plates of buffalo momos, one for each of us. Farid picked one off the plate with his fingers and popped it in his mouth.

Farid told me that one day earlier, he'd had a long conversation with Anna Howe. Anna, who helped us find Amita and facilitated my trip to Humla through D.B., had remained engaged with NGN. She and Farid had become close; Anna had been a practicing Buddhist for many years, and she and Farid had bonded over their shared beliefs.

Anna, Farid said, was leaving the ISIS Foundation. She loved the work and being with children, but she wanted to work for a smaller organization. She wanted to stay in Nepal, but she said it was unlikely she would find the perfect job. In her perfect world, she told him, she would work for an organization exactly like NGN, the very organization she had been so instrumental in helping to launch.

"Do you know any organizations like that, Conor? Which might be looking for a country director like Anna?" He was smiling now.

I couldn't believe it. I thought I might have misheard him. I put down my tea and called Anna that moment, asking her if it was true that she might want to work with us, to potentially take my place as country director. She sounded as excited as me, saying what an incredible blessing this was, and that she would be absolutely honored to take the position.

After a short conversation, I hung up and put my phone down on the table. I took a sip of my tea, and Farid and I sat in silence for a few moments.

"That's amazing," I said finally.

"It is amazing," he confirmed.

That had been just three weeks earlier. Since then, Anna, Farid, and I had spent a lot of time together. She had come with us earlier that morning, my final morning in Nepal, when I said good-bye to the children at Dhaulagiri.

At the leaving ceremony at Dhaulagiri, I had sat in a chair where I would receive a tikka and flowers. First in line were the staff. Ganesh and Devaka, the house father and mother, wished me a safe trip. Then came the cooking and cleaning *didis* who worked with us, Moti and Sunita. Then it was the children's turn. They stood in a line while I sat in place. Some were shy, handing me flowers and sloppily smushing a small tikka on my forehead before giggling and running off. They were having a grand time, as I knew they would—it was like a festival for them. Most of them had little sense that I was leaving the country.

Farid joined us for a final group photo, then it was time to leave. We were heading up to the main road when I saw Amita. She stood in the path, her arms spread wide, blocking my exit. I didn't try to get around her. I just stood in front of her in silence, waiting for her permission to leave. Her scowl faded into a reluctant smile. I took her in a big hug, picking her up. Then Kumar leaped on, and Samir and Dirgha and Bishnu, those beloved children who had started it all. Then all the kids joined in, in a massive, spontaneous thirty-person group hug that ended when we tumbled over under the sheer body weight.

We passed my apartment on the way up the road. Farid and I would travel together down to Godawari so I could say good-bye to the Little Princes. I told Farid I wanted to just stop by my apartment to take a quick shower before going to see the kids.

"I would wait to take a shower until after you see the Little Princes, Conor," Farid said thoughtfully. "The tikka the boys put on your face—it is not subtle."

"They're not covering my face with tikka this time," I assured Farid. "They can do a little bit, if they put it on the tip of their finger, like the Dhaulagiri kids, but that's it."

Farid smiled. "Ah. Yes, of course you're right, Conor. Very good plan."

◇

RAJU WAS APPLYING A fistful of tikka to my temple when I noticed that his other fist was also filled with the rice and red dye.

"Raju—no. No. No more. No more tikka, Raju."

He paused, confused. "Luck, Conor Brother!"

"I have luck already. The first tikka is luck. I don't need two tikkas for luck." I saw Santosh sneaking up behind me with another fistful of tikka. I spun around.

"Santosh! No. I'm serious. No more tikka," I said as sternly as I could.

"No tikka on your cheeks yet, Brother," he protested. "Very bad luck!"

"It's not *supposed* to be on my cheeks, Santosh. It is supposed to be a small area on my forehead. You would do this to a Nepali man? Cover his face in tikka? You would do this to Hari?"

"You are traveling very very far, Conor Brother! More luck needed!"

I stood up and went to the bathroom mirror. My forehead was covered in the thick red paste. It looked like I'd been in a car accident. I took a rag to wipe some of the excess tikka off.

"No wipe off, Brother!" Santosh was standing behind me. "You look very beautiful! And very very lucky!"

"Oh, *please*!"

"True, Brother!"

I turned to face him. He was smiling. He had surprisingly white teeth. "I don't know why I let you boys do that. I'm going to look ridiculous on the bus."

"Because we are fun, Brother! You not have much fun in America I think," said Santosh, admiring the red goop covering my face. "You come back soon to live here with your wife, Liz Sister. You may share a room with us, no problem."

"I'm not coming back to live, just to visit. But Liz and I will be back in three months, in January. We'll be here for two weeks," I told him.

"Much better that you come with your wife, Conor Brother!" Santosh said. "Liz Sister much more beautiful than you! You are a little hard to look at for me." He grew suddenly mock-thoughtful. "You need more tikka, maybe. . . ."

I put my arm around his shoulder, and we walked back into the living room. The rest of the children were gone—they were now waiting in a long line that stretched from the front door to the blue gate, leading out to the path. Farid was marshaling the affair expertly, joking with them and rearranging them until they were in the right order, youngest to oldest. Each of them was holding white and yellow flowers that they would present to me on my way out. They stood shoulder to shoulder, chatting excitedly as they always did. Somehow they never ran out of things to talk about, even though they had spent virtually every minute together that day and the day before that, stretching back almost five years, not just in this house but in the house of the child trafficker who had first taken them from Humla. Some of them had been together more than half their lives.

I didn't go out just yet. My arm still slung around Santosh, I walked through the house one last time. Santosh swung his arm around me, and his hand rested on my far shoulder. When I had first met him three years earlier he had been nine years old—he was much smaller then, and his arm had not been nearly long enough to reach all the way up to my shoulder. Suddenly he was unstuck in time, leaping forward from the nine-year-old I had carried through the hospital to become this twelve-year-old boy next to me.

Together, we walked outside, into the sunshine, to the start of the line of children. Santosh rushed off to grab his own flowers and take up his place in line between Dawa and Bikash. Bikash, at the end of the line, was also suddenly a young man, standing a full head taller than the rest of the boys. He was fifteen, old enough in Nepal to be married or a member of the staff. Raju was the first boy on the left, holding his flowers high, head down, singing quietly to himself. The boy who had hung from my neck the first moment I walked in the gate of Little Princes was gone, and I hadn't noticed until that moment. This boy, this Raju, was seven, maybe even eight years old. His face was thinner, his arms longer, his voice stronger, richer, even in mumbled song.

Nuraj elbowed Raju in the ribs and he jumped, startled, and noticed me there for the first time. "Conor Brother!" he yelled. "Flowers, Conor Brother!"

I took them and continued down the line, accepting flowers from each child and watching them transform before my eyes; I released them from the images I had kept of them as young children, just months after being rescued from Golkka, when they were still undernourished and small. They were not *supposed* to age, because I was not supposed to still be here. It was three years since I first walked through the gate, when they were so completely unknown to me that I could only tell them apart by the clothes on their backs.

I walked out the blue gate, three years older myself, and up the path. The children waved frantically, shouting my name as I walked with an armload of flowers and a face covered in tikka. But they stayed within the walls of the Little Princes, because they still had to get ready to go to the temple, where they would wash their clothes and play in the shallow pool.

◇

FARID WALKED ME UP to the road. He would be staying in Godawari for a few days. Together we waited for the minibus that would take me back to Kathmandu and the airport. We said nothing for a while, just stared up the road in the direction the bus would come from.

"I remember doing this before the revolution, one and a half years ago, standing in this spot," Farid said finally. "There was the bandha, and no traffic was moving. I had to walk for ten hours, with my bag, to the airport. That big bag I had, you remember it? It was such a bad time—you had just left back to America, I remember. They were fighting in the streets. It was not long after the Maoists had bombed the Ratna Park bus station, and the police had shot people for protesting. It was very violent out on the streets—they were arresting people breaking curfew. I did not know what to do. I had many hours to walk to the airport, and I did not want to be arrested, or to have them think I was some revolutionary and get attacked. So I put a sign on my bag. I made it from an empty page from one of the children's drawing books. I used the big pen they have, the one they love—what is the name of that?"

"A marker."

"Yes, a marker. I took the blue marker, and I wrote my big sign, and I attached it with a pin to my bag so everyone—the police and the Maoists—

could see it, and see who I was. To see *what* I was," he said. "Then I walked, for hours. I thought I would never get home. But I did, and somehow I was back in France. I thought I would not come back here for a long time."

He was looking down the road now, seeing it as he did almost two years earlier, with no cars and the airport impossibly far away. He must have thought he was going home for good, that both of us were finished with Nepal. Then there was a revolution in the streets and seven children had disappeared, and our lives were suddenly tangled up with this mountain kingdom.

The white minibus came around the corner. Farid held out his arm to stop it for me. The squeal of the brakes started immediately, we could hear it all the way down the road as the bus gradually slowed. I slung my backpack onto my back. Farid held out his hand, I took him in a hug, clapping his back. Farid never liked good-byes. The bus puttered to a rolling stop in front of me.

"What did your sign say?" I asked him. "The one you pinned to your bag?"

He smiled. "It said TOURIST."

Afterword

I GOT AN E-MAIL from Farid in the fall of 2008.

"We are bringing the Little Princes back to Humla," he told me.

This had been our dream for four years. The trip would only be a visit and would only be for nine children, a test to see how they would adapt after so many years of living in a harsh urban landscape, cut off from their families. But Humla was now safe, and the children had a two-week break from school.

◇

THE CHILDREN WERE ANXIOUS as their small prop plane set down on the dirt landing strip in the village of Simikot. Almost all of them had spent more than half their young lives far away from here. But after just a few hours of trekking slowly south along the Karnali River toward their villages, they transformed into Humli children. They ate berries and cracked open fallen walnuts on nearby rocks and ran off the trail and into the fields, fueled by an extraordinary excitement. A day later, they spotted the village of Ripa in the distance, small mud huts built on steep terraces, and memories came flooding back. They giggled madly at the surprise in store for their families, who had no idea that their prodigal children were just a few hours away.

The village erupted at the sight of them. The older children saw parents and old friends, and there were many tears. The younger ones were shy—they had stopped giggling. They wanted to remember these people who were crying over them, speaking a dialect they no longer understood, touching their faces and clothes, but they were little more than toddlers when they were taken from this place. Their families were strangers to them.

But the bonds ran deep. By the end of their first day home, all the children, young and old, were village children again. They followed their mothers and fathers across the barren winter fields, where the crops would be planted in the spring, and into the forest where they would search for herbs. Their hands may have been softer than those of their brothers and sisters, but they stood taller and stronger than even their eldest siblings, who had lived through years of drought. They slept that night not on the mattresses of the Little Princes Children's Home but on the floors of mud huts, wrapped in homemade blankets, huddled next to their mothers. There were no light switches to turn off now, nobody to shush them if they continued to chatter. When the fire died, they slept.

At the end of the two weeks, not a single child from the Little Princes wanted to leave Humla. And though they had to return to Kathmandu for now, they were changed children. They were more purposeful now; they worked even harder in school. They no longer spoke of becoming astronauts or football players, but of becoming doctors and teachers in their villages. Their destiny had been set in motion, and it was back in Humla, working the land, marrying, starting families, rebuilding their villages, and carrying on traditions that stretch back centuries, long before the Maoist rebels took over the country.

Farid paused at the end of his story, letting it sink in. I hadn't said a word in the last twenty minutes. It was March 2009; we were speaking on the phone for the first time in months. I had read his account of it at the time, months earlier, but hearing him tell it, with that familiar French accent, brought it to life.

"It's incredible, Farid. I'm stunned. I wish I could have been there to see all that," I said finally.

"Yes, you would have liked it very much, Conor. . . . Oh, and we must speak about something. I know we are already talking about moving the children's home to Simikot, so that they can be in Humla. We must do that. But after this trip, I also believe that some of the children can perhaps return home, can live with their families," he said, his voice accelerating with excitement. "Can you imagine, Conor? Imagine what it would be like, for these parents to have their children back, living with them? Becoming one family again?"

I looked across the living room at Liz. She sat in a wide armchair in our apartment in New York City, legs slung over one arm of the chair, her head resting on the other, watching me with a drowsy smile on her face. On her chest lay our three-week-old son, Finn, curled up against her shoulder like he would never let her go.

"Yeah, I think I can."

Acknowledgments

T HIS BOOK EXISTS BECAUSE a group of children in Nepal welcomed me into their world. They were my wards, my friends, my translators, my teachers, and often my lone source of entertainment when I lived in Nepal. They remain, today, my brothers and sisters, and I will be forever indebted to them. Farid Ait-Mansour was an equal (if not greater) partner in this adventure. I have never met a man with a stronger desire to do what was right for those less fortunate. He is my hero.

I want to thank the team at William Morrow for their passion, enthusiasm, and hard work in bringing this book to life. I especially want to thank my editor, Laurie Chittenden, for seeing into the heart of the story and bringing out the very best in it and in me.

Trena Keating, my agent, has been a phenomenal advocate, editor, and friend from the very beginning, and reassured me every step of the way that yes, really, honestly, there *would* be people who would want to read this book.

My mother, along with the rest of my family, was always incredibly generous, loaning me money so that I could remain in Nepal even when my savings had expired. During the writing process, my father, the poet Eamon Grennan, worked his magic during the editing process, while my stepmother, Rachel Kitzinger, an accomplished writer in her own right, lent me her apartment so I could have a quiet space to work. Itay Banayan and my other class-mates at the world's greatest business school, NYU Stern, helped me through the most intense classes each semester, knowing that I was working on this manuscript.

Last, I simply could not have written this book without the enduring love, support, and editorial assistance of my wife, Liz. May every author be so blessed to have such a companion.

About Next Generation Nepal

Next Generation Nepal

B Y PURCHASING THIS BOOK, you are already making a difference in the lives of the kids you have just read about. Through the publication of this book, we have raised crucial funds that allowed us to open a children's home in Humla, where these same children now live back in their own communities. A portion of the proceeds from the very book you hold in your hands is going toward food, clothing, educational supplies, and finding more families of trafficked children in Nepal.

If you would like to learn more about Next Generation Nepal, find ways of getting involved, or help spread the word about the plight of trafficked children in Nepal, please visit us at www.nextgenerationnepal.org. We would love to hear from you.

Index

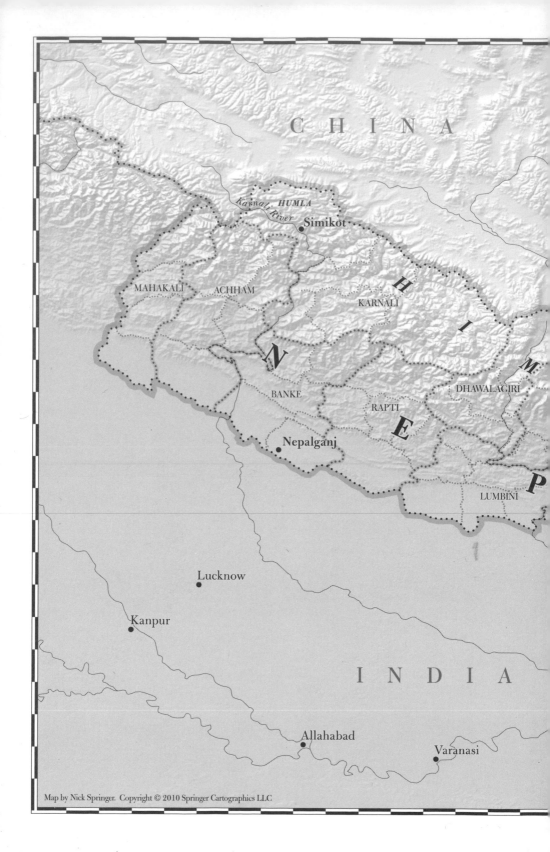

C H I N A

Karnali River HUMLA

Simikot

H I M

MAHAKALI   ACHHAM

KARNALI

N

DHAWALAGIRI

BANKE

RAPTI

E

M

Nepalganj

P

LUMBINI

Lucknow

Kanpur

I N D I A

Allahabad

Varanasi

Map by Nick Springer. Copyright © 2010 Springer Cartographics LLC